The Law Commission
(LAW COM No 324)

THE HIGH COURT'S JURISDICTION IN RELATION TO CRIMINAL PROCEEDINGS

Presented to Parliament pursuant to section 3(2) of the Law Commissions Act 1965

Ordered by The House of Commons *to be printed*
26 July 2010

HC 329   London: The Stationery Office   £35.50

THE LAW COMMISSION

The Law Commission was set up by the Law Commissions Act 1965 for the purpose of promoting the reform of the law.

The Law Commissioners are:

> The Right Honourable Lord Justice Munby, *Chairman*
> Professor Elizabeth Cooke
> Mr David Hertzell
> Professor Jeremy Horder
> Miss Frances Patterson QC

The Chief Executive of the Law Commission is Mr Mark Ormerod CB.

The Law Commission is located at Steel House, 11 Tothill Street, London SW1H 9LJ.

The terms of this report were agreed on 25 June 2010.

The text of this report is available on the Internet at:

http://www.lawcom.gov.uk/judicial_review.htm

THE LAW COMMISSION

THE HIGH COURT'S JURISDICTION IN RELATION TO CRIMINAL PROCEEDINGS

CONTENTS

PART 3: THE CONSULTATION PAPER PROPOSALS

PART 4: THE RESPONSE OF CONSULTEES (1): THE CROWN COURT IN ITS APPELLATE JURISDICTION

PART 5: THE RESPONSE OF CONSULTEES (2): THE NEW STATUTORY APPEAL AND THIRD PARTY RIGHTS

PART 6: OUR PRINCIPAL CONCLUSIONS

PART 14: RECOMMENDATIONS

GLOSSARY

TERMS USED

AFA 2006   Armed Forces Act 2006

Archbold   Archbold Criminal Pleading, Evidence and Practice 2010

appellate jurisdiction   the jurisdiction exercised by the Crown Court when hearing appeals from the magistrates' courts

Blackstone's   Blackstone's Criminal Practice 2010

CA   Court of Appeal

CAA 1968   Criminal Appeal Act 1968

CACD   Court of Appeal Criminal Division

CJA 2003   Criminal Justice Act 2003

CP 184   Law Commission Consultation Paper No 184, The High Court's Jurisdiction in relation to Criminal Proceedings

CPS   Crown Prosecution Service

the ECHR   the European Convention on Human Rights and Fundamental Freedoms

first instance jurisdiction   trial on indictment jurisdiction exercised by the Crown Court

OCJR   Office of Criminal Justice Reform

SCA 1981   Senior Courts Act 1981, formerly the Supreme Court Act 1981

section 29(3)   section 29(3) of the SCA 1981

THE LAW COMMISSION

THE HIGH COURT'S JURISDICTION IN RELATION TO CRIMINAL PROCEEDINGS

To the Right Honourable Kenneth Clarke QC, MP, Lord Chancellor and Secretary of State for Justice

PART 1
INTRODUCTION AND SUMMARY

1.1 The Crown Court sits in several different capacities: as a trial court, as a court hearing appeals from the magistrates' courts, as a sentencing court, and as a civil court, amongst others. There is a variety of ways in which decisions of the Crown Court can be challenged: by appeal to the Court of Appeal, by appeal to the High Court by way of case stated, and by application to the High Court for judicial review.

1.2 The availability of each of these appeal routes depends on the case in question. A defendant who wishes to appeal against a conviction or sentence takes that appeal to the Court of Appeal (Criminal Division) ("the CACD"). However, the prosecution or defence might be able to appeal a point of law to the High Court by way of case stated as an alternative. This is where the prosecution or defendant asks the High Court to determine an issue of law in a case set out for it by the Crown Court. Additionally, any person with sufficient legal interest in a case might be able to challenge a court's decision by way of judicial review. This is where a person asks the High Court to review a decision of the Crown Court on the grounds that it was illegal, irrational or invalidated by procedural impropriety. It is an attack on the process by which the decision was made, rather than on the merits of the decision.

1.3 The High Court has the power to hear appeals by way of case stated and applications for judicial review in respect of decisions made by the Crown Court by virtue of sections 28 and 29(3) respectively of the Senior Courts Act 1981 ("the SCA 1981"), but there is a crucial limitation on these two routes of challenge: appeal by case stated and judicial review are not permitted if the decision is in a "matter relating to trial on indictment".

1.4 We were asked to examine the criminal jurisdiction of the High Court over the Crown Court. Our focus is thus the availability of appeal by way of case stated and judicial review from the Crown Court. By a reference made to the Law Commission on 30 June 2004 we were asked to consider:

> (a) the origins and nature of, and the limitations upon, the High Court's criminal jurisdictions by case stated and judicial review over the Crown Court, as set out in sections 28 and 29 of the Supreme Court Act 1981[1] and in particular sections 28(2) and 29(3) thereof;

---

[1] Now called the Senior Courts Act 1981, and referred to in this report as "the SCA 1981".

(b) how those jurisdictions are best transferred to the Court of Appeal, simplified and, if appropriate, modified;

the implications of (a) and (b) for the High Court's criminal jurisdiction over the magistrates' court, and for courts-martial;

and to make recommendations.

THE CONTEXT OF THE PROJECT

The numbers of cases involved

1.5 It is useful at this point to give an idea of the numbers of cases involved in case stated and judicial review in criminal proceedings. In the years 2000 to 2008 the Administrative Court (a Division of the High Court) received between 246 and 337 applications for permission for judicial review in criminal cases from magistrates' courts and from the Crown Court each year. In the same time period it received between 12 and 23 appeals by way of case stated against the Crown Court each year (but five times as many cases stated against magistrates' courts). By way of comparison, the CACD receives in the region of 7000 applications each year.[2]

A changed statutory backdrop

1.6 An important feature of the context in which the project arises is the statutory changes which have taken place since 1981. First, interlocutory appeals are now available in trials on indictment in ways that were not possible at the time of the SCA 1981. Complex fraud cases, terrorism cases, and some complex, serious or lengthy cases may have a preparatory hearing at which pre-trial issues of law can be resolved, and some appeals are possible against the rulings on those issues. Secondly, the prosecution now has a right of appeal under section 58 of the Criminal Justice Act 2003 against a ruling which will bring the prosecution to an end unless the appeal succeeds. The availability of these two kinds of interlocutory appeal[3] makes it easier to see that the role for appeal by case stated or judicial review as a means of challenging decisions of the Crown Court in trials is no longer so significant, and can be abolished or curtailed.

---

[2] *Judicial and Court Statistics 2008* (2009) Cm 7697 pp16 and 27.

[3] See paras 2.29 to 2.35 below.

Lord Justice Auld's Review of the Criminal Courts

1.7 Another important aspect of the context of this project is the Review by Lord Justice Auld of the Criminal Courts of England and Wales in 2001.[4] He surveyed the whole of the appellate system, including the role of magistrates' courts, and made recommendations. He envisaged a unified criminal court consisting of three Divisions (the Crown Division, the District Division and the Magistrates' Division). The Government thought the advantages he foresaw from unification could be achieved by different means,[5] and so some of the recommendations were accepted by the Government, and have led to legislation, and some were not.

1.8 Lord Justice Auld also thought there should be a single route for criminal matters which led to the Court of Appeal (Criminal Division). One of his recommendations was to abolish appeal by way of case stated and judicial review from the Crown Court in both its trial on indictment and in its appellate jurisdiction.[6] This recommendation was accepted in principle by the Government.[7]

THE PROBLEMS WITH THE CURRENT LAW

1.9 As we note above, appeal by way of case stated and judicial review of the Crown Court in criminal proceedings are barred in respect of the Crown Court's jurisdiction "in matters relating to trial on indictment", by sections 28(2) and 29(3) of the SCA 1981. There has been considerable litigation over the meaning of the phrase. Lord Browne-Wilkinson has described it as "extremely imprecise". He continued,

> In *Smalley* ...Lord Bridge of Harwich said that it may be impossible to lay down any precise test to determine what is and what is not excluded. As a result the law has developed on a case by case basis, not always with happy results.[8]

1.10 The consequences have been uncertainty, litigation, and, in some cases, the absence of a remedy. For example, a defendant who is acquitted will generally have a costs order made in his or her favour, but if the Crown Court refuses a costs order and does so unlawfully, that defendant has no recourse against the refusal. Commenting on this particular situation, Lord Justice Waller said,

---

[4] Auld LJ, *A Review of the Criminal Courts of England and Wales* (September 2001).

[5] Justice for all (July 2002) Cm 5563 para 4.6. The Government was also not persuaded that it should introduce the new intermediate tier of District Division, as recommended by Auld LJ (para 4.19). See also The Criminal Justice Bill (2002-03) The House of Commons Research Paper 02/72, p 21.

[6] Auld LJ, *A Review of the Criminal Courts of England and Wales* (September 2001) recommendations 307.1 and 307.2.

[7] Annexe to "Justice for All" July 2002, Cm 5563, p 43. Recommendations 307.1 and 307.2 could not, in any event, be implemented in quite the way envisaged by Lord Justice Auld, because the Government did not agree to the restructuring of the criminal courts that he recommended.

[8] *R v Manchester Crown Court, ex parte Director of Public Prosecutions* [1993] 1 WLR 1524, 1528 citing *Re Smalley* [1985] AC 622, 643h.

...it is not as it seems to me altogether satisfactory that a defendant who obtains no order for costs or for that matter has an order for costs made against him after an acquittal has no remedy even if the judge was "plainly wrong".[9]

THE VALUES AT STAKE

1.11 We are conducting our review of sections 28 and 29(3) of the SCA 1981 in a different landscape from that which pertained in 1971 (when the predecessors of sections 28(2) and 29(3) of the SCA 1981 were enacted). Thirty-nine years ago trials were perhaps more commonly regarded as a contest between the prosecutor and the defendant, adjudicated by the court and decided by the magistrates or jury. That notion has been put under scrutiny in the intervening years by the increasing recognition of the importance of those other than the prosecution and defendant in criminal trials. For example, the roles of victims, witnesses and the media in the criminal justice system have become more significant in legal terms. The criminal justice system of a state must also play its part in securing the rights under the European Convention on Human Rights and Fundamental Freedoms ("the ECHR") – for victims and witnesses as well as for the accused. The result of these two trends has been significant change.

1.12 Some changes have come about through legislation, and others through the adoption of new forms of good practice in addressing the needs of victims and witnesses. We now see, for example, improved protection for witnesses in the court room to help them give their best evidence, Victim Impact Statements at the sentencing stage, and an emphasis on keeping witnesses informed about the outcomes of cases. There is a wider variety of penalties which may be imposed in order to bring greater benefit to individual victims and/or to the community generally, and a statutory right for the media to challenge orders restricting the reporting of proceedings.

1.13 The importance of the way that the interests of third parties may affect trials can be illustrated by focusing on two key issues: the avoidance of delays and the avoidance of interruptions to criminal proceedings. It is very important to keep in mind that these issues are central to doing justice in criminal cases. They are not simply "managerial" concerns with efficiency and cost.

The avoidance of delay and interruption

1.14 The avoidance of delay in criminal trials has long been recognised as the core principle underlying sections 28 and 29(3) of the SCA 1981. In our Consultation Paper ("CP 184") we endorsed the principle of minimum delay and said,

---

[9] *R v Canterbury Crown Court, ex parte Regentford* [2001] HRLR 18 at [19]; [2000] All ER (D) 2415.

One of the aims of effective case management is the elimination of unnecessary delay in the conduct of criminal proceedings. Delay to criminal trials can seriously compromise the interests of justice, especially when the trial is before a jury. If it cannot be accurately predicted when a trial before a jury will be ready to commence, the interests of defendants, victims, and witnesses may be adversely affected. The passage of time can affect the ability of witnesses to recall events. The greater the delay in a jury starting to hear the evidence, the greater the strain on defendants, victims and witnesses. A trial the start of which is delayed may have a disproportionate effect on a defendant who is in custody awaiting his or her trial. In addition, delay in starting one trial may have a knock-on effect if it delays the start of other trials.[10]

1.15 In CP 184 we also emphasised what we called the "minimal interruption" principle:

The "minimal interruption" principle is meant to ensure that once a jury has been sworn and starts to hear the evidence, the proceedings should be subject to minimal interruption. The rationale underlying the "minimal interruption" principle is more complex than that underpinning the 'minimum delay' principle. Both principles seek to ensure that the interests of defendants, victims and witnesses should not be adversely affected. If it cannot be accurately predicted how long a trial will last because there is no way of knowing how much time will be taken up by adjournments, the interests of defendants, victims and witnesses will be adversely affected. They should all be entitled to know, within reason, approximately how long it will last. As we have previously said, a trial that overruns may also have a knock-on effect by delaying the start of other trials.

However, there is a further rationale for the "minimal interruption" principle. Once a trial has begun to run in the sense of the jury hearing evidence, it is important that, as far as possible, the jury hears all the evidence without interruption. If the "thread" of each side's case cannot adequately be maintained during the course of the trial, because of constant or lengthy interruptions, there is a risk that some members of the jury will not attain or retain an adequate grasp of the evidence or the issues.[11]

1.16 In that regard, we endorse the following observations of Justice Frankfurter in the United States Supreme Court in *Cobbledick v United States*[12] on the danger of delay:

---

[10] The High Court's Jurisdiction in Relation to Criminal Proceedings (2007) Law Commission Consultation Paper No 184, para 5.18.

[11] CP 184, paras 5.24 and 5.25.

[12] *Cobbledick v United States* (1940) 309 US 323.

These considerations of policy [that is, against interlocutory appeals] are especially compelling in the administration of justice ... . An accused is entitled to scrupulous observance of constitutional safeguards. But encouragement of delay is fatal to the vindication of the criminal law. Bearing the discomfiture and cost of a prosecution for crime even by an innocent person is one of the painful obligations of citizenship. The correctness of a trial court's rejection even of a constitutional claim made by the accused in the process of prosecution must await his conviction before its reconsideration by an appellate tribunal.[13]

Balancing the avoidance of delay against giving effect to ECHR rights

1.17 As we note above, the criminal justice system has a role to play in helping citizens secure their ECHR rights. Most obviously in the context of a criminal trial, the court will always have in mind the right of the accused to a fair trial under Article 6, but the court may well have to take account of another ECHR right, whether the right to life under Article 2, the right to liberty under Article 5, or some other ECHR right. In that regard, we emphasise that the perspective of the courts is not restricted to the rights of defendants but also includes the rights of third parties, such as a witness who is remanded in custody during the trial.

1.18 Thus although the rules and procedures at issue in this project are in some senses narrow and technical, behind them is the significant value of promoting just procedures and the need to bring about a just result. That means seeking to secure a difficult balance between avoiding delay and interruption to criminal proceedings whilst also, in a proportionate way giving effect to human rights considerations and allowing for the legitimate interests of third parties.

OUR CONSULTATION

1.19 We published a Scoping Paper in 2005,[14] and CP 184 in October 2007.

1.20 We gave an account of the origins of the High Court's jurisdictions by case stated and judicial review over the Crown Court in Part 1 of the CP. We describe the main features of the current law in Part 2 below. A detailed description can be found in Part 2 of CP 184.

1.21 The proposals in the CP are described in Part 3 below. Their broad outlines are as follows.

---

[13] *Cobbledick v United States* (1940) 309 US 323, 325.

[14] Judicial Review of Decisions of the High Court (2005) Law Commission Scoping Paper.

Remove case stated and judicial review and replace with a new statutory appeal

1.22 The general thrust of the proposals was to remove case stated and judicial review for criminal matters in the Crown Court and to provide a new statutory appeal, on judicial review-type grounds,[15] to the CACD. In all cases it would only be available if there was no other adequate remedy (such as an existing statutory appeal) and the leave of the Crown Court would be required. It would be available to persons directly affected as well as to the defendant and, in some circumstances, the prosecution.

Appellate jurisdiction

1.23 With regard to the appellate jurisdiction, we proposed that the Criminal Appeal Act 1968 should be extended to allow an appeal, with leave, to the CACD from the Crown Court. We made associated proposals in relation to extending interlocutory prosecution appeals to cover cases being heard on appeal at the Crown Court, but removing the prosecution's right of appeal otherwise. We also made proposals in relation to rulings before the conclusion of the case.

First instance jurisdiction

1.24 With regard to the first instance jurisdiction of the Crown Court, the new statutory appeal would be available on different bases depending on the stage reached in the proceedings, whether before the jury had been sworn, after it had been sworn but before it had been discharged, or after it had been discharged.

1.25 The most generous regime applied after the jury had been discharged: this right of appeal would be available to any person directly affected by the order of the Crown Court.

1.26 The next most generous regime was that applying before the jury was sworn: it would be available to the defendant or a directly affected third party, but not the prosecution, and as well as showing that the grounds were made out, the appellant would have to show either that he or she would have no other adequate remedy or that, even if there was some remedy available, the potential advantages of permitting the appeal were such as to make it the right course.

1.27 The tightest regime applied after the jury had been sworn and before it had been discharged – broadly speaking, during trial. In this situation, the defendant or directly affected third party would have to show that the judicial review-type grounds were made out, that he or she would have no adequate remedy without the appeal, *and* that the ruling in question affected his or her liberty or was one which he or she alleged was unlawful because it contravened a right under the ECHR.

---

[15] In other words, not an appeal on the merits, but a challenge to the way in which the decision was made.

The response to CP 184

1.28 We list those whom we consulted at Appendix B to this report, and we are grateful to them for their help. We describe the response on consultation in detail in Parts 4 and 5 below but, in brief, consultees did not object to the removal of case stated as proposed, but some were concerned about the removal of judicial review as proposed, and all had serious concerns about the new statutory appeal that was proposed. The arguments put caused us to reconsider the proposals carefully. We concluded that we could not proceed with the new statutory appeal, nor remove judicial review of criminal proceedings in the Crown Court in all circumstances.

THIS REPORT

1.29 Part 6, where we set out the principles governing our recommendations, is the pivot between the CP proposals and the recommendations in this report. The policy decisions in this report represent a point of balance between the competing values, identified above, of: the need to avoid delay; the need to give effect to rights of third parties; and the need to ensure a fair trial. The recommendations are the outcome of this balancing exercise.

1.30 We set out our recommendations for reform in Parts 7 to 11, and we attach a Bill to the report which would give legislative effect to those recommendations. In this report we also draw out the implications of our recommendations for the High Court's criminal jurisdiction over the magistrates' courts (in Part 12), and over the Court Martial (in Part 13).

1.31 In Appendix C we collect together suggestions for improvements made to us by consultees which do not relate directly to our recommendations but which are worth pointing out. The Impact Assessment is Appendix D.

OUR RECOMMENDATIONS

1.32 We have concluded that appeal by case stated from the Crown Court in a criminal cause or matter should be abolished. The simplification of the routes of appeal from the Crown Court which this would bring about can be seen from the flow charts on pages 10 and 11 below.

1.33 We have also concluded that generally speaking, trials should not be interrupted by appeals or judicial review, but challenges to rulings made after the end of the trial do not risk interrupting trials, and do not run the same risk of delaying the conclusion of the proceedings. The objection to permitting a challenge by way of appeal or review is not as strong once the defendant has been sentenced or acquitted, or the trial has ended in some other way. Therefore, judicial review ought not to be permissible from the point a case is sent to the Crown Court for trial up to the end of the trial, but judicial review should be possible for rulings made after sentence or acquittal.

1.34 We recommend that section 29(3) of the SCA 1981 is amended accordingly.

1.35 This conclusion will allow, for example, a defendant who has been acquitted but refused an order for costs, to challenge that refusal by way of judicial review, which is not possible under the current law.

1.36   There are, however, three situations in which the potential harm cannot be undone by a post-trial appeal, an ECHR right is engaged, and the consequences of letting an unlawful decision go unchallenged justify delay and interruption to trial proceedings. They are:

(a) in some circumstances where bail is refused;

(b) where the ruling will lead to the identification of a child or young person in the trial; and

(c) where the ruling could lead to a real and immediate threat to a person's life.

1.37   In the case of the refusal of bail, we recommend that judicial review should be available to any defendant or witness who is remanded in custody and who has no other way in which to challenge the loss of liberty.

1.38   In situation (b) we recommend that there should be a new statutory appeal on the merits which can be exercised by the child or young person, with leave.

1.39   In situation (c) we recommend that there should be a new statutory appeal which can be exercised by the person whose life is threatened, with leave, and, if a person who is not a party can satisfy the court that the ruling or proposed ruling could lead to a real and immediate threat to his or her life, then the court should hear representations by him or her before making the ruling.

CURRENT STRUCTURE OF APPEALS IN THE CRIMINAL COURTS

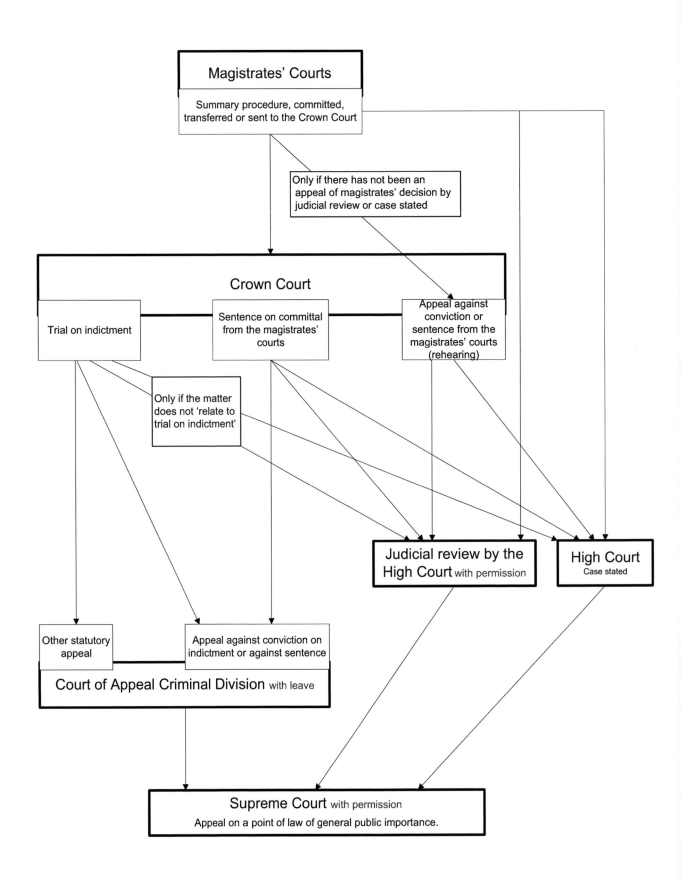

PROPOSED STRUCTURE OF APPEALS FROM CRIMINAL CASES IN THE CROWN COURT

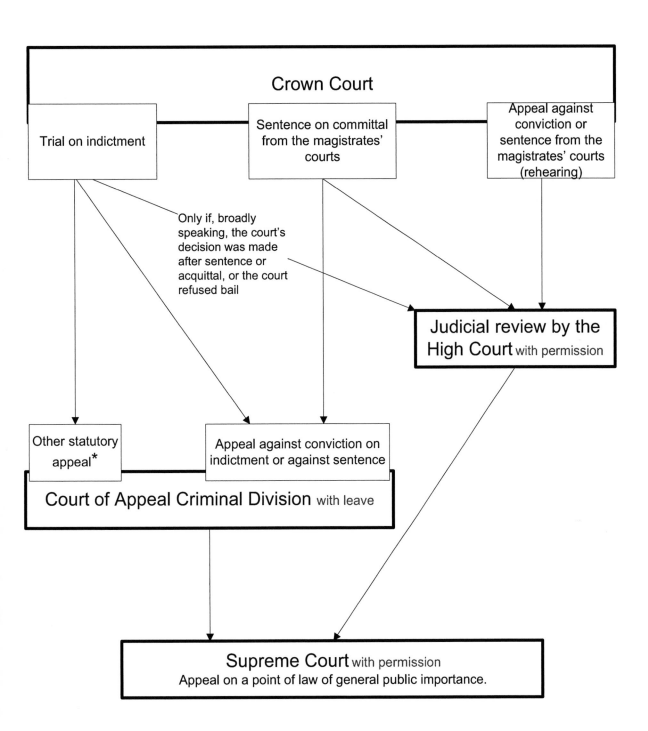

* 'Other statutory appeal' includes existing statutory appeals and the two new, specific, appeals recommended in Parts 10 and 11. Not all of these appeals can go to the Supreme Court.

PART 2
THE CURRENT LAW

2.1 This project is about the statutory provisions which permit and restrict appeal by way of case stated against, and judicial review of, a ruling by the Crown Court in criminal proceedings (sections 28 and 29(3) of the Senior Courts Act 1981 ("the SCA 1981")). These provisions cannot, however, be considered in isolation from other procedures which permit challenges to rulings of the Crown Court. (By "challenges" we mean judicial review as well as appeals.)

2.2 In Part 2 of CP 184 we gave a detailed description of the ways in which decisions can be challenged, including challenges to magistrates' decisions (a flowchart of the current structure of appeals in the criminal courts was included at page 59 of the CP). Here is a brief overview.

CHALLENGING DECISIONS OF THE MAGISTRATES' COURTS IN CRIMINAL MATTERS

2.3 A defendant who is convicted and sentenced in a magistrates' court has three potential avenues for challenging the conviction and/or sentence:

(1) an appeal to the Crown Court against conviction and/or sentence;

(2) an appeal to the High Court by way of case stated;

(3) an application to the High Court for judicial review.

Only the third of these requires leave of the court.

2.4 There is a significant difference between route (1) and routes (2) and (3). An appeal to the Crown Court is by way of rehearing; it may be on issues of law, fact, or both. By contrast, appeal by way of case stated and judicial review are challenges on issues of law, not of fact. An appeal to the High Court by way of case stated may be made on the grounds that the conviction and/or sentence "is wrong in law or in excess of jurisdiction". In judicial review proceedings, the High Court's function is to examine the magistrates' decision, not to retry the case (though it may receive evidence).

2.5 In contrast to a defendant who is challenging a conviction by a magistrates' court, the prosecution cannot seek to challenge an acquittal by appealing to the Crown Court. However, the prosecution can challenge the acquittal by:

(1) appealing to the High Court by case stated;

(2) (in limited circumstances) applying to the High Court for judicial review.

2.6 From the High Court, appeal lies only to the Supreme Court (whether on application by the prosecution or the defence). It is necessary to obtain leave of the Supreme Court or the High Court. Leave will not be granted unless the High Court certifies that a point of law of general public importance is involved in its decision and it appears to that Court or the Supreme Court that the point is one that ought to be considered by the Supreme Court. There is no appeal to the Court of Appeal (Criminal Division) ("CACD") from the High Court in this context.

CROWN COURT JURISDICTION

2.7 The Crown Court has jurisdiction in some civil matters. We are concerned only with its jurisdiction in criminal matters. In CP 184 we identified three jurisdictions of the Crown Court as particularly relevant to this project: (1) its appellate jurisdiction, (2) what we called its "first instance" jurisdiction, where it deals with a charge to be tried on indictment, and (3) its committal for sentence jurisdiction.

Appellate jurisdiction

2.8 A defendant convicted in the magistrates' court can appeal against conviction and/or sentence to the Crown Court.[1] When the Crown Court hears an appeal from a magistrates' court against conviction and/or sentence, the Crown Court is acting in its appellate capacity. The proceedings are by way of rehearing before a judge and justices of the peace and the trial is not on indictment.

2.9 In addition to a defendant's right to appeal to the Crown Court, the prosecution may have a specific right of appeal, as provided by, for example, section 147(3) of the Customs and Excise Management Act 1979,[2] and by section 14A(5A) of the Football Spectators Act 1989 which the prosecutor may rely on if the magistrates refuse to make a football banning order.

2.10 For other circumstances in which the Crown Court may be acting in an appellate capacity, see rule 63.1 of the Criminal Procedure Rules.

---

[1] Magistrates' Courts Act 1980, s 108.

[2] Which provides "In the case of proceedings in England or Wales, without prejudice to any right to require the statement of a case for the opinion of the High Court, the prosecutor may appeal to the Crown Court against any decision of a magistrates' court in proceedings for an offence under the customs and excise Acts."

On indictment

2.11 Proceedings on indictment may only be brought before the Crown Court and not before any other court, by virtue of section 46 of the SCA 1981. An offence may be on indictment because it may only be tried by way of indictment ("indictable only offences"), or because it could be tried summarily or on indictment and the decision has been made that it shall be tried on indictment ("either way offences").[3] The phrase "indictable offence" encompasses both indictable only offences and either way offences.[4] In addition, it exercises this jurisdiction in cases where a youth court has declined jurisdiction in relation to a child or young person. Where the Crown Court exercises its first instance jurisdiction, the trial is on indictment before a judge and jury.

Where a defendant is unfit to plead

2.12 A defendant who appears before the Crown Court in its trial on indictment jurisdiction may suffer from a disability such that it would be unfair for him or her to be tried in the usual way. When there is a question whether the defendant is fit to plead, the judge determines the issue.

2.13 If the judge determines that the defendant is fit to plead, the trial proceeds as a trial on indictment in the normal way. If a judge determines that the defendant is unfit to plead, the proceedings continue, and they are still criminal proceedings, but no longer a trial on indictment. Judicial review is therefore available under section 29(3) and appeal by way of case stated is available by virtue of section 28(1) of the SCA 1981. The trial is then of the question whether the defendant did the act or made the omission charged, pursuant to section 4A of the Criminal Procedure (Insanity) Act 1964.[5]

2.14 Until there has been a finding of unfitness, the case continues to fall within the trial on indictment jurisdiction.[6]

2.15 Very exceptionally, the Crown Court may make a hospital order for a defendant even though there has not been a finding that the defendant is unfit to plead and to be tried.[7] Such a hospital order can be challenged by way of judicial review.[8]

---

[3] If an offence may be tried on indictment or summarily, the court may have to go through the "mode of trial" procedures, by which it is decided where trial will take place.

[4] When dealing with indictable offences, the Crown Court may also deal with summary offences which have been sent or committed to it under ss 40 and 41 of the Criminal Justice Act 1988.

[5] *Grant* [2001] EWCA Crim 2611, [2002] QB 1030 – this was an appeal by way of case stated. See also *R (Young) v Central Criminal Court*, [2002] EWHC 548 (Admin), [2002] All ER 268, *R (Kenneally) v Crown Court at Snaresbrook* [2001] EWHC Admin 968, [2002] 2 WLR 1430, and *South West Yorkshire NHS Trust v Bradford Crown Court* [2003] EWHC 640 (Admin), [2003] All ER 411.

[6] See *Bradford Crown Court, ex parte Bottomley* [1994] Criminal Law Review 753 in which it was held that, where there had been a finding that the defendant was fit to plead, a refusal to hold a trial on the issue of fitness to plead was a matter relating to trial on indictment.

[7] Under s 51(5) of the Mental Health Act 1983.

[8] *R (Kenneally) v Crown Court at Snaresbrook* [2001] EWHC Admin 968, [2002] QB 1169.

Cases committed for sentence

2.16 Cases may be committed to the Crown Court by the magistrates' courts for sentencing where the defendant has been convicted following a trial or guilty plea in the magistrates' court.

CHALLENGING DECISIONS OF THE CROWN COURT

Challenging decisions of the Crown Court made in its appellate jurisdiction

2.17 Both the prosecution and the defence can challenge a ruling by

(1) appealing by way of case stated to the High Court on the basis that the ruling was wrong in law or in excess of jurisdiction under section 28 of the SCA 1981, or by

(2) applying to the High Court for judicial review under section 29(3) of the SCA 1981.

2.18 There is no appeal to the Court of Appeal available to either party. The rationale for this is that, by the conclusion of the appeal in the Crown Court, there have already been two hearings of the facts. If the magistrates made an error of law, that is irrelevant because the hearing starts afresh in the Crown Court. If the Crown Court made an error of law that may be challenged by going to the High Court (see paragraph 2.17 above).

Challenging decisions of the Crown Court made in its committal for sentence jurisdiction

2.19 The defendant may appeal against the sentence to the Court of Appeal, with leave. (This will be the first opportunity for appeal as no sentence will have been passed in the magistrates' court which committed the defendant to the Crown Court.) Appeal by way of case stated is possible, and judicial review may be entertained of a ruling prior to sentence, but such an application would be very rare.

Miscellaneous statutory rights of appeal

2.20 There are statutory rights of appeal to the CACD from the Crown Court in the following instances:

(1) against an order restricting or preventing reports of proceedings or restricting public access to proceedings;[9]

(2) by the prosecution against a failure or refusal to make a Football Banning Order;[10]

(3) against finding of and sentence for contempt of court;[11]

---

[9] Pursuant to s 159 of the Criminal Justice Act 1988.

[10] Pursuant to s 14A(5A) of the Football and Spectators Act 1989.

[11] Pursuant to s 13 of the Administration of Justice Act 1960.

(4)   against a restraining order made following a conviction or following an acquittal;[12]

(5)   against the making, variation or non-variation of a Serious Crime Prevention Order;[13]

(6)   for a third party against a third party costs order;[14] and

(7)   against a Wasted Costs Order.[15]

Where there is a finding of unfitness to plead or to be tried

2.21   Where a defendant is found unfit to plead, and there is also a finding that D did the act or made the omission,[16] the defendant may appeal to the CA against either or both of these findings under section 15 of the Criminal Appeal Act 1968 ("the CAA 1968").

2.22   If there is a finding that D did the act or made the omission, this is not a conviction. The court may make a hospital order or interim hospital order or a supervision order. The defendant then has a right of appeal to the CA against any of these orders under section 16A of the CAA 1968. The defendant needs leave from the CA or a certificate from the trial judge.

Challenging decisions of the Crown Court made in its trial on indictment jurisdiction

CHALLENGING CONVICTIONS, ACQUITTAL AND SENTENCE

2.23   The defendant can appeal against a conviction and/or sentence under the CAA 1968.[17] Leave must be obtained. The single ground for the Court of Appeal to quash a conviction is that the conviction is unsafe. There is no rehearing.

2.24   The prosecution can make an Attorney-General's reference in respect of a point of law where the defendant was acquitted.[18] The acquittal is unaffected, but the Court of Appeal then has the opportunity to settle the point of law for future cases.

---

[12] Pursuant to ss 5 and 5A respectively of the Protection from Harassment Act 1997.

[13] Pursuant to s 24 of the Serious Crime Act 2007.

[14] Pursuant to regulation 3H in Part IIB of the Costs in Criminal Cases (General) Regulations 1986 SI 1986 No 1335.

[15] Pursuant to regulation 3C in Part IIA of the Costs in Criminal Cases (General) Regulations 1986 SI 1986 No 1335.

[16] See para 2.13 above.

[17] The statutory right of appeal against sentence encompasses appeals against confiscation orders, against sentences which have been reviewed under s 74 of the Serious Organised Crime and Police Act 2005, and appeals by a parent or guardian of a defendant against a penalty imposed on the parent or guardian.

[18] Criminal Justice Act 1972, s 36.

2.25   In limited cases, the prosecution can apply to the Court of Appeal for an order quashing an acquittal and for a retrial under Part 10 of the Criminal Justice Act 2003 ("CJA 2003"). Part 10 is entitled "Retrial for Serious Offences" and concerns cases where, amongst other conditions, new and compelling evidence incriminating the acquitted person is available.

2.26   The prosecution can also challenge an unduly lenient sentence, with leave, by way of an Attorney-General's reference to the Court of Appeal.[19] The Court of Appeal may alter the sentence.

CHALLENGING PRE-VERDICT RULINGS

2.27   To explain the different ways in which a ruling of the Crown Court made before or during the course of a trial may be challenged, we need to set out something of pre-trial procedure.

Plea and Case Management Hearings

2.28   All cases tried on indictment are preceded by a Plea and Case Management Hearing ("PCMH"). They are held before a jury is empanelled. They do not constitute the start of the trial. At PCMHs the judge may make rulings. They are more usually concerned with management of the case (such as setting a timetable) and not the kind of ruling which would give rise to a challenge. They may, however, be the subject of a prosecution appeal under section 58 of the CJA 2003.[20]

Preparatory hearings

2.29   "Preparatory hearings" are confined to certain trials on indictment. The hearing, which must take place before the jury is sworn, marks the beginning of the trial. Unless he or she has previously done so, the defendant enters a plea to the charge at the start of the hearing.

2.30   A preparatory hearing must be held in a terrorism case.[21] It may be held in serious or complex fraud cases,[22] in cases to be heard without a jury,[23] and in complex, serious or lengthy cases,[24] provided that the judge is satisfied that: "substantial benefits" will accrue from holding the hearing "for one or more specified purposes".[25]

---

[19]   Criminal Justice Act 1988, s 36.

[20]   See paras 2.33 to 2.35 below.

[21]   Criminal Procedure and Investigations Act 1996, s 29(1B). "Terrorism offence" is defined in s 29(6).

[22]   Criminal Justice Act 1987, s 7(1).

[23]   Criminal Procedure and Investigations Act 1996, s 29(1A).

[24]   Criminal Procedure and Investigations Act 1996, s 29(1).

[25]   Criminal Justice Act 1987, s 7(1) and Criminal Procedure and Investigations Act 1996, s 29(2).

2.31   The preparatory hearing regime has its own appeal procedure. This procedure enables both the prosecution and the defendant, with leave, to appeal to the Court of Appeal against certain rulings and orders made by the judge in the course of a preparatory hearing. Pending the determination of the appeal, the judge can continue with the preparatory hearing, but no jury can be sworn until the appeal has been determined (or abandoned).

2.32   The case law on the interpretation of the specified purposes, on what rulings can be made as part of a preparatory hearing, and on which rulings may be appealed, is far from straightforward.

Section 58 appeals[26]

2.33   Section 58 of the CJA 2003 enables the prosecution to appeal to the Court of Appeal against judicial rulings made in trials on indictment (including at a preparatory hearing and a PCMH). Conditions in section 58 need to be complied with. There is no right of appeal unless the undertaking – that the defendant will be acquitted if the appeal is not successful – is given at the time and on the occasion prescribed in the statute.[27] If the prosecution is unsuccessful in its appeal the effect is to terminate the trial in respect of the offence in respect of which the appeal is made. Consequently the prosecution tend not to appeal under this section unless the ruling in question has the effect of leading to an acquittal. Such rulings are often referred to as "terminating rulings", but the phrase does not appear in the statute and the Court of Appeal has said the phrase should be avoided.[28]

2.34   The appeal under section 58 is, broadly speaking, for the kinds of ruling which formally end the trial, such as a ruling that there is no case to answer, or which have the de facto effect of terminating the trial. Seeking an Attorney-General's reference will allow an error of law to be corrected for future cases (see paragraph 2.24 above), but appealing under section 58 allows the instant prosecution to proceed if the Crown is successful.

2.35   There is provision in the CJA 2003 for a similar right of appeal in relation to evidentiary rulings, but this has not been brought into force.

Appeal against an order for trial without a jury of sample counts

2.36   An application for an order for trial without a jury of sample counts pursuant to section 17 of the Domestic Violence, Crime and Victims Act 2004 must be made at a preparatory hearing. An appeal against it may be made in the same way as an appeal against a ruling in a preparatory hearing.[29]

---

[26] This route of appeal followed on recommendations by the Law Commission in its report on Prosecution Appeals, Double Jeopardy and Prosecution Appeals (2001) Law Com No 267 Cm 5048.

[27] See *R v NT* [2010] EWCA Crim 711.

[28] *Y* [2008] EWCA Crim 10; [2008] 1 Cr App R 34 at [20].

[29] Domestic Violence, Crime and Victims Act 2004, s 18(5).

Appeal against an order for trial without a jury in cases of fraud and jury tampering

2.37 An application may be made for trial without a jury in serious and complex fraud cases or, put briefly, where jury tampering is likely to distort the trial, under sections 43 and 44 of the CJA 2003 respectively. Such applications must be made at a preparatory hearing, and appeals against orders for trial without a jury are to be made in the same way as appeals against rulings in preparatory hearings.

Appeal against an order that a trial is to continue without a jury due to jury tampering

2.38 If a judge becomes so concerned that there has been jury tampering that he or she decides to end the trial, he or she may order that the trial may continue without a jury or that a new trial without a jury shall take place.[30] In either event, there is a right of appeal against such an order to the CA, with leave of the judge or of the CA.[31]

APPEAL BY WAY OF CASE STATED AND JUDICIAL REVIEW

2.39 We noted above (paragraph 2.17) that case stated and judicial review are available for challenging rulings made by the Crown Court in its appellate jurisdiction. The circumstances in which these procedures are available to challenge rulings of the Crown Court in its trial on indictment jurisdiction are less certain.

2.40 With regard to case stated, jurisdiction is granted by section 28(1) of the SCA 1981, while a limitation on that jurisdiction is contained in subsection (2). Section 28(1) is headed "Appeals from Crown Court and inferior courts" and reads,

> (1) Subject to subsection (2), any order, judgment or other decision of the Crown Court may be questioned by any party to the proceedings, on the ground that it is wrong in law or is in excess of jurisdiction, by applying to the Crown Court to have a case stated by that court for the opinion of the High Court.

2.41 Subsection (2) provides:

> Subsection (1) shall not apply to −
>
> (a) a judgment or decision of the Crown Court relating to trial on indictment; or…

2.42 With regard to judicial review, the granting of jurisdiction and the limitation on that jurisdiction are all contained in the one provision, section 29(3) of the SCA 1981:

---

[30] Sections 46(3) and 46(5) respectively of the CJA 2003.

[31] Section 47 CJA 2003.

In relation to the jurisdiction of the Crown Court, other than its jurisdiction in matters relating to trial on indictment, the High Court shall have all such jurisdiction to make mandatory, prohibiting or quashing orders as the High Court possesses in relation to the jurisdiction of an inferior court.[32]

2.43 There is a helpful explanation of the relative positions of the High Court and the Crown Court in *R v Chelmsford Crown Court ex parte Chief Constable of Essex*:

> The argument is this: the power of this court [the High Court] to supervise by way of judicial review is exercisable over inferior courts and tribunals but not over superior courts. The Crown Court is a superior court of record[33] and therefore, as a general proposition, this court has no supervisory power in relation to the Crown Court exercising its jurisdiction.
>
> ...
>
> Sections 28 and 29(3) of the Supreme Court Act 1981 therefore expressly granted to this court powers which it would not otherwise have to supervise the decisions of the Crown Court in relation to matters there defined.... It is wrong... to regard s 29(3) as imposing a limitation. On the contrary, what ss 28 and 29(3) did was to grant to this court jurisdiction and powers which this court otherwise would not have had... .[34]

2.44 Thus, the High Court can entertain appeals by way of case stated and applications for judicial review in respect of decisions made by the Crown Court, even though the latter is a superior court of record, and it has thus a general jurisdiction to review decisions of the Crown Court when exercising its appellate jurisdiction, but it has no jurisdiction in relation to a decision made by the Crown Court when exercising its first instance jurisdiction if the decision is in *a matter relating to trial on indictment*.[35]

2.45 The exclusion in section 29(3) and 28(2) serves to avoid delay to trials, and interruption of trials. There is also the general view that satellite litigation in criminal proceedings is undesirable.[36]

---

[32] A similar, though not identical, provision covers rulings by Courts Martial. See Part 7 of CP 184.

[33] See s 1(1) Courts Act 1971 which became s 45(1) of the SCA 1981. (fn added)

[34] [1994] 1 All ER 325, 333 to 334: submissions by counsel acting as amicus curiae which were accepted by Glidewell LJ at 336.

[35] In *R v DPP ex p Kebilene* [2000] 2 AC 236 counsel identified a presumption in the common law against permitting judicial review in criminal cases where a point may be pursued within the ordinary criminal trial and appeal processes, although the court was cautious in what it said about the presumption. See [2000] 2 AC 236, 370 to 371. See also *R (Securiplan Plc) v Security Industry Authority* [2008] EWHC 1762 (Admin), [2009] 2 All ER 211, [23] to [24].

[36] See Lord Steyn's comments in *R v DPP ex parte Kebilene* [2000] 2 AC 236, 371.

Interpretation in the case law of section 29(3)

2.46 The exclusions in sections 29(3) and 28(2) are in almost identical terms. Almost all the case law has been on the interpretation of section 29(3). Section 28, and the reforms of it which we seek, is discussed more fully in Part 7 below.

2.47 The exclusionary bar applies only to decisions of the Crown Court; it does not affect the High Court's jurisdiction over other bodies, tribunals or courts.[37]

The "pointers"

2.48 The case law provides various "pointers" to interpretation of section 29(3). The pointers indicate that review of a decision should be excluded if the decision:

> affected the conduct of the trial in any way;[38]

> was an integral part of the trial process;[39]

> was an issue arising between the Crown and defendant formulated by the indictment;[40]

> was not truly collateral to the trial;[41] or

> is in substance the answer to some issue between the prosecution and the defence arising during a trial on indictment.[42]

2.49 The fullest recent explanation of the scope of section 29(3) is that given by Lord Browne-Wilkinson in *R v Manchester Crown Court, ex parte DPP*, which concerned the quashing of an indictment. He said,

---

[37] See Laws LJ in the Divisional Court decision in *R v DPP ex p Kebilene* [1999] 4 All ER 801, 819, and Lord Steyn at [2000] 2 AC 326, 369.

[38] *Re Smalley* [1985] AC 622, 642 to 643 by Lord Bridge, and *Re Ashton* [1994] 1 AC 9, 20 by Lord Slynn.

[39] *Re Sampson* [1987] 1 WLR 194, 196 to 198 by Lord Bridge.

[40] *R v Manchester Crown Court, ex p DPP* [1993] 1 WLR 1524, 1530 by Lord Browne-Wilkinson.

[41] *R v Manchester Crown Court, ex p DPP* [1993] 1 WLR 1524, 1530 by Lord Browne-Wilkinson.

[42] *R v DPP, ex p Kebilene* [2000] 2 AC 326, 394 by Lord Hobhouse.

With one possible exception (to which I will return) the only decisions of the Crown Court which have been held to be reviewable are those in which either the order was made under a wholly different jurisdiction eg binding over an acquitted defendant (*R v Inner London Crown Court, Ex parte Benjamin* (1986) 85 Cr App R 267) or the order sought to be reviewed has been made against someone other than the defendant. Thus the Divisional Court has been held to have jurisdiction to review decisions estreating a recognisance given by a third party (*Smalley*), ordering solicitors to pay costs thrown away (*per* Megaw LJ in *R v Smith (Martin)* [1975] QB 531, 544–545, approved by Lord Bridge in *In re Smalley* [1985] AC 622, 644) for an order forfeiting a motor car belonging to someone other than the defendant which had been used by the defendant in the course of drug dealing: *Reg v Maidstone Crown Court, Ex parte Gill* [1986] 1 WLR 1405. It may therefore be a helpful further pointer to the true construction of the section to ask the question, "Is the decision sought to be reviewed one arising in the issue between the Crown and the defendant formulated by the indictment (including the costs of such issue)?" If the answer is "Yes," then to permit the decision to be challenged by judicial review may lead to delay in the trial: the matter is therefore probably excluded from review by the section. If the answer is "No," the decision of the Crown Court is truly collateral to the indictment of the defendant and judicial review of that decision will not delay his trial: therefore it may well not be excluded by the section.[43]

Difficulties with the interpretation of section 29(3)

2.50 As we stated in CP 184, the interpretation in the case law has been problematic. Even the "pointers" given by the House of Lords have not always helped the courts: in *Lipinski*[44] Mr Justice Stanley Burnton thought that the pointers went in opposing directions. He said that in *Smalley*[45] the pointer tended to indicate "that matters of procedure, as well as substance, are within the expression",[46] but Lord Browne-Wilkinson's formulation in *DPP v Manchester Crown Court*[47] "would seem to indicate that procedural matters might be outside the exclusion".[48]

2.51 The law has developed on a case by case by case basis within the parameters of the "pointers" expressed by the House of Lords. The following are matters that have been held to relate to trial on indictment and, therefore, are not reviewable:

---

[43] *R v Manchester Crown Court, ex parte DPP* [1993] 1 WLR 1524, 1530.

[44] [2005] EWHC 1950 (Admin), [2005] All ER 62.

[45] [1985] AC 622.

[46] *R (Lipinski) v Wolverhampton Crown Court* [2005] EWHC 1950 (Admin), [2005] All ER 62 at [11].

[47] [1993] 1 WLR 1524.

[48] *R (Lipinski) v Wolverhampton Crown Court* [2005] EWHC 1950 (Admin), [2005] All ER 62 at [13].

(1)   a refusal to award an acquitted defendant his or her costs out of central funds;[49]

(2)   a refusal to award costs in respect of costs incurred as a result of an unnecessary or improper act or omission by, or on behalf of, another party to the proceedings;[50]

(3)   an order discharging a jury;[51]

(4)   an order in relation to the taking of steps to vet a jury panel;[52]

(5)   an order that an indictment lie on the file marked "not to be proceeded with without leave";[53]

(6)   the refusal of a Crown Court judge to grant legal aid;[54]

(7)   the decision of a Crown Court judge to order a defence solicitor personally to pay the costs occasioned by the granting of a defence application for an adjournment;[55]

(8)   a refusal to fix a date for trial until a certain event occurred, such as the trial of another matter;[56]

(9)   a decision to quash an indictment for want of jurisdiction to try an offence;[57]

(10)   an order to stay criminal proceedings on the grounds of abuse of process;[58]

(11)   an order refusing to stay criminal proceedings on the grounds of abuse of process;[59]

(12)   the issue of a witness summons under section 2(1) of the Criminal Procedure (Attendance of Witnesses) Act 1965;[60]

---

[49] *Re Meredith* [1973] 1 WLR 435, *R v Canterbury Crown Court, ex parte Regentford Ltd* [2000] All ER 2415, and *R v Harrow Crown Court ex parte Perkins* (1998) 162 Justice of the Peace 527. See CP 184, paras 3.13, 3.17 to 3.19, and 5.36.

[50] *R (Commissioners for Customs and Excise) v Leicester Crown Court* [2001] EWHC Admin 33.

[51] *Ex parte Marlowe* [1973] Criminal Law Review 294.

[52] *R v Sheffield Crown Court ex parte Brownlow* [1980] QB 530.

[53] *Ex parte Raymond* [1986] 1 WLR 710.

[54] *Ex parte Abodunrin* (1984) 79 Cr App Rep 293. See CP 184, para 5.79.

[55] *Smith* [1975] QB 531. However, see now s 50(3) of the Solicitors Act 1974.

[56] *Ex parte Ward* [1996] Criminal Law Review 123.

[57] *R v Manchester Crown Court ex parte DPP* [1993] 1 WLR 1524.

[58] *Re Ashton* [1994] 1 AC 9. See CP 184, para 2.102(9) and 5.23.

[59] *R (Salubi) v Bow Street Magistrates' Court* [2002] EWHC 919, [2002] 1 WLR 3073.

[60] *Ex parte Rees, The Times* 7 May 1986.

(13) a decision pursuant to section 4(3) of the Criminal Procedure (Attendance of Witnesses) Act 1965 to remand a witness in custody until such time as the court may appoint for receiving his or her evidence;[61]

(14) a refusal to grant a further extension of time in which to prefer a bill of indictment;[62]

(15) a legal aid contribution order made at the conclusion of a trial;[63]

(16) a decision not to dismiss a charge which had been sent for trial under section 51 of the Crime and Disorder Act 1998;[64]

(17) a decision not to allow an individual to appear in person as the prosecutor;[65]

(18) refusal of a representation order by the Crown Court for a confiscation hearing following a defendant's conviction on indictment,[66]

(19) the failure to make a compensation order by reason of error of law,[67] or

(20) the designation of a local authority as the supervising authority in the course of sentencing.[68]

[61] *R (TH) v Wood Green Crown Court* [2006] EWHC 2683 (Admin), [2007] 1 WLR 1670. See CP 184, paras 2.102(12), 3.14 and 5.58.

[62] *R v Isleworth Crown Court, ex parte King* [1992] COD 298.

[63] *Re Sampson* [1987] 1 WLR 194. Lord Bridge also stated (at 198) that "any other order with regard to costs which the Crown Court may make at the conclusion of a trial on indictment" relates to trial on indictment and cannot be challenged.

[64] *R (Snelgrove) v Woolwich Crown Court* [2004] EWHC 2172 (Admin), [2005] 1 WLR 3223; *R (O) v Central Criminal Court* [2006] EWHC 256 (Admin), [2006] All ER 201. Subsequently, the Court of Appeal has held that a decision to dismiss a charge sent for trial under s 51 cannot be appealed by the prosecution to the Court of Appeal under s 58 of the CJA 2003: *Thompson and Hanson* [2006] EWCA Crim 2849, [2007] 1 ELR 1123. The prosecution's remedy is to prefer a voluntary bill of indictment. See CP 184, para 2.102(15), and paras 8.13 to 8.15 below.

[65] *R v Southwark Crown Court ex parte Tawfick* (1995) 7 Admin Law Review 410.

[66] *R (Ludlam) v Leicester Crown Court* [2008] EWHC 2884 (Admin).

[67] *R (Faithfull) v Ipswich Crown Court* [2007] EWHC 2763 (Admin), [2008] 1 WLR 1636.

[68] *R (Kirklees Metropolitan Council) v Preston Crown Court* [2001] EWHC Admin 510, [2001] All ER 308.

2.52 It does not necessarily follow that a mode of challenge ought to be available in all the above cases, but it is not always easy to see why judicial review is not available in those cases, but is available in respect of the following matters:

(1) an order for forfeiture of a surety's recognizance for bail where a defendant failed to surrender to his trial at the Crown Court;[69]

(2) a forfeiture order under section 27 of the Misuse of Drugs Act 1971 made against the owner of property who was not a defendant in the criminal proceedings;[70]

(3) an order committing an acquitted defendant to prison unless he agrees to be bound over;[71]

(4) following conviction, orders made under section 39 of the Children and Young Persons Act 1933 to protect the anonymity of a child who was a defendant in the proceedings or an order discharging such an order;[72]

(5) an order that a defendant convicted on indictment whose legal representation was publicly funded should pay some or all of the costs of his or her representation;[73]

(6) a bail decision "at an early stage of criminal proceedings";[74]

(7) a bail decision following conviction;[75]

(8) a decision as to the manner in which the Crown Court deals with an application for bail (for example, whether or not to sit in public);[76]

(9) decisions and orders made following a finding of unfitness to plead;[77]

(10) a decision or order made without jurisdiction;[78]

---

[69] *Re Smalley* [1985] AC 622.

[70] *R v Maidstone Crown Court ex parte Gill* [1986] 1 WLR 1405. See CP 184, paras 2.103(2) and 5.38.

[71] *R v Inner London Crown Court ex parte Benjamin* [1987] 85 Cr App Rep 267. See CP 184, paras 2.103(3) and 5.36.

[72] *R v Manchester Crown Court ex parte H* [2000] 1 WLR 760. See para 10.24 below.

[73] *Patel* [2005] EWCA Crim 977. See CP 184, para 2.103(5).

[74] *R (M) v Isleworth Crown Court and Her Majesty's Customs and Excise* [2005] EWHC 363 (Admin), [2005] All ER 42. See CP 184, para 2.103(6) and 2.109.

[75] *R (Galliano) v Manchester Crown Court* [2005] EWHC 1125 (Admin), [2005] EWHC 1125; *R (Groves) v Newcastle Crown Court* [2008] EWHC 3123 (Admin).

[76] *R (Malik) v Central Crown Court and another* [2006] EWHC 1539 (Admin), [2006] 4 All ER 1141. See CP 184, para 2.103(7).

[77] *R v H, R v M, R v Kerr* [2001] EWCA Crim 2024, [2002] 1 WLR 824 at [17]; *R v Grant* [2001] EWCA Crim 2611, [2002] QB 1030 at [10]. See CP 184, para 2.103(8).

[78] *R v Maidstone Crown Court, ex parte Harrow London Borough Council* [2000] QB 719. See CP 184, paras 2.103(9) and 2.112.

(11)   the refusal of a judge to recuse himself on hearing a wasted costs application;[79] and

(12)   a third party application for a declaration.[80]

[79]   *R (AB) v X Crown Court* [2009] EWHC 1149 (Admin), [2009] All ER 230.

[80]   *R (TB) v The Combined Court at Stafford* [2006] EWHC 1645 (Admin), [2007] 1 WLR 1524. See CP 184, paras 2.103(10) and 2.126.

PART 3
THE CONSULTATION PAPER PROPOSALS

3.1 The complexity of the current possibilities for appeal and review are evident from the description of the current law in the previous Part. The overall objectives of the proposals were to clarify and simplify the routes of appeal/review and to provide a new means of appeal to prevent breaches of rights under the European Convention on Human Rights.

REMOVE CASE STATED AND JUDICIAL REVIEW

3.2 The general thrust of the proposals was to remove case stated and judicial review for criminal matters in the Crown Court and to provide new means of statutory appeal to the CACD.

3.3 We proposed a wholly new statutory appeal, as described at paragraphs 3.5 to 3.10 below. As regards the appellate jurisdiction of the Crown Court, we also proposed extending some existing statutory rights of appeal to the CA as described at paragraphs 3.11 to 3.19 below.

JUDICIAL REVIEW AND THE FIRST INSTANCE JURISDICTION

3.4 We thought that repealing section 29(3) and thus removing the possibility of judicial review in relation to the whole of the first instance jurisdiction was too simplistic a solution. We concluded that "the Court of Appeal will require a means of performing the role, whether or not enhanced, that the High Court currently performs when it hears applications for judicial review of decisions and rulings made by the Crown Court when exercising its first instance jurisdiction".[1] We thought there were instead two options: giving the power to the CA to hear all applications for judicial review which would currently be heard by the High Court, or creating a new statutory appeal to the CA, based on judicial review principles. We thought the second of these was to be preferred, and so we developed the proposed new statutory appeal in the CP to replace judicial review in criminal proceedings.

THE NEW STATUTORY APPEAL

3.5 The new statutory appeal was to have the following features:

It would not be available in respect of any conviction, acquittal or sentence, nor for any ruling for which a statutory right of appeal already existed.

An appellant would have to obtain the leave of the Crown Court.

It was not a simple merits-based appeal, but was to be available only if the ruling in question was:

wrong in law;

involved a serious procedural or other irregularity; or

---

[1] Para 4.53 of CP 184.

was one that no competent and reasonable tribunal could properly have made.[2]

The CA was to have the power to confirm, reverse or vary the ruling or remit it to the Crown Court with its opinion.

The new statutory appeal and the first instance jurisdiction

3.6 The basis on which the new statutory appeal could be made would differ depending on one of three different stages reached in the proceedings: (1) whether before the jury had been sworn, (2) after it had been sworn but before it had been discharged, or (3) after it had been discharged.

3.7 We also put before consultees the possibility of using a different cut-off point: instead of the swearing of the jury, using the point on or after the day on which the trial proper was listed to start.

After the jury had been discharged

3.8 The most generous regime applied after the jury had been discharged: this right of appeal would be available to any person directly affected by the order of the Crown Court (including the prosecution as well as third parties).

Before the jury was sworn

3.9 The next most generous regime was that applying before the jury was sworn: it was to be available to the defendant or a directly affected third party, but not the prosecution. As well as showing that the grounds were made out, the appellant would have to show either that he or she would have no other adequate remedy or that, even if there was some remedy available, the potential advantages of permitting the appeal were such as to make it the right course.

After the jury was sworn but before it was discharged

3.10 The most restrictive regime applied after the jury had been sworn and before it had been discharged – broadly speaking, during trial. In this situation, the defendant or directly affected third party would have to show that the judicial review-type grounds were made out, that he or she would have no adequate remedy without the appeal, *and* that the ruling in question affected his or her liberty or was one which was unlawful because it contravened a right ("a Convention Right") under the European Convention on Human Rights (ECHR). Again, this regime was not going to benefit the prosecution.

THE CROWN COURT'S APPELLATE JURISDICTION

3.11 With regard to the appellate jurisdiction, we proposed that the CAA 1968 should be extended to allow an appeal by the defendant, with leave, to the CACD from the Crown Court. This route of appeal would replace case stated and judicial review in relation to the appellate jurisdiction.

---

[2] What we call "judicial review-type grounds".

3.12   The effect would be that appeals against conviction and/or sentence following a rehearing at the Crown Court would be heard by Lord Justices of Appeal instead of the High Court, and that the basis on which a defendant could appeal against sentence would be slightly relaxed. The appeal to the CA would require the leave of the CA.

Appeals by the prosecution

3.13   The appeal to the CA which we proposed was also to be available to the prosecution against "perverse guilty" verdicts following a rehearing, and against acquittals which resulted from court rulings. Again, this route of appeal would replace case stated and judicial review. It would have required the leave of the CA, and would have resulted in the issue coming before the CA instead of the High Court.

3.14   The appeal to the CA which we proposed would not permit the prosecution to appeal against acquittal following the rehearing at the Crown Court (except where it followed a "terminating ruling"). In that respect, the proposals reduced the rights of appeal available to the prosecution. We proposed instead that the Attorney-General should be able to refer a point of law to the CA, as it can do following an acquittal at a trial on indictment, and that section 36 of the Criminal Justice Act 1972 should be extended accordingly.

3.15   The appeal to the CA which we proposed would also not permit the prosecution to appeal against a sentence following a rehearing, which it may currently do by way of case stated.

The new statutory appeal and the appellate jurisdiction

3.16   We proposed that the new statutory appeal should be available in respect of rulings made by the Crown Court in its appellate jurisdiction along similar lines to the proposals for the appeal and the first instance jurisdiction.

3.17   It was to have the same common features as described above (paragraph 3.5).

Before the determination of an appeal by way of rehearing

3.18   A defendant or directly affected third party would be able to appeal (with leave) if he or she could show that the judicial review-type grounds were made out, that there would be no adequate remedy without the appeal, *and* that the ruling in question affected his or her liberty or was one which was unlawful because it contravened a Convention right.

After the determination of an appeal by way of rehearing

3.19   Any person directly affected by a ruling would be able to appeal on the judicial review-type grounds, subject to obtaining leave and to there being no other statutory appeal available.

DISCUSSION OF THE IMPLICATIONS FOR THE COURT MARTIAL AND MAGISTRATES' COURTS

3.20 We did not make any provisional proposals in relation to magistrates' courts and the Court Martial. However, in accordance with our terms of reference, we outlined the implications of our proposals in relation for decisions of the Crown Court for both magistrates' courts and the Court Martial.

CONSULTATION

3.21 Thirteen written responses to the CP were received and we also held meetings with various consultees (see Appendix B). We very much appreciate the time and thought consultees gave to the problem.

PART 4
THE RESPONSE OF CONSULTEES (1): THE CROWN COURT IN ITS APPELLATE JURISDICTION

4.1 Some of the proposals in the CP were about the appellate jurisdiction of the Crown Court. The difficulties which consultees identified in those particular proposals affect the CP proposals as a whole. This is because some consultees doubted that the proposed scheme was "worth the candle", and if the proposals on appellate jurisdiction are removed, that argument is even stronger. We therefore discuss the proposals relating to the appellate jurisdiction in this Part, before considering the proposed new statutory appeal in the round in the next Part.

SUMMARY OF THE PROPOSALS IN THE CONSULTATION PAPER

4.2 We provisionally proposed abolishing appeal by case stated and judicial review as means of challenging decisions made by the Crown Court in criminal proceedings, including decisions made when exercising its appellate jurisdiction. We proposed that appeals against conviction or sentence should, broadly speaking, be made to the CACD in the same way as appeals against conviction or sentence resulting from a trial on indictment. Where the judge made a ruling which was not susceptible to appeal in that way, the defendant or a directly affected third party would be able to make use of the proposed new statutory form of appeal.

A SIGNIFICANT BACKGROUND DEVELOPMENT

4.3 It is appropriate at this point to recall part of the context in which this reference came to the Commission. Eminent judges had referred to the difficulties in interpreting section 29(3) of the SCA 1981 and their views inspired the reference, but another important part of the background was Lord Justice Auld's review of the criminal courts. He looked at the system as a whole and recommended streamlining the criminal process. He would have preferred to see only one route of appeal from the "Magistrates' Division" (magistrates' court), to a judge only at the Crown Division (Crown Court), subject to permission. From the Crown Division, appeal would lie to the Court of Appeal.[1] He also recommended that the only appeal from the Crown Division acting in its appellate capacity should be to the Court of Appeal (with permission and only in special circumstances), removing case stated and judicial review.

---

[1] Auld LJ, *Review of the Criminal Courts of England and Wales* (September 2001) ch12, para 30.

4.4   One of the difficulties with the proposals in the CP to remove case stated and judicial review in respect of the Crown Court's appellate jurisdiction and to extend the CAA 1968 instead, is that, without Lord Justice Auld's recommendations as regards magistrates' courts being effected, the result would be to introduce an *additional* layer of appeal. Such a result would be contrary to one of the principles which Lord Justice Auld adopted, "that only one level of appeal should be the norm",[2] and also to one of the aims of this project, namely, to simplify the appeals process.

4.5   This warrants further explanation: Lord Justice Auld envisaged one route of appeal from the magistrates – to the Crown Division – and a limited means of challenge thereafter. Lord Justice Auld recommended that the defendant's right of appeal to the Crown Court from the magistrates by way of rehearing should be abolished and replaced by a right of appeal, with leave, to the Crown Court constituted by a judge sitting alone on the ground that the conviction was unsafe.[3] The proposals in the CP would, necessarily,[4] leave in place all three existing routes of challenge to magistrates' cases – judicial review, case stated and appeal by way of rehearing – and provide in addition a route of appeal (with leave) to the CACD on the ground that the conviction was unsafe, a *less* limited basis than is currently possible.

GENERAL RESPONSE ON CONSULTATION

4.6   We asked consultees whether they thought the new statutory appeal and the extended appeal rights we proposed in place of judicial review and case stated would be an adequate substitute for case stated and judicial review.[5]

4.7   The Law Reform Committee of the Bar Council did not wish to see judicial review abolished for criminal proceedings of the Crown Court, in this context or any other.

4.8   The OCJR and the CPS were concerned that, as regards the appellate jurisdiction, the proposals entailed reducing the options for challenge open to the prosecution. They thought rather that the prosecution should be able to challenge acquittal and sentence.

4.9   Master Venne, Registrar of Criminal Appeals and Master of the Crown Office, agreed with this aspect of the proposals in relation to convictions, with some reservations, but not in relation to sentence, and we now turn to that important issue.

---

[2]   Auld LJ, *Review of the Criminal Courts of England and Wales* (September 2001) ch12, para 37.

[3]   This recommendation was not accepted by the Government.

[4]   Because magistrates' courts are outside our remit.

[5]   We discuss case stated in Part 7 below.

APPEAL AGAINST SENTENCE

By the defendant

4.10   Under the current law, a defendant in any of the following categories may, subject to obtaining leave or on certificate from the Crown Court,[6] appeal to the Court of Appeal against the sentence imposed. The categories are:

(1)   one who is convicted in a trial on indictment;[7]

(2)   one who is sentenced by the Crown Court having been committed to that court for sentence by the magistrates' court;[8] or

(3)   one who is dealt with by the Crown Court for breach of an earlier sentence, such as a conditional discharge or a suspended sentence.[9]

4.11   An appeal may succeed if:

the sentence is not justified by law;

the sentence has been passed on the wrong factual basis;

irrelevant matters have been taken into account or relevant matters have not been taken into account; or

the sentence is manifestly excessive or wrong in principle.

Following an appeal by way of rehearing in the Crown Court

4.12   Defendants whose cases are originally heard in the magistrates' court do not, under the current law, have access to the Court of Appeal as just described. A defendant who is sentenced by the Crown Court when exercising its appellate jurisdiction may not appeal against the sentence to the Court of Appeal.[10] A defendant wishing to appeal against such a sentence must apply to the High Court for judicial review or appeal to the High Court by case stated on the grounds that the sentence "is wrong in law or is in excess of jurisdiction".[11] This is a more demanding test to satisfy than having to show that a sentence is "manifestly excessive".

4.13   Our proposal was to move all appeals from the High Court to the CACD, extending the Criminal Appeal Act 1968. Thus one effect of the proposal would be a slight change in the test applicable to defendants challenging sentences by the Crown Court in its appellate jurisdiction, the change being in the defendant's favour.

---

[6]   Criminal Appeal Act 1968, s 11(1) and 11(1A).

[7]   CAA 1968, s 9.

[8]   CAA 1968, s 10(2)(a) and (3).

[9]   CAA 1968, s 10(2)(b) and (3).

[10]   CAA 1968, s 10(1).

[11]   SCA 1981, s 28(1).

Comments by consultees

4.14 Master Venne disagreed with the proposals to extend the CAA 1968 in relation to sentence appeals. He said:

> It seems to me that there is a real possibility that we would have a lot of sentence appeals from the Crown Court sitting in its appellate jurisdiction. My particular concerns are driving matters especially drink driving and "totting" procedures. It is also right that the magistrates' courts deal with a very wide range of offences – tacographs, axle weights etc. It is not appropriate in my view that the CACD should be required to deal with the minutiae of these offences. Moreover the lawyers in the Criminal Appeal Office would need to have the kind of extensive knowledge that magistrates' court legal advisers have in relation to summary offences and their sentences. The right to an appeal against sentence to the CACD would amount to a third bite of the cherry.

4.15 Another consultee also referred to this last point. He questioned the wisdom of the proposals that allowed for an appeal against a sentence passed by the Crown Court when exercising its appellate jurisdiction. His view was that this would only serve to permit a convicted defendant to have a second go at securing a reduction in sentence (putting a defendant who had been convicted in the magistrates' court in a better position than one convicted in the Crown Court).

4.16 We find these arguments persuasive. Whereas at present the High Court has only a supervisory jurisdiction over sentences imposed following a rehearing, under the provisional proposals the defendant would have a right to have the sentence reconsidered subject only to the requirement to obtain leave.

4.17 The Criminal Appeal Office noted that, particularly in driving matters, it was highly likely that defendants would appeal sentence if they thought there was any chance of avoiding a disqualification, for example. It could be anticipated that there would be a fair number of such appeals,[12] and defendants would also be quite likely to appeal against a refusal of leave.

4.18 The Criminal Appeal Office also made the important point that sentences imposed by the appellate Crown Court are bound to be short, and therefore, for an appeal against sentence to be worthwhile, it would have to be heard urgently, and that would have a knock-on effect on other work of the CACD. If the list is disturbed in order to deal with an urgent case, cases which were expected to be heard are delayed, extra administrative work is created by the need to redraw the list, and work is duplicated as those preparing for one list of cases will need to re-read the material when those delayed cases are finally heard.

---

[12] In 2006, there were 160,664 disqualifications ordered by magistrates' courts for all motor vehicle related offences. In the Crown Court, there were 5,744 disqualifications ordered. See tables 13 and 14 at pages 37 and 38 in R Fiti, D Perry, W Giraud and M Ayres, *Offences Relating to Motor Vehicles, England and Wales 2006, Supplementary Tables*, Office for Criminal Justice Reform (Ministry of Justice) (April 2008). Accessed at http://www.justice.gov.uk/about/docs/offences-relating-to-motor-vehicles-2006-ii.pdf (last visited 9 March 2010). We have been unable to locate data stating the specific number of appeals from a disqualification order.

4.19 A further concern was the possibility of any increase in applications for leave needing to be heard by Court of Appeal judges. The provisional proposal envisaged a requirement to obtain leave from the Court of Appeal, as for appeals against conviction or sentence on indictment. The acute point of the process in criminal appeals is the leave stage. There are too few judges available to deal with applications for leave. Any increase at all in this workload would put undue pressure on the staff and judges, and would have to be resourced[13] (which is unlikely: see, for example the OCJR's comments on costs at paragraph 5.50 below).

4.20 If we accept the points made by consultees, in particular by those who process criminal appeals, then it seems that this aspect of our proposals must be abandoned. If this is so, then one of the advantages of our proposals – that they would streamline the criminal appeals procedures – is weakened.

4.21 A further consequence is that, if a challenge to sentence imposed after rehearing is not transferred to the CACD, then there is far less purpose in transferring appeals against conviction to the CACD: a defendant might wish to appeal against both the conviction at the Crown Court and the sentence, and it would not make sense to have to pursue two separate routes of appeal simultaneously.

APPEAL AGAINST CONVICTION FOLLOWING REHEARING AT THE CROWN COURT

4.22 We proposed removing the possibilities of appeal by way of judicial review and case stated, and providing for appeals against conviction, following appeal at the Crown Court, to be dealt with by the Court of Appeal.[14] The effect of our proposals was that all such matters would be heard by the CACD and not by the High Court.

4.23 The current grounds on which a defendant may appeal against a conviction following a rehearing are traditional judicial review grounds or, if applying by way of case stated, that the conviction was wrong in law or in excess of jurisdiction.[15] Switching the route of challenge to the Court of Appeal, and aligning the appeal with appeals against conviction after trial on indictment, would mean the basis of the challenge was that the conviction was "unsafe".[16]

4.24 Tony Edwards and the CPS agreed with these proposals. The Law Reform Committee of the Bar Council was content to see case stated abolished but thought judicial review should remain. The OCJR supported the principle of moving appeals against conviction from the High Court to the CACD, and agreed with the proposal to that extent, but wanted to see prosecution and third party rights of challenge preserved.

4.25 Master Venne commented that the Court of Appeal:

[13] As well as the direct costs there would be the additional judicial time that would have to be made available: each application for leave considered on the papers might take between 30 and 60 minutes of a judge's time.

[14] Proposals 8.1, 8.5 and 8.6.

[15] See para 2.17 above.

[16] CAA 1968, s 2.

would require a reasoned judgement akin to a summing up (reminding themselves of the law, their powers and the evidence) in order to enable this Court to see how the decision was made. This could potentially result in an increase in the work of Crown Court judges.

4.26 Such an increase in workload would not be welcomed. If a reasoned judgment were only required after leave to appeal had been given, that would mean a delay between the case being heard at the Crown Court and the judgment being put in a form suitable for the Court of Appeal, with the concomitant difficulties. If it were required in order for the leave decision to be made, then it would be required in a large number of cases. To give an idea of the number of cases, we note that between 2000 and 2007 the Crown Court received between 4,480 and 5,821 appeals against verdict in the magistrates' court. Of those, between 1,390 and 1,840 were unsuccessful.[17] We cannot say what proportion of those defendants might seek leave to appeal against the dismissal of their appeal.

Leave for an appeal from a rehearing

4.27 If there is a rehearing in the Crown Court from a magistrates' court trial and a defendant is convicted again, under the current law he or she does not need leave to state a case (though the Crown Court might refuse to state a case if it thinks the appeal wholly ill-founded). We proposed that leave should be required.[18] While this entails a new stage in the case which would not otherwise have been required for some cases, the imposition of a leave requirement may mean that some appeals which would have had to be heard under the case stated route would not be heard because they would not be granted leave. Those consultees who commented were content with this suggestion.

4.28 We put forward for consultees' consideration the possibility of an enhanced leave requirement where a person is appealing a conviction where the Crown Court was exercising its appellate jurisdiction.[19] We did not ourselves favour the enhanced leave requirement. The CPS was the only respondent who did favour it. Tony Edwards thought it would introduce an unnecessary complication, as did the OCJR.

4.29 Master Venne thought it arguable that the test should be the same as in appeals from the Crown Court in its trial jurisdiction. This is because appeals heard by the Crown Court start afresh – proceeding by way of rehearing – and so the issues may not be the same as the issues at the original trial.

4.30 We therefore conclude that, if this proposal were pursued, there would be no need for an enhanced leave requirement, as it would only be an unnecessary complication.

---

[17] See table 6.10 of *Judicial and Court Statistics 2007* (September 2008) Cm 7467. See, however, table 6.1 of *Judicial and Court Statistics 2008* (September 2009) Cm 7697, which gives a different picture. Far higher figures appear, though they represent all appeals against decisions in the magistrates' courts; appeals against conviction, sentence or any other kind of appeal are undifferentiated.

[18] Proposal 8.2.

[19] Paragraphs 4.21 and following and question 9.6 in CP 184.

CONCLUSION

4.31   If challenges to sentence should not be brought within the ambit of the CAA 1968, for the reasons expounded by Master Venne, judicial review would have to remain (though case stated could be removed, as discussed in Part 7 below).

4.32   If challenges to conviction on rehearing also cannot be brought within the ambit of the CAA 1968 – because it does not make sense to split them off from challenges to sentence – then judicial review again has to remain for that purpose.

4.33   In CP 184, because we were proposing removing the prosecution's right to appeal by way of case stated, we proposed extending the Attorney-General's reference on a point of law[20] and the prosecution appeal under section 58 of the CJA 2003.[21] If judicial review remains for rulings in the appellate jurisdiction, then it should be available to the prosecution too, as now, and there is no need to alter the provisions regarding the Attorney-General's reference or section 58 appeals.

4.34   It is then evidently advantageous to leave judicial review available as a means of challenge to interlocutory rulings in the appellate jurisdiction.

4.35   The overall conclusion is that the case for abolishing judicial review in relation to the appellate jurisdiction is not made out. This weakens any argument for removing judicial review in respect of any other jurisdiction of the Crown Court.

---

[20]   Proposal 8.4.

[21]   Proposal 8.3. Such appeals are described at paras 2.33 to 2.35 above.

PART 5
THE RESPONSE OF CONSULTEES (2): THE NEW STATUTORY APPEAL AND THIRD PARTY RIGHTS

5.1 As described in the previous Part, queries were raised by some consultees on the proposals about the appellate jurisdiction of the Crown Court and, on considering the difficulties they pointed out, we have concluded that we should not proceed with those CP proposals. The consequence is that one of the advantages of the CP proposals – that they would streamline the criminal appeals procedures – was weakened.

5.2 In this Part we consider consultees' responses to the new statutory appeal we proposed in CP 184.[1] Following consultation, we have decided that we also should not proceed with those proposals in the form described in the CP, as we now explain.

THE OBJECTIONS TO THE NEW STATUTORY APPEAL

5.3 Respondents had serious concerns about the proposed new statutory appeal. Their objections were based on the conceptual difficulty of "no adequate remedy", on principle, on the leave aspect of the proposals, and on practical grounds, and we now discuss each of them in turn.

The conceptual difficulty of "no adequate remedy"

5.4 The concept of "adequate remedy" was employed in CP 184 in two specific contexts: in the new statutory appeal proposed for trials on indictment before the jury is sworn,[2] and in the new statutory appeal proposed for trials on indictment after the jury is sworn and before it is discharged,[3] – in other words in relation to the new statutory appeal pre-trial and during trial. Those proposals were then used as the foundation of other proposals.[4]

5.5 The concept of "adequate remedy" was to act as an exclusionary test in the proposals in the following way. If a defendant or third party sought to appeal a determination, judgment, order or ruling ("the decision") before the jury was sworn, or after it was sworn but before it was discharged, he or she would have to show, amongst other things, that he or she would have no adequate remedy in respect of the decision without the proposed right of appeal.

---

[1] It is described at paras 3.5 to 3.10 above.

[2] Proposals 8.15 and, in the alternative, 8.16 of CP 184 which proposed the listing of the trial as an alternative cut-off point to the time when the jury is sworn, but was otherwise the same as 8.15.

[3] Proposals 8.13 and, in the alternative, 8.14, of CP 184.

[4] Such as proposal 8.17 of CP 184 (treating decisions about the composition of the jury as being ones made after the jury has been sworn), and, where the Crown Court is acting in its appellate capacity, in the proposal about appeals against decisions and rulings before the appeal is determined (proposal 8.20).

5.6 The Criminal Sub-Committee of the Council of HM Circuit Judges wrote, "we consider that the concept of 'no adequate remedy' is imprecise and could potentially give rise to problems. It is important to bear in mind that unintended consequences may flow from measures introduced with the best of intentions", and that as a result it would "encourage satellite litigation and delay". The OCJR's view was "... the question of what is an 'adequate remedy' is in itself fraught with difficulty and any definition seems likely to generate legal argument". Given that part of the difficulty with the present law is that its lack of clarity has generated legal argument, we accept that any reform should make the law clearer.

5.7 We tried, in the CP, to pin down the concept of "adequate remedy" by asking the following question:[5]

> Do consultees agree that a defendant or third party has an "adequate" remedy in respect of a determination, judgment, order or ruling if:
>
> (1) he or she can resort to a specific statutory appeal in respect of the determination, judgment, order or ruling; or
>
> (2) no adverse effect:
>
>> (a) would materialise from the determination, judgment, order or ruling in the event of the defendant being acquitted; and
>>
>> (b) no adverse effect, other than any sentence passed following conviction, would materialise from the determination, judgment, order or ruling if the appeal against conviction was successful?

5.8 Tony Edwards, the CPS, Master Venne (Registrar of Criminal Appeals and Master of the Crown Office) and the LRC of the Bar Council all agreed with this question. The OCJR noted that it did not support a "no adequate remedy" limb, and added "that aside, it would seem likely that in most cases limb (1) would not apply. It follows that the court would have to apply limb (2). This would engage it in a case by case decision about whether the particular circumstances were to be regarded as having an 'adverse effect'. This would generate further unnecessary litigation."

5.9 Edward Rees QC raised the specific issue of whether a post-conviction right of appeal is an adequate remedy. This issue leads us to the objection in principle of some consultees to the new statutory appeal, to which we now turn.

Wrong in principle

5.10 The OCJR and HM Circuit Judges and Master Venne thought the new statutory appeal wrong in principle because the defendant has a post-conviction right of appeal. If a post-conviction appeal will provide an opportunity for a decision to be challenged, and corrected if appropriate, then there is no justification for an earlier challenge, delaying or interrupting the trial.

---

[5] Question 9.21 of CP 184.

5.11 We expressed this view in our report on Prosecution Appeals.[6] The issue was also raised in Parliament during the passage of the Bill which became the Criminal Justice Act 2003. The Government was seeking to enact provisions which would give the prosecution the right of interlocutory appeal in circumstances where they did not exist at that time. The opposition introduced amendments which would have extended the right of interlocutory appeal to the defence. The Attorney General said, in relation to the amendments: "the attempt to create the direct equivalent of a prosecution appeal which the amendments envisage is wrong in principle".[7] He referred to the fact that "there is no direct equivalent for the defence of a de facto terminating ruling. There is no ruling that a judge is capable of making which would end the trial in the prosecution's favour with the defendant's conviction."[8] The nearest equivalent is a ruling on a point of law to the effect that a set of facts can or cannot amount in law to an offence, or to a defence. Such a ruling can be decisive for a defendant. In that event, "if a defendant thinks that whether or not he pleaded guilty depends solely on a point of law, he has already the right to appeal."[9]

5.12 The issue of whether a post-conviction appeal can give effect to a defendant's right to a fair trial under Article 6 was canvassed in *R (Shields) v Liverpool Crown Court*[10] where the question was posed, "is English law entitled to require a litigant in a trial on indictment in the Crown Court to pursue any complaint of breach of his Convention rights before the appeal court after the trial has taken place, or is the law obliged to provide a remedy by way of judicial review at an earlier stage?".[11] Lord Justice Brooke was clear that English law complies with the Convention where it refuses judicial review at an interlocutory stage.[12]

5.13 One might, however, hesitate before saying that the defendant has an *adequate* remedy. As Professor Spencer has written, in some circumstances a defendant may win the point on appeal (in other words, satisfy the Court of Appeal that the judge made a wrong ruling) but still lose the appeal.[13] Had the defendant won the point at an earlier stage, he or she might have been acquitted.

5.14 This is a difficult issue, but on balance, we respectfully agree with Lord Justice Brooke that a defendant's Article 6 right to a fair trial is given effect by the trial and appellate system as it stands, because the CACD concentrates on the most important question: whether the conviction is unsafe.

---

[6] Double Jeopardy and Prosecution Appeals (2001) Law Com 267, Cm 5048, para 7.41.

[7] *Hansard* (HL), 30 October 2003, vol 654, col 443.

[8] *Hansard* (HL), 30 October 2003, vol 654, col 443.

[9] *Hansard* (HL), 30 October 2003, vol 654, col 443.

[10] [2001] EWHC Admin 90, [2001] All ER 190.

[11] *R (Shields) v Liverpool Crown Court* [2001] EWHC Admin 90, [2001] All ER 190 at [20].

[12] *R (Shields) v Liverpool Crown Court* [2001] EWHC Admin 90, [2001] All ER 190 at [34] and [35].

[13] J R Spencer, "Quashing Convictions, and Squashing the Court of Appeal" (2006) 170 Justice of the Peace 790, 791 to 792.

5.15 The defendant's post-conviction right of appeal clearly is of no avail to defendants who are acquitted, to the prosecution, or to third parties. It is also irrelevant to convicted defendants in some circumstances. For these people, a post-conviction right of appeal cannot be an adequate remedy.

The absence of any appeal against a refusal of leave to appeal

5.16 A third objection to the new statutory appeal which some consultees raised was the absence of any appeal against a refusal of leave to appeal.

5.17 The exercise of the proposed new statutory appeal depended on the appellant obtaining leave. We proposed that the Crown Court should give leave to appeal against the ruling in question and, if leave was refused, that would be the end of the matter.[14] Only one respondent (the CPS) agreed with this proposal. Those who disagreed did so strongly. There was a general view that the proposal was contrary to the usual practice in criminal justice and possibly non-compliant with the Human Rights Act 1998. Respondents argued that there would need to be a way of appealing against a refusal of leave, and that appeal would have to go to a level senior to the Crown Court judge who had refused leave. We accept these criticisms.

5.18 In some cases, the judge who made the decision will be prepared to grant leave for it to be challenged. Given that likelihood, there does not seem to us any advantage in requiring leave *always* to be sought at a higher level. It therefore seems more practical to suggest that leave may be given in the first instance by the trial judge, but with a right to appeal to a single judge of the CACD if leave is refused.

The practical consequences of the proposed new statutory appeal

5.19 Various practical consequences of the proposed new statutory appeal gave rise to potential problems. In brief, it appeared that it would be used against a wide range of rulings, repeatedly, and it could be used by people other than parties to the proceedings. It would undermine the existing preparatory hearing regime. Lastly, it would increase the burden on the criminal justice system. We now describe consultees' objections on these grounds.

The breadth of the proposed appeal

5.20 A major cause for concern amongst consultees was the potential breadth of issues which could be the source of challenges during trial, and the consequent risk of increased satellite litigation. Consultees pointed out that applications for adjournments, decisions about reporting restrictions, about special measures,[15] could all generate applications to make use of the new statutory appeal.

5.21 A second major cause for concern was the fact that the proposed appeal would be available not just to the parties, but also to victims, witnesses and any directly affected third party. We discuss the position of third parties in detail at paragraphs 5.60 to 5.87 below.

---

[14] Proposal 8.8, question 9.24 of CP 184. See also paras 5.52 and 5.53 of CP 184.

[15] "Special measures" are steps which a court can require to make it easier for a witness to give evidence.

The difficulties created by having different rules for pre-trial appeals from appeals after the start of the trial

5.22 Our proposals in the CP distinguished between rulings made at three different stages of a trial on indictment: before the jury was sworn, after it was sworn and before it was discharged, and rulings made after the jury was discharged. Consultees thought that if the rules governing pre-trial appeals were different from those governing appeals after the trial had started, that would have a number of undesirable effects.

5.23 First, it would lead to inconsistent decisions across courts. Secondly, pressure to resolve matters "pre-trial" would conflict with the target for trials to be effective.[16] Thirdly, if there is significance in a cut-off point – namely the likelihood of being able to obtain a review is greater on one side of the cut-off point than the other – that not only puts pressure on parties and the judge to have an issue discussed at a particular point in the process, but it also creates a new point against which an appeal may be taken.

5.24 If the reality were that pre-trial issues are in fact addressed in advance of the trial being listed, then the possibility of a challenge would not derail the trial to the same extent. Feedback from discussion with the CPS and Crown Court judges suggests it is not, however, the reality. Courts are unwilling to assign judges far in advance of a trial date to particular cases; judges are unwilling to make rulings which bind their successors; counsel is unwilling to seek a ruling which will bind the advocate who is going to conduct the trial. So in practice, issues which should be addressed before the date a trial is listed are not. Further, practice varies a great deal around England and Wales.

5.25 We accept that it is not desirable to have different rules pre-trial from those which apply during a trial.

The impact of the proposed new statutory appeal on existing interlocutory appeals

5.26 There already exists a variety of interlocutory appeals, available in a range of circumstances and for different purposes.[17] For example, one of the functions of the preparatory hearing regime is to fix the trial judge as having conduct of the hearing. Another purpose is to allow for the possibility of interlocutory appeals, but in restricted circumstances. What, it might be asked, would be the point of the preparatory regime if it became possible to appeal rulings made outside it? If the proposals in the CP were taken forward, the effect would be to undo the boundary between cases where there is or could be an appeal from a preparatory hearing and those where there is not. The justification for opening up pre-trial potential challenges in this way would, in the light of consultees' disquiet, have to be very strong.

---

[16] The target for trials to be effective encourages a party to move to the point where the jury is sworn.

[17] See paras 2.27 to 2.38 above.

5.27 We conclude that Professor Ormerod is right when he says that "the solution to these problems [on the interpretation of the statutory provisions governing the preparatory hearing regimes] must now lie with Parliament"[18] and that the pre-trial appeals need to be reviewed as a whole. We would add that the routes of interlocutory appeals – and in particular whether they should go all the way to the Supreme Court – is also a question worth exploring. It may be that in due course the Supreme Court will indicate which kinds of interlocutory appeal generally are appropriate for it to hear, but we do not consider that our current terms of reference extend that far.

The disruptive effect

THE PRE-TRIAL APPEAL

5.28 We proposed that, pre-trial, a defendant or directly affected third party may appeal on the grounds that the determination was wrong in law, involved a serious procedural or other irregularity, or was one that no competent and reasonable tribunal could properly have made if,

> (a) being unable to appeal forthwith, he or she would have no adequate remedy in respect of the determination, judgment, order or ruling; or

> (b) he or she, even if unable to appeal forthwith, would have an adequate remedy in respect of the determination, judgment, order or ruling but the potential advantages of permitting an appeal forthwith are such as to make it the right course (proposal 8.15).

5.29 As explained above, the right to appeal following conviction is only relevant to defendants, so limb (a) is no bar to third parties. Even as regards defendants, limb (a) may not serve as a bar if it is irrelevant in some situations (such as in relation to bail, or where his or her life is endangered as a consequence of a court ruling).

5.30 In some cases, establishing whether there is in law another remedy open to a defendant could in itself be difficult: it will be necessary for a court to decide first whether a ruling is or is not one which may be appealed under the preparatory hearing regime, which may not be an easy question to answer.[19]

Limb (b)

5.31 There is still the effect of limb (b) to consider. Whereas the current law is conservative in terms of pre-trial appeals, limb (b), in effect, had the potential to extend the possibility of appeal to:

> cases where there has not been and is not going to be a preparatory hearing;

> cases where there has been a preparatory hearing but the ruling may not be appealed within that regime; and

---

[18] D Ormerod, [2007] Criminal Law Review 731, 735.

[19] See *H* as described at paras 2.70 to 2.89 of CP 184.

to cases where the judge has rejected an application for a ruling which, if acceded to, would bring the trial to an end.

5.32 The effect would be that the prohibition on appealing some rulings from ordinary pre-trial hearings could be side-stepped; and the defence would have an equivalent of the prosecution appeal against "terminating rulings" open to it in some circumstances.[20]

5.33 With regard to pre-trial appeals, Edward Rees QC and the Circuit Judges both thought that, in cases serious enough to have a preparatory hearing, there is already a right of appeal and it did not seem necessary to have an additional right of immediate appeal.

THE APPEAL AFTER THE TRIAL HAD STARTED

5.34 We proposed that an appeal could be made after the trial had started, on judicial review-type grounds, where there was no alternative remedy or where the ruling affected a person's liberty or it was argued that the ruling breached a Convention right.

5.35 Consultees were very worried by the prospect of immediate challenges to rulings made during the course of a trial. HM Council of Circuit Judges wrote, "we believe that the introduction of such a general and imprecise basis for challenge during trial is quite unnecessary and undesirable. The consequences are likely to result in disruption and uncertainty. It would open Pandora's Box."[21]

5.36 Our view in the CP was that the number of appeals which would be possible under this proposal was small, but consultees did not agree. The OCJR, for example, wrote that there was "potentially no limit to the number of decisions it would render appealable".

5.37 Consultees impressed upon us the practical difficulties caused if a jury was required to "stand by" while the Court of Appeal adjudicated on the propriety of a ruling made by the trial judge. There would be a considerable risk that the jury would have to be discharged and the trial restarted. It was quite possible that it would be a matter of weeks rather than days before the Court of Appeal would be able to hear the challenge, and any appeal received at short notice would have a knock-on effect on the appeals already lodged with the Court of Appeal.

5.38 Master Venne wrote,

---

[20] See the comments of the Attorney General cited at para 5.11 above.

[21] Some respondents pointed out ramifications of this proposal, such as the CPS who suggested that a defendant who was in custody would be able to use this proposal to challenge, say, a ruling rejecting a submission of no case to answer, because the consequence of the decision is that the case continues, and a consequence of the case continuing is that the defendant is not at liberty.

I have very great reservations about any proposal to confer what is in effect a new interlocutory right of appeal. Such challenges will inevitably disrupt a trial, thus causing delay and the requirement for additional resources (the jury will have to await the appeal being dealt with by CACD, the defendant may have to be accommodated for a longer period than if the trial proper were to continue, the application will have to be prepared by CACD lawyer/admin staff and then listed before the CACD, thus using Court and judiciary time) when the application may in fact be academic. ... If however the defendant is not convicted, the appeal would have been academic but would have a) disrupted the trial process and possibly incurring unnecessary delay and additional cost; and b) utilised resources of CACD unnecessarily.

5.39 If a refusal of leave may itself be appealed to a judge of the Court of Appeal, then not only is further delay likely, and further cost, but also the workload on judges at that level is likely to increase. In the CP we saw the leave requirement as acting as a filter, to keep out unmeritorious appeals. If a party (including a third party) is refused leave, he or she may continue to litigate by appealing that refusal, whether meritorious or not.

5.40 If a trial has to be delayed or suspended, or stopped so that the jury is discharged and a retrial ordered, there are significant practical consequences for the defendant, for complainants, for witnesses for all parties, and for the professionals involved. The cost is financial – and borne by the public as well as by individuals – and emotional.

Increased workload and resource implications

5.41 Judges of all levels to whom we spoke were worried about their workload. There would inevitably be an increase in the workload of the judges and staff of the CACD, and there was considerable concern at this prospect.[22] Applications for leave to appeal are considered by a judge of the Court of Appeal, frequently in "unallocated" time, or in other words, outside working hours. There is already concern about pressures of work on the Administrative Court.[23] We note also that the administrative burden on senior Crown Court judges has increased.[24] We appreciate that any recommendations which would lead to an increase in workload at any level would be unwelcome.

[22] As regards the CACD, while the 2006-07 and 2007-08 Reviews of the Legal Year of the CACD were positive about the court's ability to reduce waiting times, it referred to the additional pressure created by prosecution appeals under section 58 of the CJA 2003. See paras 2.33 to 2.35 above for a brief description of these appeals. See Court of Appeal Criminal Division, *Review of the Legal Year 2006-07* (October 2006/September 2007), para 1.7 and Court of Appeal Criminal Division, *Review of the Legal Year 2006-07* (October 2007/September 2008), para 10.1.

[23] The Lord Chief Justice's Review of the Administration of Justice in the Courts (March 2008) HC 448, para 5.67.

[24] See Judges Council, *First Progress Report of the Standing Committee of the Judges' Council: Judicial Support and Welfare* (December 2007) and in particular "A Presider's View" at Annex A.

5.42   Transferring work from the High Court to the CACD is highly unlikely to be cost-neutral.[25] (It seems that this is still likely to be the case, even if the new statutory appeal were pursued in an amended form.) The Administrative Court Office noted that the number of cases which they would cease to deal with, under the proposals, was not high enough to be likely to generate savings.

5.43   The Administrative Court might even find it had more cases coming through: in discussion with the Administrative Court Office it appeared that, if magistrates' decisions are unaffected while all Crown Court challenges have to go via the CACD – a consequence of our proposals – then there might be an incentive for defendants to use case stated/judicial review as a means of challenge to the magistrates' courts rather than to appeal to the Crown Court.[26] The result would be an increase in the numbers of case stated/judicial review of magistrates' court decisions.

5.44   For any new appeal, whether pre-trial, during trial or post-verdict, there are potential cost implications for the court service, the Criminal Defence Service, the prosecuting authorities, and for witnesses and defendants. As the Criminal Appeal Office noted, it is impossible to assess the potential impact without knowing roughly what number of cases might be affected.

5.45   The Criminal Appeal Office, which would be receiving additional cases under the proposals, noted cost implications arising from new procedures, IT initiatives, training, demands on staff (possibly additional staff). They also thought it particularly difficult to be sure what the impact would be because the number of cases which the new statutory appeal would generate was so hard to estimate.

5.46   The OCJR attempted to estimate the number of cases that might be generated. As a basis for the calculations, the OCJR used data for the number of appeals from the magistrates' courts to the High Court on the basis of existing appeal rights by way of case stated and judicial review. These data were considered to "bear some resemblance" to the proposals given these appeals "are interlocutory, open to some third parties, and available before, during and after a trial in the magistrates' court". A final figure of 640 additional appeals per year from the Crown Court was achieved via a number of steps:

[25]   The issue of the effect on the respective caseloads of the Administrative Court and of the CACD was raised in our Scoping Paper – Judicial Review of Decisions of the Crown Court (2005) Law Commission. Most respondents to that paper felt unable to say what the effect would be. The Criminal Bar Association thought a corresponding transfer of staff and resources from the Administrative Court Office to the CACD ought to suffice – a natural assumption, but one which was not borne out in discussions with the Administrative Court Office or the Criminal Appeal Office.

[26]   This is because the options for challenging decisions of the Crown Court might be perceived as more limited, although a party who appeals by way of case stated loses the right of appeal to the Crown Court (Magistrates' Courts Act 1980, s 111(4)).

5.47   First, there were found to be 251 applications for leave to appeal to the High Court in criminal cases in 2005, with approximately 150 applications[27] for leave to appeal a year from the magistrates' court to the High Court.[28]

5.48   There were 47,200 convictions after a trial in the magistrates' court in 2006; in the Crown Court a third of a total of 75,000 cases were contested, resulting in 25,233 trials on indictment. If one divides the number of convictions after trial in the magistrates' court by the number of applications for leave to appeal from that court, then that means approximately one application for leave to appeal for every 314 cases in the magistrates' court. Accordingly, applying that calculation directly to the Crown Court, "the number of additional applications/appeals would be approximately 25,233 ÷ 314 = 80 a year".

5.49   Finally, the number of 80 cases a year was multiplied by eight, given that cases in the Crown Court "are perhaps 8 times more likely to be contested than cases in the magistrates' court".[29] The OCJR wrote,

> A more realistic figure for the additional number of appeals resulting from the statutory appeals in their proposed form would be, not 80 a year but 80 X 8 (the greater likelihood of a Crown Court case being contested) = 640 a year. Taking "a" as the unit cost of an appeal in court time and "b" as the unit cost in legal aid time, it may be calculated that the proposals would cost approximately 640 X a + 640 X b per annum to implement. HM Courts Service may be able to supply unit costs for a and b in Court of Appeal cases. It will also be necessary to factor in a greater number of appeals to the House of Lords, and prosecution costs.
>
> As noted, these estimates relate only to contested cases. The proposed appeal rights extend beyond the trial itself, applying both after and, more importantly, before the trial, so all 75,000 Crown Court cases are potentially caught. It seems unlikely that there would be many appeals before the trial, but the possibility cannot be excluded. Furthermore, the availability of the potential for delay and disruption may encourage defendants who would otherwise plead guilty to contest cases.

[27]   The OCJR referred to table D at the end of CP 184, which indicated that fewer than 100 of the 251 applications were from the Crown Court. It was therefore assumed that the remainder were from the magistrates' courts in criminal matters, and thus there were 150 applications for leave to appeal from the magistrates' courts to the High Court.

[28]   Citing Judicial Statistics (Revised) England and Wales for the Year 2005 (August 2006) Cm 6903, 31.

[29]   This calculation was based on the fact that "only about 1 in 20 to 1 in 25 cases in the magistrates' court results in a trial and conviction, compared with about 1 in 3 contested cases in the Crown Court".

5.50   One of the principal reasons for the OCJR not agreeing with all the proposals was the "principle in the current difficult financial climate that any change in this area should not generate a net overall increase in costs". In the light of that opposition, we would have to show strong justification for recommendations which were going to increase costs. The responses from other consultees, particularly from the judiciary, do not disclose that kind of justification for the proposals as they stood.

A disproportionate solution

5.51   There was a general view amongst consultees that the changes would not bring enough benefits to make them worthwhile, and the proposed appeal was not a proportionate response to the problems of the current law.

THE PROPOSALS WOULD NOT ACHIEVE THE AIM OF SIMPLIFYING THE SYSTEM

5.52   It is acknowledged by the judiciary and by academics that the range and structure of appeal possibilities in the criminal justice system is "incoherent and unsatisfactory".[30] It could be argued that the provisional proposals did not do enough to make the scheme of criminal appeals coherent, and there was a significant risk that they would introduce more complexity.

5.53   While it is true that the proposals would have simplified appeal options by getting rid of case stated and judicial review in relation to rulings by the Crown Court, much complexity would have remained. For example, the significance and scope of prosecution appeals under section 58 CJA 2003 is still being worked out[31] – and the case law has already established that such appeals are not open to the prosecution in some situations.[32] Additionally, as noted above, a party wishing to appeal pre-trial would have to show that he or she could not appeal under the preparatory hearing regime before beginning an appeal under the new statutory appeal.[33]

The difficulties in repealing section 29(3)

5.54   Section 29(3) provides a power of review where it would not otherwise exist. We proposed removing it.[34] This would have the unwelcome consequence of removing it without providing a substitute form of challenge in relation to two areas (at least).

---

[30]   D Ormerod [2008] Criminal Law Review 466, 469, commenting on Y [2008] EWCA Crim 10, [2008] 1 WLR 1683 and referring to J Spencer, "Does Our Present Criminal Appeal System Make Sense?" [2006] Criminal Law Review 677, 689, which in turn refers to the report of Auld LJ: Review of the Criminal Courts of England and Wales (September 2001).

[31]   See, eg, D Ormerod's commentary on O, J and S in [2008] Criminal Law Review 892; R v Al-Ali [2008] EWCA Crim 2186, [2009] 1 WLR 1661.

[32]   Namely, where charges are sent for trial under the Crime and Disorder Act 1998 rather than committed for trial: Thompson and Hanson [2006] EWCA Crim 2849, [2007] All ER 205.

[33]   This would entail working through H's "thicket", as described by Lord Scott: H [2007] UKHL 7, [2007] 2 AC 270 at [30]. See D Ormerod [2007] Criminal Law Review 731.

[34]   Proposal 8.6 of CP 184.

5.55   First, judicial review and appeal by case stated are currently available in respect of rulings after there has been a finding (by the court) that a defendant is unfit to plead. We proposed removing both those avenues of challenge, but the new statutory appeal which we proposed would not have covered cases after a finding of unfitness.

5.56   Secondly, the Crown Court has jurisdiction in some civil matters, such as appeals in licensing matters, the grant/issue of firearms certificates, or civil contempts. The effect would be to remove judicial review of Crown Court rulings made in its civil jurisdiction, which we did not intend.

The High Court would still have jurisdiction in criminal matters

5.57   The High Court has jurisdiction in many criminal matters. In addition to hearing appeals by way of case stated from and judicial reviews of cases in the Crown Court, it has the power to:

> hear applications for judicial review of magistrates' courts' decisions;
>
> hear appeals by way of case stated from magistrates' courts;
>
> entertain applications for judicial review in respect of criminal cases where it is not the judge's ruling which is being challenged – it may be the decision of a prosecuting authority, of the police, of the Criminal Cases Review Commission, or of the Secretary of State;
>
> give leave to the prosecutor to serve a draft indictment (a voluntary bill of indictment);[35]
>
> review control orders under the Prevention of Terrorism Act 2005;
>
> hear challenges arising out of extradition proceedings;[36]
>
> make ancillary orders such as in relation to the Bankers' Books Evidence Act 1879; and to
>
> hear appeals from Summary Appeal Courts.

5.58   It also has jurisdiction in proceedings which are classified as "civil" but which are related to criminal matters, such as in relation to Serious Crime Prevention Orders,[37] or in a claim brought under the Human Rights Act 1998 in relation to judicial acts, which includes judicial decisions in criminal cases.

5.59   Thus, the High Court would still have jurisdiction in all the above situations even if the CP proposals were taken forward.

---

[35]   Administration of Justice (Miscellaneous Provisions) Act 1933, s 2(2)(b).

[36]   See paras 6.43 to 6.46 of CP 184. They are heard at the magistrates' court, and appeals go to the High Court. They are criminal proceedings for the purposes of legal representation under s 12(2)(c) of the Access to Justice Act 1999.

[37]   Serious Crime Act 2007, s 1.

THIRD PARTIES

5.60 The potential impact of providing a statutory right of appeal to persons other than the defendant or prosecution, as proposed in the CP, alarmed consultees. We now review the position of third parties under the current law so we can see how the proposals would affect the current position. We then set out the response to the third party aspect of the proposals in the CP. At the end we conclude that a general right of appeal for a directly affected third party is not the right way forward, but that where a ruling does directly affect a fundamental right, it may be appropriate for the person affected to be able to challenge that ruling.

The current law

5.61 The current law gives rights of challenge to persons other than the prosecution and defendant in criminal proceedings in some circumstances:

(1) The case stated procedure is open to a "person aggrieved" in respect of a ruling in the magistrates' courts.[38]

(2) Judicial review is open to a person who has a sufficient interest in the proceedings (subject to the exclusion in section 29(3) of the SCA 1981).

Whether a victim of a crime has sufficient interest to bring judicial review proceedings in relation to a Crown Court ruling is not a settled point. In the recent case of *R (Faithfull) v Ipswich Crown Court*[39] the point was not directly considered. Lord Justice Richards noted that the question of standing of the victim had been raised but, in view of the court ruling against him on a different point, the court did not have to consider it.[40]

5.62 Various statutory provisions give third parties a right or a voice in specific circumstances.

Other statutory provisions

5.63 A third party may have a right of appeal:

against an order restricting the reporting of proceedings,[41]

against a costs order,[42]

against a Wasted Costs order,[43]

---

[38] Magistrates' Courts Act 1980, s 111.

[39] [2007] EWHC 2763 (Admin), [2008] 1 WLR 1636.

[40] *R (Faithfull) v Ipswich Crown Court* [2007] EWHC 2763 (Admin), [2008] 1 WLR 1636 at [43].

[41] Criminal Justice Act 1988, s 159(1).

[42] Regulation 3H of the Costs in Criminal Cases (General) Regulations 1986 and Part 68 of Criminal Procedure Rules.

[43] Regulation 3C of the Costs in Criminal Cases (General) Regulations 1986 and Part 68 of the Criminal Procedure Rules. As regards orders made against solicitors, see s 50(3) of the Solicitors Act 1974 (inserted by ss 147 and 152(4) of, and Sch 7 to the SCA 1981).

where a person is liable for payment of a penalty imposed on another (such as when a parent, guardian or local authority is liable for a fine, surcharge, costs or compensation order imposed on a child), or is bound over in respect of a child or young person who has been convicted of an offence, that parent or guardian may appeal to the CA against the order as if it were a sentence passed on him or her;[44]

in relation to a decision of the Crown Court to make, to vary, or not to vary a serious crime prevention order, if the person had a right to make representations at the time of the making of the order.[45]

5.64 Alternatively, a third party may have no right of appeal, but instead a right to apply for an order to be varied, discharged or withdrawn.[46] In other cases, a third party may have only a right to make representations, but not to appeal.[47] In some cases the third party simply has a right to be notified of a proposed order, but that right then triggers the possibility of an application to the court by that person.[48]

The proposals in the CP

5.65 The CP proposed that a right of appeal should be available to the defendant and to "a directly affected third party" or "a person directly affected".[49] We noted that "Parliament has provided only limited rights of appeal to third parties in relation to criminal proceedings in the Crown Court".[50] We cited the example of section 159 of the Criminal Justice Act 1988 under which a third party may appeal against an order restricting the reporting of proceedings. We then said, "we believe that third parties should enjoy the same level of protection as defendants against erroneous decisions. ...."[51]

---

[44] Powers of Criminal Courts (Sentencing) Act 2000, s 137(7) and s 150(9).

[45] Serious Crime Act 2007, s 24. See also 50.3(2) and Part 68 of the Criminal Procedure Rules.

[46] As in relation to a restraining order under s 5 of the Protection from Harassment Act 1997 following conviction, or under s 5A of the same Act following an acquittal; or where the court requires a witness to produce a document, the witness may apply for the order to be withdrawn: Criminal Procedure (Attendance of Witnesses) Act 1965 and Part 28 of the Criminal Procedure Rules.

[47] As in the following examples (1) Where a defendant is convicted of a sexual or violent offence, in some circumstances the victim may be entitled to make representations on appropriate licence conditions or supervision requirements: ss 35 to 44 of the Domestic Violence, Crime and Victims Act 2004. (2) Where the court makes a Serious Crime Prevention Order (SCPO), if the Crown Court considers that the making or variation of a SCPO "would be likely to have a significant adverse effect" on a person, it must hear representations by that person: Serious Crime Act 2007, s 9(4) and Part 68 of the Criminal Procedure Rules. (3) Where the court makes a compensation order and the defendant applies for it to be reviewed, the beneficiary may be heard by the court.

[48] Such as a surety, who has to be notified if the court is thinking of forfeiting a recognizance: Criminal Procedure Rules 19.23(2) and 19.24(2); or a witness, where the court requires a witness to produce a document: Criminal Procedure (Attendance of Witnesses) Act 1965 and rule 28.5 of the Criminal Procedure Rules.

[49] Proposals 8.12, 8.13, 8.14, 8.15, 8.16, 8.19 and 8.20.

[50] Para 5.56 of CP 184.

[51] Para 5.57 of CP 184.

5.66 The possibility that a non-party might exercise a right of challenge in circumstances where it is not currently possible provoked much comment from consultees.

The impact of the provisional proposals

5.67 The right provided by our proposals did not come into play if there was any other statutory appeal available, and therefore the existing rights of challenge by a third party would continue to be available even if our provisional proposal were pursued.

5.68 Our provisional proposal would have provided a right of appeal in the following situations (and possibly in others):

where a court refused the use of a special measure to help a witness,

where a court refused an order protecting a person's anonymity,

where a court attached a condition to the bail granted to the defendant,

where a court made an order for the protection of members of the jury,[52]

where a court refused to impose reporting restrictions,

where the court designated a particular authority as the supervising authority in a sentencing matter, or

where the court refused or failed to make a compensation order.

The views of respondents

5.69 Respondents' concerns fell, broadly speaking, into two categories: how the phrase "directly affected third party" would be interpreted, and the increase in litigation which would result from the extension of rights.

5.70 Master Venne commented that, "it is arguable that a clear definition of 'a person directly affected' is required as it potentially has a very wide application". The CPS was also unclear about the breadth of the phrase: "we would also welcome clarification on the term 'third party'. The prosecution sometimes represents the interests of victims and witnesses in court. Does the term 'third party' include victims and witnesses – as distinct from, for example, a publisher or a campaigning group?"

5.71 The Newspaper Society welcomed the proposals insofar as they widened the doors of the courts to members of the media, and said that the media should have "the opportunity for immediate reversal of open justice restrictions in all circumstances".

---

[52] Eg, that they should be referred to by number rather than by name: *Comerford* [1998] 1 WLR 191 at 199.

5.72 The OCJR accepted that, just as in some cases a person who is not party to the proceedings might have sufficient standing to apply for judicial review, so a third party might justifiably wish to challenge a court's decision, but it did not wish to see any extension of that right. It said:

> Although the parties to criminal proceedings are the prosecutor and defendant alone, third party appeal rights are acceptable within the parameters imposed by section 29(3) [of the SCA 1981] in its current form. General third party appeal rights against any Crown Court decision relating to trial on indictment, as proposed in the paper, are likely to give rise to delay and disruption to proceedings.

5.73 As regards interlocutory appeals, the OCJR said, "… the general principle against interlocutory appeals in relation to trial on indictment should apply to prosecutors, defendants and third parties alike". The OCJR also put forward the broader argument:

> …There is an enduring principle that the parties to criminal trials are the prosecutor and the defendant alone. Against this background, one might argue that judicial review is essentially a civil procedure, that multi-party issues are a feature of the civil not the criminal law, and that the third party element of the judicial review jurisdiction should be abolished when the statutory appeal is created.

> On the other hand, some people might think that this would be an excessively radical move and one going beyond the remit of the current exercise. Our preferred approach at the moment is to preserve without extending the judicial review test in the statutory appeal, namely that the applicant must have a sufficient interest in the matter. It appears that the terminology "a directly affected third party" (and "any person directly affected" …) is intended to re-work this definition. We have some doubts as to the desirability of attempting to rewrite the judicial review test for standing in the context of the present exercise. It raises issues all of its own and has wider implications.

5.74 Some Crown Court Judges and Court of Appeal judges were concerned at the inclusion of third parties, particularly in relation to compensation orders and the plethora of appeals which would be the probable result, as they saw it.

5.75 The Criminal Sub-Committee of the Council of HM Circuit Judges, however, recognised that

> there are, from time to time, some cases where a third party might wish to intervene and *R (TB) v The Combined Court at Stafford* [2006] EWHC 1645 (Admin) is a good example of that.[53]

---

[53] *R (TB) v The Combined Court at Stafford* [2006] EWHC 1645, [2007] 1 WLR 1524. In that case the court had ordered disclosure of a witness's medical records, without hearing representations from the witness, and she sought a declaration in relation to that order.

Policy reasons for restricting challenges by third parties

5.76   On a case-by-case basis, there is already provision in a number of situations for a person who is directly affected by an order of the court (other than the prosecutor and defendant) to challenge it. Our provisional proposal would have extended this right significantly.

5.77   The policy reasons that victims and third parties do not generally play a role directly in criminal proceedings have been explained in the case law, and are worth setting out here.

The Crown represents the public interest

5.78   There is a strong tradition in the common law that the prosecution and the defence are the only proper parties to criminal proceedings. Some of the policy reasons for excluding victims are that a challenge might threaten the need for adequate punishment, lead to disparities in sentence, lead to media pressure on victims to seek compensation, or undermine the courts' responsibility to uphold the rule of law. In *R (Bulger) v The Lord Chief Justice*[54] the father of a victim sought judicial review to challenge the tariff set for the perpetrators of the crime. On the question of whether he had standing to make this challenge, Lord Justice Rose said this:

> ...in the present matter the traditional and invariable parties to criminal proceedings, namely the Crown and the defendant, are both able to, and do, challenge those judicial decisions which are susceptible to judicial review as, for example, the many authorities on the meaning of the words "relating to trial on indictment" in section 29(3) of the Supreme Court Act 1981 amply illustrate.

> It follows that in criminal cases there is no need for a third party to seek to intervene to uphold the rule of law. Nor, in my judgment, would such intervention generally be desirable. If the family of a victim could challenge the sentencing process, why not the family of the defendant? Should the Official Solicitor be permitted to represent the interests of children adversely affected by the imprisonment of their mother? Should organisations representing victims or offenders be permitted to intervene? In my judgment, the answer in all these cases is that the Crown and the defendant are the only proper parties to criminal proceedings. A proper discharge of judicial functions in relation to sentencing requires that the judge take into account (as the Lord Chief Justice said he did in this case) the impact of the offence and the sentence on the public generally, and on individuals, including the victim and the victim's family and the defendant and the defendant's family. The nature of that impact is properly channelled through prosecution or defence.[55]

---

[54]   [2001] All ER 203.

[55]   *R (Bulger) v The Lord Chief Justice* [2001] EWHC Admin 119, [2001] 3 All ER 449 at [20] and [21].

5.79   A sentence serves to punish, to deter, to rehabilitate, and to prevent more crimes being committed. Those elements of a sentence engage the public interest, and we agree that a third party – even the victim of the offence – should not have standing to challenge a sentence in the name of the public interest.

5.80   While it is true that the prosecution represents the general public interest, there are limits to the extent to which it is acting on behalf of the complainant. It is not obvious either that the state is acting for a particular victim, nor that the interests of a particular individual ought always to be subsumed into the general public interest.

5.81   Further, while the policy considerations which Lord Justice Rose sets out are very powerful, they are not relevant in all cases, and where they are not under threat, it could be argued that the affected party should be able to challenge the decision, in particular where his or her fundamental rights will be affected and there is no other adequate remedy.

The avoidance of delay and interruption

5.82   The need to avoid delay to the proceedings as a whole, and interruption to stages involving oral evidence, is recognised in many authorities and we acknowledge it.

Complexity of the issues and suitability of the criminal court

5.83   Third party rights on occasion throw up complex legal and factual problems which are inappropriate for a Crown Court sentencing process.[56]

Third party rights: conclusion

5.84   Under the current law, rights for third parties have been provided in some specific circumstances, and not at all in others. We acknowledge that in recent years, statutory provisions on matters of procedure affecting third parties have not provided for appeals.

5.85   We note also that a third party may be able to bring a civil action, or have a right to compensation under the statutory compensation scheme. We note also that where the court has simply made an error at the sentencing stage, the length of time within which a party can bring a matter back to the Crown Court for the error to be corrected has been extended relatively recently.[57]

---

[56]   As in *Bewick* [2007] EWCA Crim 3297, [2008] 2 Criminal Appeal Reports (Sentencing) 31.

[57]   See s 155 of the Powers of Criminal Courts (Sentencing) Act 2000.

5.86 The effect of the proposals in the CP would have been to provide rights in all areas where they do not currently exist. We now think that where there are gaps which give rise to injustice, they are best corrected on a case-by-case basis, and not by a general right of appeal (or of review). This approach would allow the right to be tailored as appropriate. For example, in some situations all the third party might need would be to be heard on an application made by others, whereas in other situations a full right of appeal might be appropriate.[58]

5.87 We also conclude that if a judge makes a ruling which directly affects a fundamental right of a person it may be justifiable for that person to be able to challenge the decision even if he or she is not a party to the proceedings.

OVERALL CONCLUSION

5.88 If the objections to the proposals in relation to the Crown Court's appellate jurisdiction are heeded, then the scope of our proposed new statutory appeal could only apply in relation to the first instance jurisdiction of the Crown Court. We must also take account of the fact that the High Court would retain jurisdiction in sundry other criminal matters, and therefore, even if we discounted those objections, we still would not succeed in simplifying the system of appeals and review in the way we wished.

5.89 It follows that one of the main benefits of the new statutory appeal is lost, and in consequence it is hard to argue for a new statutory appeal along the lines in the CP. In particular, the interpretation of section 58 of the CJA 2003 and the existing statutory appeals against rulings in preparatory hearings[59] mean that we cannot find secure ground for our "no alternative remedy" stance.

5.90 We accept that the practical consequences of the new statutory appeal that we proposed would be undesirable and unpredictable.

5.91 Our proposals were intended to be relatively minor changes within a larger system. That system is itself beset by arbitrariness and uncertainty[60] and we have therefore concluded that it is not possible to recommend changes made in isolation which will be worth the cost and effort without a broader overhaul of the whole appellate system. We are not therefore pursuing the CP proposals, and specifically we do not recommend the new statutory appeal in the general form in which it appeared in the CP.

5.92 His Honour Judge Murphy wrote, "… the answer lies in refining the remedy in narrow and specific terms, so that it cannot be abused easily, but is available in proper cases". We have taken up that challenge and looked at the issues afresh.

---

[58] Procedural rules and guidance can help a third party to benefit from existing court powers. For example, in relation to compensation orders, part of the Prosecutor's Pledge (in effect October 2005) requires the prosecutor to apply for compensation on behalf of the victim and the Joint police/CPS Witness Care Unit must explain to victims the meaning and effect of the sentence given to the offender in their case: The Code of Practice for Victims of Crime (2005), para 6.8.

[59] See paras 2.29 to 2.32 above and para 2.78 and following of CP 184.

[60] See footnote 30 above.

PART 6
OUR PRINCIPAL CONCLUSIONS

6.1 The general problem at the heart of this report is whether the High Court and the CA should be able to review or change rulings made by the Crown Court in a trial on indictment and, if so, in what circumstances. In this Part we examine the policy considerations which underpin our answer to that question, and we reach conclusions about when a right of challenge to a Crown Court ruling is justified. We discuss the differences between judicial review and appeal to the CACD. We conclude by explaining in which circumstances we think there should be a right to challenge a ruling in a trial on indictment, and whether that should be by way of judicial review or by appeal to the CACD.

THE POLICY CONSIDERATIONS

6.2 We have seen in Parts 4 and 5 above that the solutions we proposed in the CP will not work. In reconsidering the problem, we need to return to the underlying justifications for the statutory bar, because they will inform any viable solution. The justifications for the statutory bar are clear from the case law. They are, in themselves, uncontentious: the avoidance of delay to proceedings, and the provision of a remedy where there is none. These policy considerations may work against each other.

The "no delay" criterion

6.3 If a trial is held too speedily, then the quality of evidence may suffer and justice will be impaired. However, there is an important difference between unfairness caused by hastily conducted trials which in themselves are uninterrupted, and unfairness caused by excessive or unnecessary delay to a trial otherwise being conducted at the right pace. We are concerned with the latter. Delay is undesirable for a number of reasons, as we have set out at paragraph 1.14 above. To those reasons we might add that delay affects the willingness of witnesses to give evidence, usually adds to the total cost of proceedings, and can be particularly harmful in cases where children or vulnerable people are involved (as witnesses or as defendants). Further, if the defendant is remanded in custody, but is acquitted or does not receive a custodial sentence at the end of the proceedings, then delay means additional and unnecessary time in custody.

6.4 There is a general view evident in the case law and in the responses to the CP that delay to criminal trials is to be avoided. Fair procedure entails minimal delay. As the Sub-Committee of HM Council of Circuit Judges put it in their response, "the rights of all involved in the process to a conclusion of the proceedings within a reasonable time" need to be weighed in the balance. We accept that expedition is a process consideration. If a right of challenge is going to cause delay then, in order to be justifiable, that right of challenge must be essential to give effect to a fundamental right or freedom of the individual.

6.5   One reason that a right of challenge might justifiably be permitted, even though it causes delay, can be in the interests of what we called in the CP "waste avoidance": the more serious, complex or lengthy a trial, the more important it is to ensure that the time, effort and resources devoted to it are not wasted through failure to correct an error made early in the proceedings, before those proceedings continue.

6.6   It would not be appropriate to permit challenges according simply to whether there will in fact be delay to the trial in any particular case, because that would be a question of fact which would vary from one case to another, thus introducing uncertainty and inconsistency. If delay in the instant case was the only criterion then, for example, a highly unfair decision might not be reviewed because the trial was imminent, while in a different case a decision with less serious consequences could be challenged simply because the trial date was further off.

6.7   Another question is whether it is delay of a particular kind of hearing or of the ultimate determination of the issue which is the concern. It might be argued that delay is bad because it causes inconvenience to defendants and jurors, and in particular to witnesses. In that event, it is especially the kinds of hearings in which witnesses will be involved which should not be delayed, namely, any hearing at which evidence falls to be called. This would encompass: a trial before a jury (including retrial), a trial of the issue of fitness to plead,[1] a hearing to determine whether D did the act or made the omission charged where D is unfit to plead, a *Newton* hearing,[2] or a trial without a jury.

6.8   By way of contrast, cases where a challenge could not delay a hearing at which evidence falls to be called would be where:

        (1)   the trial has already been completed;

        (2)   there is not going to be a trial because the prosecution offers no evidence (whether a jury has been sworn or not);

        (3)   there is not going to be a trial because the defendant has indicated guilty pleas (and any other counts are not going to be proceeded with).[3]

---

[1]   Heard by a judge, but likely to entail the calling of evidence.

[2]   A hearing which takes place after a guilty plea, when the facts on which the defendant is to be sentenced are in dispute.

[3]   D is supposed to enter a plea or give an indication of plea at the first hearing in the Crown Court, if not before: Criminal Procedure Rules 3.8(2)(b).

6.9   However, if the distinction were drawn according to whether there was going to be a hearing at which evidence would be called, there would be two potential difficulties. There could be a circular problem: whether that kind of hearing will be delayed might depend on whether the court accepts jurisdiction or not.[4]

6.10   Leaving the practical problem of possible circularity to one side, it is submitted that there is a principled objection to treating hearings at which evidence falls to be called as the only hearings which ought not to be held up. This is that the proceedings as a whole ought not to be delayed, for the sake of the complainant, the defendant, witnesses, and the public interest generally. Delay in concluding proceedings can eventually lead to a breach of Article 6(1) of the ECHR: the state is required to secure "determination" of a criminal charge "within a reasonable time".[5] There is a public interest in finality of proceedings.

The need for an opportunity to appeal or review a decision

6.11   The second policy consideration discerned in the purpose of section 29(3) of the SCA 1981 is that of providing a remedy where there is none.

6.12   We have already discussed the difficulties consultees had with the test of "no alternative remedy", and explained why, in some circumstances, we think that a post-conviction right of appeal is an adequate remedy.[6] If the person directly affected by the ruling has an opportunity to have its lawfulness reviewed, whether post-conviction appeal or otherwise, we consider that he or she has an adequate remedy.

Conclusion

6.13   Interruption to and delay of hearings which involve jurors or witnesses are particularly undesirable but the proceedings as a whole should be concluded as speedily as is consistent with a just outcome. We conclude that the policy considerations behind the bar in section 29(3) do not apply with anything like the same force to rulings made after the end of the trial (whether by acquittal, sentence or in some other way) as to those which are made before that point.

APPEAL OR REVIEW?

6.14   In order to explain our view on whether the High Court or the Court of Appeal might be the more appropriate court to hear a challenge to a ruling of the Crown Court, it is worth investigating how the roles of the High Court and the Court of Appeal differ.

---

[4]   Eg, in *R (Hasani) v Blackfriars Crown Court* [2005] EWHC 3016 (Admin), [2006] 1 WLR 1992, the defendant had been found unfit to plead. Some time later it appeared that he was fit to plead and the Crown Court ordered that he be arraigned. It had not, however, held a fitness hearing and determined the issue of fitness. If the order was quashed then a hearing would follow (a fitness hearing) – if the order was not quashed then the defendant sought an absolute discharge, which might have necessitated a court hearing, but not necessarily one at which evidence would be called. In the event, the High Court granted judicial review and quashed the Crown Court's order.

[5]   See, eg, *Archbold* (2010) 16-73: Article 6(1) is "directed primarily towards excessive procedural delays in the conduct of a prosecution, including any appeal".

[6]   See paras 5.4 to 5.14 above.

Review

6.15   Generally speaking, the High Court's function on judicial review is supervisory. The court is restricted in the basis on which it may intervene:

> It is important to remember always that this is judicial review of, and not an appeal against, the judge's decision. We can only intervene if persuaded that his decision was perverse or that there was some failure to have regard to material considerations or that account was taken of immaterial considerations or that there was some material misdirection.[7]

6.16   Where, however, a challenge is based upon an alleged infringement of a Convention right, this statement must be modified, as we now discuss.

The role of the reviewing court where violation of a Convention right is alleged

6.17   The courts have considered their role where it is alleged that a Convention right has been breached in a number of cases since the introduction of the Human Rights Act 1998. The role will vary, depending on the Convention right in question (absolute or qualified), whether it is a negative or positive obligation under the right which arises, and on the kind of decision-maker whose decision is under examination.

6.18   The leading authority is now taken to be *Huang*,[8] as explained in *Re E*.[9] *Re E* was a review of the approach taken by the Royal Ulster Constabulary to harassment by one group of people in Belfast of another group of people going about their lawful business, which included children going to school. The Convention right in issue was Article 3 (the prohibition against inhuman or degrading treatment or punishment) and what the police ought to have done in light of the positive obligation which arises under it. Lady Hale summarised the position as follows:

> It is now clear that, under the Human Rights Act, the court must make its own assessment of whether a public authority has acted incompatibly with the convention rights. That said, as Lord Bingham said in *Huang*, para 16, the court has to "give appropriate weight to the judgment of a person with responsibility for a given subject matter and access to special sources of knowledge and advice".[10]

6.19   Lord Carswell, with whom their Lordships agreed, set out the development of the law out in some detail. He returned to the statement of Lord Bingham in *R (SB) v Governors of Denbigh High School*:[11]

---

[7]   *R v Manchester Crown Court ex parte McDonald* [1999] 1 WLR 841, 855 by Lord Bingham.

[8]   [2007] UKHL 11, [2007] 2 AC 167.

[9]   [2008] UKHL 66, [2009] 1 AC 536.

[10]   [2008] UKHL 66, [2009] 1 AC 536 at [13] quoting *Huang* [2007] UKHL 11, [2007] 2 AC 167 at [16] by Lord Bingham.

[11]   [2006] UKHL 15, [2007] 1 AC 100.

The domestic court must now make a value judgment, an evaluation, by reference to the circumstances prevailing at the relevant time ... . Proportionality must be judged objectively, by the court ... .[12]

6.20 Lord Carswell noted also that Lord Bingham "further observed at para 31 that what matters 'is the practical outcome, not the quality of the decision-making process that led to it'."[13]

6.21 In summary, the courts would, we submit, approach the issues as follows. There is a range of conclusions which the Crown Court might reach in response to an application. Within that range, there will be a band of reasonable conclusions. Where a Convention right is engaged, that band may be narrower, and the decision-making court's approach more constrained, than where no Convention right is engaged. The reviewing court will not decide the matter afresh, but will make its own assessment of how one right is weighed against another, and the intensity of the review will increase if an absolute Convention right or an unqualified obligation is engaged. *Archbold* puts it thus:

The High Court will not simply substitute its own view, but it will subject the decision under review to a degree of scrutiny appropriate to the interest to be protected. In particular, it will need to be satisfied as to the proportionality of the decision.[14]

Appeal

6.22 Appeal may be as of right, or with leave, and the grounds on which it may be made are likely to be set out in statute. Appeal may denote a rehearing and the court may be able to reach its own conclusions as to the facts (as, for example, in an appeal to the Crown Court from the magistrates' court) and determine the outcome of the case.

The CACD

6.23 The CACD cannot be simply categorised as either an appellate court or as a supervisory court. In some circumstances the CACD is careful not to substitute its own view for that of the jury or of the judge, while in others it is empowered to substitute its view for that of the Crown Court.

---

[12] *Re E* [2008] UKHL 66, [2009] 1 AC 536 at [52] citing *R (SB) v Governors of Denbigh High School* [2006] UKHL 15, [2007] 1 AC 100 at [30].

[13] *Re E* [2008] UKHL 66, [2009] 1 AC 536 at [52] citing *R (SB) v Governors of Denbigh High School* [2006] UKHL 15, [2007] 1 AC 100 at [31]. See also *R (Nasseri) v Secretary of State for the Home Department* [2009] UKHL 23, [2010] AC 1 at [12] where Lord Bingham's observations were relied upon. An example from a different context again shows the High Court needing to go into the merits of the decision, as in *R (Wilkinson) v Broadmoor Special Hospital Authority* [2001] EWCA Civ 1545, [2002] 1 WLR 419 where the Convention right in issue was Article 5 (the right to liberty and security of persons). See also *R (JB) v Haddock* [2006] EWCA Civ 961, [2006] All ER 137 at [63] to [65] by Auld LJ.

[14] *Archbold* (2010) 7-13.

6.24 On an appeal against conviction to the CACD there is no rehearing. The court shall allow the appeal if it finds that the conviction is unsafe.[15] The court does not substitute its own view of whether the offence is proved, and the "appeal" is not therefore an appeal in the pure sense. As the Court of Appeal itself has said, "the Criminal Division is perhaps more accurately described as a court of review".[16]

6.25 As a court of review, it does not generally make findings of fact or hear evidence. Where the trial judge has made a finding of fact,

> 1. the Court of Appeal will not intervene merely because the members of the court disagree with the way the trial judge decided; but
>
> 2. will do so even if no specific error can be identified, if no reasonable judge could have reached the conclusion to which the trial judge came.[17]

6.26 When the Court of Appeal reviews the correctness of a point of law, similarly, it does not simply substitute its own view for that of the judge.[18] Thus the CACD, when dealing with an appeal against conviction, is carrying out a function which is closer to that of a reviewing court. However, the CACD also hears other kinds of appeals, such as a prosecution appeal against a ruling of the Crown Court,[19] or a ruling in a preparatory hearing.[20] In relation to these kinds of appeal the CACD may "confirm, reverse or vary" the ruling or decision in question.[21] In these kinds of appeals, the CACD is carrying out an appellate function because it may substitute its own view for that of the Crown Court.

---

[15] Section 2 of the Criminal Appeal Act 1968 (as amended by the Criminal Appeal Act 1995) says,
> (1) Subject to the provisions of this Act, the Court of Appeal-
>> (a) shall allow an appeal against conviction if they think that the conviction is unsafe; and
>> (b) shall dismiss such an appeal in any other case.

[16] *McIlkenny* [1992] 2 All ER 417, 425 by Lords Lloyd, Mustill and Farquharson. Since this judgment, procedure on appeals in civil cases has been modified by the Civil Procedure Rules (introduced in 1999 and amended since). The position in civil law may not now, therefore, be quite as described in this judgment, but there is still a significant difference between appeals to the Civil Division of the CA from appeals to the Criminal Division of the CA.

[17] R Pattenden, "The standards of review for mistake of fact in the Court of Appeal, Criminal Division" [2009] Criminal Law Review 15, 19.

[18] See, eg, *Koc* [2008] EWCA Crim 77 [2008] All Er 127 at [27].

[19] CJA 2003, ss 58 to 61.

[20] See paras 2.29 to 2.32 above. The governing provisions are s 35(3) of the Criminal Procedure and Investigations Act 1996 or s 9(14) of the Criminal Justice Act 1987. A detailed description is given at paras 2.70 to 2.89 of CP 184.

[21] See s 61(1) of the CJA 2003, s 35(3) of the Criminal Procedure and Investigations Act 1996, and s 9(14) of the Criminal Justice Act 1987.

What we proposed in the CP

6.27   We proposed a hybrid between review and appeal: we proposed a right of appeal to the CACD on judicial review-type grounds but that the CACD would have appellate powers, meaning the power to substitute its own view for that of the Crown Court judge.

The arguments

6.28   The trial judge is frequently best-placed to make a decision, having had conduct of the case, and sometimes having heard evidence on the point at issue. If the CACD is exercising a supervisory function – ensuring that fair procedures are followed – then supervisory powers are sufficient.

6.29   It could also be argued that if the CACD had the power to produce a different result then that in itself would make an application to it more attractive and thus make litigation more likely.

6.30   Against these arguments it may be said that it is the grounds which are key, and so long as the grounds on which a challenge may be made are restricted to judicial review grounds and no appeal on the merits is permitted, then it does not really matter if the reviewing/appellate court has the freedom to make whatever order it thinks fit. It could even be said that such freedom is more likely to lead to just decisions and to save resources by avoiding the need to remit cases to the originating court.

6.31   If it is positively desirable that the "supervising court" should be able to substitute its own view for that of the Crown Court in a case in which infringement of a Convention right does not arise, then the court to which the application needs to be made will be the CACD.

6.32   If, on the other hand, the "supervising court" should have a flexible range of powers which stops short of permitting that court to substitute its own view for that of the Crown Court, then the question as to whether the High Court or the CACD is the appropriate reviewing court remains open.

6.33   Further, in a case where infringement of a Convention right is alleged, it may not matter which court hears the challenge because they will both look to the substance of the decision and not just the decision-making process.

6.34   We now turn to the practical advantages and disadvantages of the supervisory jurisdiction remaining in the hands of the High Court or transferring to the CACD.

In favour of the CACD

6.35 Lord Justice Auld wrote, "there should be a single form of appeal and procedure combining the best of both jurisdictions. The only question is to what court should it go?"[22] It would certainly be preferable for criminal matters to have a single path for appeals but as we have already noted, this is not going to be possible. Lord Justice Auld's recommendations for streamlining in respect of cases on appeal from the magistrates have been rejected by the Government, and so the High Court will retain jurisdiction for case stated from and judicial review of magistrates' cases for the time being.[23]

In favour of judicial review

6.36 The Law Reform Committee of the Bar Council feared the loss of judicial review. They thought that transferring the judicial review functions to the CACD is unnecessary, and worse, that it is potentially dangerous. They wrote:

> Judicial review has … proved to be a useful protection of the individual, in particular see the run of cases concerning custody time limits.[24] Although it is difficult to see why these arguments could not have been run in the Court of Appeal, and no great prejudice would result from the proposed changes which would in future require an appellant to go to the Court of Appeal rather than the High Court, we are firmly of the view that it would be wrong to abolish judicial review so far as it relates to the Crown Court. We have already seen the erosion of habeas corpus, to abolish judicial review as well would in our view be potentially dangerous.
>
> …
>
> It is noted that the Law Commission recognises at para 4.47 [of CP 184] that the position is far less straightforward in relation to the High Court's supervisory powers in judicial review than case stated. We share the Law Commission's caution but not its conclusion. Whilst it is recognised that the number of judicial reviews of decisions of the Crown Court are not large we are strongly opposed to any proposal to abolish this route.

---

[22] Auld LJ, *Review of the Criminal Courts of England and Wales* (September 2001) ch 12, para 37.

[23] See paras 4.3 to 4.5 above.

[24] *R v Manchester Crown Court, ex p McDonald* [1999] 1 Criminal Appeal Reports 409; *R v Sheffield Crown Court, ex p Headley* [2000] 2 Criminal Appeal Reports 1.

The supervisory role of the High Court as a protection of the individual's common law rights is a fundamental bulwark of our legal system. The current arrangements properly prevent the High Court from interfering with the trial process whilst at the same time allowing the High Court to prevent the Crown Court from exceeding its powers or acting procedurally improperly. We note that the Law Commission is not proposing to abolish these safeguards but to transfer them from the High Court to the Court of Appeal. This is unnecessary. The current arrangements whereby a two-member Divisional Court hears judicial reviews in criminal causes or matters works well and would not be improved by the proposed transfer. We therefore oppose the provisional proposal to abolish section 29(3) of the Supreme Court Act 1981.

6.37 A highly significant feature of moving the jurisdiction to the CACD from the High Court is that the Court of Appeal is a creature of statute, and would have only those powers conferred on it by statute,[25] unlike the High Court, which exercises an inherent jurisdiction as well as statutory powers and has considerable flexibility.[26] The Court of Appeal would have less flexibility to manage cases which fell at the margins of its statutory powers. The flexibility of the High Court seems to us a significant advantage.

6.38 A practical advantage of retaining judicial review is that the solution to the problem might be simpler,[27] and, given the scale of the problem,[28] complicated legislative solutions could be disproportionate.

Conclusion

6.39 The essential difference between the traditional functions of appeal and review is whether the reviewing/appellate court has the power to substitute its own view for that of the court being reviewed. However, the role of the Court of Appeal can be described as supervisory in some circumstances, and conversely, the High Court goes beyond a supervisory review in some circumstances.

---

[25] "The Court of Appeal is a creature of statute and has no jurisdiction other than that accorded by statute or that which is ancillary to such jurisdiction by reason of implication" *G v Secretary of State* [2004] EWCA Civ 265, [2004] 1 WLR 1349 at [13] by Lord Phillips. This would include "the ability, like any other court of record, in certain areas to control its own procedure": *Taylor on Appeals* (2000) 10-032.

[26] As recently discussed in *T-Mobile and Telefonica O2 v Ofcom* [2008] EWCA Civ 1373, [2009] 1 WLR 1565 at [18] to [20] and *IBA Healthcare Ltd v Office of Fair Trading* [2004] EWCA Civ 142, [2004] All ER 1103 at [100].

[27] For example, it is inherent in judicial review proceedings that such proceedings are not appropriate if another remedy is available. See, eg, Lord Bingham's dictum in *Kay v Lambeth LBC* [2006] UKHL 10, [2006] 2 AC 465 at [30]: "if other means of redress are conveniently and effectively available to a party they ought ordinarily to be used before resort to judicial review".

[28] See para 1.5 above.

6.40   If the whole of the High Court's criminal jurisdiction were to be transferred to the CACD, we could see that it would be beneficial for the "supervisory" jurisdiction currently afforded by section 29(3) of the SCA 1981 to be passed to the CACD, although we would have some reservations about the possible loss of flexibility. Such a transfer would be better as part of a wholesale reform of the system of appeals in criminal proceedings. We do not see this as a realistic possibility in light of the responses we received on consultation and therefore conclude that it is best to retain and reform judicial review.

REDUCING THE SCOPE FOR DELAY AND INTERRUPTION TO TRIALS

6.41   In our recommendations we aim to balance the provision of a right of challenge where it is needed against the avoidance of delay or interruption to trials. Our view is that, generally, the High Court ought to be precluded from having jurisdiction over the Crown Court in its trial on indictment jurisdiction, whether by way of case stated or by way of judicial review.

6.42   We therefore conclude that, in the interests of simplifying criminal procedure, appeal by way of case stated from the Crown Court in criminal causes or matters should be abolished. We so recommend in Part 7 below.

6.43   It is clear that the case for excluding judicial review of a trial on indictment once it has reached the Crown Court is strong, and the terms of the exclusionary bar – the statutory provision which prevents the High Court having judicial review jurisdiction over the Crown Court – need to be made clearer. Once, however, the trial has ended, whether with an acquittal, sentence or in some other way, then a challenge by way of judicial review does not have the same disruptive potential. We conclude that there should be a right of review for rulings made following the verdict, other than sentence, where there is no existing right of review or appeal, so long as there is no other remedy. This is the function of our recommendation in Part 8 below.

In what circumstances is a right of challenge before the end of the trial justified?

6.44   There is still the question of whether any circumstances justify a right of challenge before the end of a trial on indictment, in addition to those which already exist.[29] We have considered whether there are any specific situations where the need to challenge a ruling, and the absence of any alternative way of doing so, do justify delay and interruption to proceedings. We examined the following specific cases:

(1)   where the court rules that a defendant should be handcuffed before the court;

(2)   where the decision leads to the release of information which cannot be retrieved, resulting in an invasion of privacy;

(3)   where the decision leads to the identification of a child or young person;

---

[29]   The various possibilities for an interlocutory appeal under the current law are described in Part 2 above.

(4)   where a person is remanded in custody pending trial or the completion of the trial; and

(5)   where the decision results in a real and immediate threat to a person's life.

Interruption to a trial is not justified in the following situations

6.45   While we recognise that others may draw the line in a different place, we have concluded that in the first two situations, a right of challenge which can be exercised before the end of the trial is not justified.

HANDCUFFING IN COURT

6.46   In our view, where the court orders that a defendant should be handcuffed in court, other remedies are sufficient. For example, if the complaint is that the handcuffing gave rise to prejudice in the jury's minds which led them to convict unfairly, the post-conviction appeal is, in our view, an appropriate remedy.[30]

THE RELEASE OF INFORMATION WHICH CANNOT BE RETRIEVED, RESULTING IN A POTENTIAL BREACH OF ARTICLE 8

6.47   There is a variety of judicial decisions which could lead to interference with a person's rights under Article 8 of the ECHR.[31] Such a decision might be:

(1)   an order for disclosure of personal records or documents or confidential information,

(2)   a refusal to allow proceedings to be held in camera, or

(3)   a ruling permitting publication of the proceedings.

---

[30]   See, eg *Horden* [2009] EWCA Crim 388, (2009) 173 Justice of the Peace and Local Government Law 254, where the CACD held that the decision to allow handcuffs in the dock was wrong, but in the circumstances it had not had an adverse effect on the conviction, which was allowed to stand. Handcuffing a defendant is permissible and does not breach Article 3 of the ECHR if it is done only where reasonably necessary to prevent an escape or a violent breach of the peace: *Cambridge Justices, ex p Peacock* (1992) 156 Justice of the Peace and Local Government Law 895. If it is done to humiliate the individual then there will be a breach of Article 3: *Raninen v Finland* (1997) 26 EHRR 563; *Henaf v France* (2005) 40 EHRR 990. See *R (Faizovas) v Secretary of State for Justice* [2008] EWHC 1197 (Admin), [2008] ACD 345(82) QBD.

[31]   See para 10.3 below for the terms of Art 8.

6.48   We are mindful of the needs of victims, witnesses and defendants to have the trial proceed without undue delay. Interference with a person's Article 8 rights may be justified under Article 8(2), and give effect to other Convention rights. We note that, as we described in CP 184, even if the original decision breaches a person's Convention rights in some way, the fact that the decision is not amenable to challenge does not give rise to a further breach.[32] We have therefore concluded that it would be disproportionate to introduce a new general right of challenge to any decision which engages Article 8. We have, however, examined specific instances in which Article 8 may be engaged, as we now explain.

Challenging an order that personal records or confidential information be disclosed

6.49   We have considered specifically the position of witnesses who are compelled to disclose medical records or similar personal information, and concluded that their position is now protected following amendment to the Criminal Procedure Rules. There should be less need for challenge,[33] as compared with the law which obtained in *R (TB) v The Combined Court at Stafford*).[34] We think it is a pertinent point that the right to intervene and have one's concerns taken into account of at the time the court makes its ruling is more use than a possible right of appeal or review after an order has been made.

Challenging a refusal to order that proceedings be held in private

6.50   There are various statutory powers which enable a court to exclude the public,[35] and the court has an inherent jurisdiction to do so.[36]

6.51   Section 159(1)(b) of the Criminal Justice Act 1988 allows any "person aggrieved" to appeal against any order restricting the access of the public to the whole or any part of a trial on indictment or to any proceedings ancillary to such a trial.

6.52   The Act does *not* provide a right of appeal where an order is refused altogether. In so ruling, the Court of Appeal has said,

---

[32]   See Part 3 of CP 184.

[33]   By virtue of rule 28.5(3) an application for a witness to produce a document or to give evidence about information apparently held in confidence must be served on the proposed witness and on a person to whom the proposed evidence relates. 28.5(4) provides time for representations to be made. It also prevents the court from issuing a witness summons under rule 28 unless the court is satisfied that "it has been able to take adequate account of the duties and rights, including rights of confidentiality, of the proposed witness and of any person to whom the proposed evidence relates". Rule 28.6 allows a person served to object to the proposed summons, and rule 28.7 allows him or her to ask the court to withdraw the summons.

[34]   [2006] EWHC 1645, [2007] 1 WLR 1524. In this case, TB, aged 14, was the main witness in a trial on indictment. She had a history of mental illness which, the defence argued, was relevant to her credibility. The judge ordered the relevant NHS Trust to disclose her medical records to the defence. She was neither notified of that hearing nor represented at it. The Criminal Procedure Rules were changed by Statutory Instrument in 2007.

[35]   Eg, on a review of a sentence under s 74 of the Serious Organised Crime and Police Act 2005: s 75(2)(a).

[36]   See, eg, *Wang Yam* [2008] EWCA Crim 269, [2008] All ER (D) 212 (Jan).

That the power of the court should be so limited is unsurprising. After all, appeals of the type contemplated in this case would be productive of inconvenience and delay. There are powerful policy reasons against such appeals.[37]

We agree.

Challenging a ruling permitting publication of reports of proceedings

6.53 There is a variety of court powers to restrict publication of reports of proceedings and identification of participants in the proceedings. Some of those powers serve to protect particular groups of people, such as complainants where sexual offences are alleged, or children and young people. Section 159(1) of the CJA 1988 allows a "person aggrieved" to appeal, with leave, against an order restricting publication. Section 159(1) does not provide a right of appeal against a refusal to make an order restricting publication; Parliament thought this was not needed.[38]

6.54 There are evident policy reasons for not having a right of appeal against a refusal to restrict reporting of proceedings: such appeals would be common; reporting is, generally speaking, in the public interest; delay and cost would be increased. We have thus concluded that, with one exception, no general right of challenge to rulings about reporting of proceedings before or during trial should be introduced.

6.55 The exception is the court's power to restrict the reporting of any matter which would lead to the identification of a child or young person concerned in the proceedings. Section 39 of the Children and Young Persons Act 1933 provides a protection for children and young people against their identification in reports of court proceedings. We describe this provision, and the reasons that we think there should be a right of challenge to a refusal to prohibit publication in these circumstances in Part 10 below. We wish to highlight here, however, a possible consequence of the fact that the law makes special provision for children and young people in this context.

6.56 The statutory protection for children and young people against identification in reports of proceedings, of long-standing in English law, accords with Articles 3.1[39] and 40(2)(b)[40] of the United Nations Convention on the Rights of the Child.[41] The House of Lords has explained the status of this Convention in UK law as follows:

---

[37] *Salih* [1995] 2 Criminal Appeal Reports 347 at 349 by Steyn LJ.

[38] See *Hansard* HL 23 Nov 1987 vol 490, col 523.

[39] "In all actions concerning children, whether undertaken by public or private social welfare institutions, courts of law, administrative authorities or legislative bodies, the best interests of the child shall be a primary consideration."

[40] "Every child alleged as or accused of having infringed the penal law has at least the following guarantees:... To have his or her privacy fully respected at all stages of the proceedings."

[41] Ratified by the UK, though not incorporated into domestic law.

This is not only binding in international law; it is reflected in the interpretation and application by the European Court of Human Rights of the rights guaranteed by the European Convention: see, for example, *V v United Kingdom* (1999) 30 EHRR 131; to that extent at least, therefore, it must be taken into account in the interpretation and application of those rights in our national law.[42]

6.57   The protection afforded to a child or young person is not available in the same way to others, such as a vulnerable adult. The courts have the power to make orders prohibiting the publication of details identifying adults concerned in proceedings, but the onus is on the person seeking to restrict publication, whereas in the case of a child or young person the onus is on the party seeking to permit publication. Notwithstanding the special position of a minor, there could be a violation of Article 14 (freedom of discrimination) of the ECHR, in conjunction with violation of a person's right to privacy under Article 8 if a state was found to provide a right to one class of individuals but not to others and the distinction could not be justified.[43] It may be that the different treatment of children and young people could be justified, but we recognise that, if it could not, then the consequence of our approach is that the complaint of a breach of Articles 8 and 14 could not be litigated in the domestic courts, but would have to be litigated before the European Court of Human Rights.

Circumstances which do justify delay and interruption of a trial

6.58   In the three cases listed at paragraph 6.44 (3) to (5), however, we take a different view. In each of them there is no other way of challenging the Crown Court ruling, and the consequences of the ruling are serious and, most importantly, cannot be undone by a post-conviction right of appeal.

6.59   We therefore think that, while judicial review should be prohibited before the end of a trial on indictment, the lawfulness of a Crown Court ruling in a trial should be subject to review or appeal:

   (1)   if the ruling is a denial of bail and there will be no other opportunity to challenge the lawfulness of the remand in custody; or

   (2)   if the ruling is one which, in the opinion of the court, could entail an immediate and serious risk to a person's life from the criminal act of another.

   (3)   There should also be a right to challenge a refusal to make reporting restrictions for the protection of a child or young person.

6.60   These three situations are ones where, in our view, the decisions of the Crown Court should be subject to the supervision of either High Court or the Court of Appeal even after the trial has started, and these situations are described in detail in Parts 9 to 11 below.

---

[42] *R v Durham Constabulary ex parte R (FC)* [2005] UKHL 21 [26]. *V v UK* is also reported at (2000) 30 EHRR 121.

[43] See Lester, Pannick and Herberg *Human Rights Law and Practice* (3rd ed) 4.14.12.

6.61   In the case of (1) we recommend that the challenge should be by way of judicial review, as an exception to the prohibition on judicial review once the Crown Court is seised of a trial on indictment, because the court's role is supervisory.

6.62   In the case of (2) and (3) we recommend that there should be a new statutory appeal for each, to go to the CACD, because the CACD should be able to substitute its own view for that of the Crown Court. We would argue that (2) and (3) represent reforms which would be worthwhile on their own, but we see them as an integral part of the whole.

PART 7
REMOVAL OF APPEAL BY WAY OF CASE STATED

7.1 Appeal by way of case stated is a mode of challenge available to parties to the proceedings against court rulings and decisions. In the CP, in the context of proposing a new statutory appeal, we proposed abolishing it (proposal 8.5). In this Part, we recommend abolishing appeal by way of case stated from the Crown Court in criminal causes or matters.

THE CURRENT LAW

7.2 The procedure of appeal by way of case stated was recently described by Lord Justice Leveson as, "a request to the court to determine issues of law raised in a case stated by the magistrates after both sides have had an opportunity to comment upon it. Such an appeal is freestanding and depends only upon the facts found by the court."[1] A case may of course be stated by the Crown Court as well as by the magistrates.

7.3 Case stated in the Crown Court is governed by section 28 of the SCA 1981. Section 28 appears in Part II of the Act, which is headed "Jurisdiction". The section is headed, "Appeals from Crown Court and inferior courts" and reads:

> (1) Subject to subsection (2), any order, judgment or other decision of the Crown Court may be questioned by any party to the proceedings, on the ground that it is wrong in law or is in excess of jurisdiction, by applying to the Crown Court to have a case stated by that court for the opinion of the High Court.
>
> (2) Subsection (1) shall not apply to—
>
> > (a) a judgment or other decision of the Crown Court relating to trial on indictment; or
> >
> > (b) any decision of that court under . . . the Local Government (Miscellaneous Provisions) Act 1982 which, by any provision of any of those Acts, is to be final.
>
> (3) Subject to the provisions of this Act and to rules of court, the High Court shall, in accordance with section 19(2), have jurisdiction to hear and determine—
>
> > (c) any application, or any appeal (whether by way of case stated or otherwise), which it has power to hear and determine under or by virtue of this or any other Act; and
> >
> > (d) all such other appeals as it had jurisdiction to hear and determine immediately before the commencement of this Act.

---

[1] *M v DPP* [2009] EWHC 752 (Admin), [2009] All ER 272 at [2].

(4) In subsection (2)(a) the reference to a decision of the Crown Court relating to trial on indictment does not include a decision relating to an order under section 17 of the Access to Justice Act 1999.

7.4 The effect of subsection (4) is that if the Crown Court makes an order requiring a publicly funded defendant to pay some or all of the costs of his or her representation (a Recovery of Defence Costs Order), then an appeal by way of case stated against it is still possible.

7.5 Where a case is stated by the Crown Court, section 28A of the SCA 1981 applies, by virtue of section 28A(1)(b). It reads:

> 28A. Proceedings on case stated by magistrates' court or Crown Court
>
> (1) This section applies where a case is stated for the opinion of the High Court—
>
> (a) by a magistrates' court under section 111 of the Magistrates' Courts Act 1980; or
>
> (b) by the Crown Court under section 28(1) of this Act.
>
> (2) The High Court may, if it thinks fit, cause the case to be sent back for amendment and, where it does so, the case shall be amended accordingly.
>
> (3) The High Court shall hear and determine the question arising on the case (or the case as amended) and shall—
>
> (a) reverse, affirm or amend the determination in respect of which the case has been stated; or
>
> (b) remit the matter to the magistrates' court, or the Crown Court, with the opinion of the High Court,
>
> and may make such other order in relation to the matter (including as to costs) as it thinks fit.
>
> (4) Except as provided by the Administration of Justice Act 1960 (right of appeal to the Supreme Court in criminal cases), a decision of the High Court under this section is final.

7.6 Appeal by way of case stated is available in respect of decisions made by magistrates' courts under a separate statutory provision.[2]

7.7 Only parties to the proceedings can bring a case stated in relation to a ruling of the Crown Court.

---

[2]   Magistrates' Courts Act 1980, s 111.

7.8   A case stated may not be brought before the conclusion of the proceedings.[3] It must be made within 21 days after the date of the decision complained of.[4] There is no power to extend that time limit.[5]

7.9   The grounds on which a case may be stated are restricted to those where the court is said to have made an error of law or acted in excess of jurisdiction.

7.10   An application is made to the court whose decision the applicant seeks to challenge. Thus, in relation to decisions of the Crown Court, an application is made to the Crown Court to state a case, following rule 64.6 of the Criminal Procedure Rules.

The scope of section 28 of the SCA 1981

7.11   As with section 29(3) of the SCA 1981, section 28 of the SCA 1981 extends to appeals against rulings of the Crown Court made in the exercise of its civil jurisdiction. A case may also be stated for the High Court by other courts such as magistrates' courts and the Summary Appeal Court under other statutory provisions.[6] The High Court may also have a case stated for it by a judicial body other than a court, such as a Commons Commissioner.[7] Our remit extends only to cases stated by the Crown Court, and then within that category, only to criminal proceedings.

7.12   The jurisdiction of the Crown Court derives from the Courts Act 1971.[8] That Act transferred to the Crown Court all appellate and other jurisdictions formerly exercised by a court of quarter session.[9] The Crown Court's appellate role still extends beyond criminal matters. There is a right of appeal against certain orders from a magistrates' court.[10] There is also a right of appeal against certain decisions of licensing justices and other decisions of magistrates' courts on licensing matters. There is also power to bind a person over.

7.13   The Crown Court also has the jurisdiction to hear appeals against some decisions of local and other authorities.[11]

---

[3] *Loade v DPP* [1990] 1 QB 1052.

[4] *Criminal Procedure Rules* r 64.6(1).

[5] *Chief Constable of Cleveland v Vaughan* [2009] All ER 123.

[6] Section 111 of the Magistrates' Courts Act 1980 and s 149(2) of the Armed Forces Act 2006 respectively.

[7] Under s 18 of the Commons Registration Act 1965. That provision has been repealed but the repeal has not yet been brought into force. See Commons Act 2006, s 53, Sch 6, Pt 1.

[8] See also SCA 1981, s 45.

[9] Courts Act 1971, s 56(2) and Sch 9.

[10] Eg, s 67(2) of the Public Health (Control of Disease) Act 1984; s 102(1) of the Children and Young Persons Act 1933; against the making of a football banning order on a complaint or against the refusal to make such an order: s 14D(1) and s 14D(1A) of the Football Spectators Act 1989 as amended.

[11] Such as certain decisions of a police authority in relation to police pensions, and certain decisions of a chief officer of police in relation to firearms certificates.

7.14 We note also that appeal by way of case stated is available in respect of decisions made by magistrates' courts, and our recommendations cannot directly affect that procedure.

7.15 Appeals against decisions of the Crown Court by way of case stated are infrequent: in recent years there have not been more than 23 each year.

THE PROPOSAL IN THE CP (PROPOSAL 8.5 (QUESTION 9.1))

7.16 We provisionally proposed that section 28(1) of the SCA 1981 be amended so as to preclude all orders, judgments or other decisions of the Crown Court made in criminal proceedings being challenged by way of appeal by case stated to the High Court.

7.17 We were seeking to widen the exclusion in section 28(2)(a) to all judgments or other decisions of the Crown Court in criminal proceedings where the Crown Court is acting as a court of first instance, in its appellate (criminal) capacity, and where a person has been committed to the Crown Court for sentence.

The views of respondents

7.18 All respondents who commented on this proposal and question were content. As the Law Reform Committee of the Bar Council commented, "we believe that case stated in particular to be an unsatisfactory route of appeal and as the paper demonstrates it is rarely invoked".

The merits

7.19 A party may be faced with choosing between judicial review and appeal by case stated. That in itself complicates criminal procedure. If the case stated process is not serving a distinct purpose, then abolishing it could usefully simplify criminal procedure.[12]

7.20 Whereas appeal by way of case stated would have been an important right at the time of the SCA 1981, judicial review has developed enormously since then and has in effect supplanted case stated.

7.21 Different time limits apply for appealing by way of case stated from applying for judicial review. A party may seek judicial review if it is out of time for case stated, but the court may refuse the remedy if it takes the view that the application was not made promptly and judicial review is being sought as a solution to being out of time for case stated.

---

[12] We note that appeal by way of case stated has recently been removed in relation to family proceedings in a magistrates' court: s 111(7) of the Magistrates' Courts Act 1980.

The disadvantages

(1) Getting the facts before the High Court

7.22   The courts have said that it is advantageous in some cases if the appellant proceeds by way of case stated because the factual basis is clearer for the court.[13] In *R v Morpeth Justices ex parte Ward*, which concerned a challenge to a decision by magistrates to bind over the applicant and others, Lord Justice Brooke said:

> Our task in this case was made unnecessarily difficult because the applicants did not adopt the procedure prescribed by Parliament for referring a point of law which has arisen in a magistrates' court to the High Court for decision. If the justices had stated a case for our opinion, we would have known what their findings of fact had been and their reasons for the decisions they took and they would have identified the relevant points of law for our decision in the familiar way.[14]

We query whether this is in practice a frequent problem as regards cases coming from the Crown Court.

7.23   Secondly, it seems to us that this difficulty could be mitigated by the adoption of suitable rules. This is not a matter for us, but, for example, Part 54 of the Civil Procedure Rules (which apply in respect of judicial review rather than the Criminal Procedure Rules) could be adapted if necessary.[15]

7.24   Alternatively, the matter might proceed by way of case law. There is recent guidance available from the Divisional Court on how judicial review should proceed where there are complicated legal and factual issues, especially where they concern the interpretation of Articles of the ECHR.[16]

(2) Is judicial review always going to be adequate or appropriate?

7.25   We have considered whether there are cases which could be appealed by way of case stated but which could not be brought within the scope of the legal bases for judicial review. We have not found any where this was the case, nor were any suggested to us on consultation.

---

[13]   See, eg *R v Crown Court at Ipswich ex parte Baldwin* [1981] 1 All ER 596 in which Baldwin was convicted before the magistrates, appealed to the Crown Court and lost the case at the Crown Court. He then sought judicial review, but the court said case stated would be much more appropriate "because then we can get at the facts" (at 596 by Donaldson LJ).

[14]   (1992) 95 Criminal Appeal Reports 215 at 221.

[15]   For example, if in an application for permission for judicial review in a criminal cause or matter the applicant were required also to state any relevant facts including the facts found by the Crown Court, (as in rule 64.6(13) of the *Criminal Procedure Rules* in relation to an appeal to the High Court by way of case stated) then the High Court could be provided with the facts it needs.

[16]   *R (Al-Sweady) v Secretary of State (No 2)* [2009] EWHC 2387 (Admin), *The Times* 14 October 2009.

(3) Is it worth the change?

7.26   In the Scoping Paper (July 2005) we said we had not identified any significant problems with the working of section 28(2)(a) of the SCA 1981 and therefore saw no need to simplify this jurisdiction. We did think that the bar on interlocutory case stated could do with being made express in legislation.

7.27   We note that we are not recommending that appeal by way of case stated be abolished altogether. Appeals from the magistrates by way of case stated and appeals from the Crown Court in its civil jurisdiction are outside our terms of reference and would remain. Consultees were content to see case stated removed and we also conclude that it would be a worthwhile simplification.

RECOMMENDATION

7.28   In the interests of simplifying criminal procedure, **we recommend that section 28(2) of the Senior Courts Act 1981 be amended so as to preclude all orders, judgments or other decisions of the Crown Court made in any criminal cause or matter being challenged by way of appeal by case stated to the High Court.**

7.29   The impact of the recommendation is to remove appeal by way of case stated from the Crown Court where it is acting in its appellate capacity, where a defendant was committed to it for sentence, and in any other criminal cause or matter.

7.30   The recommendation is reflected in clause 1 of the Bill. If enacted, this clause would amend section 28(1) and (2) of the SCA 1981 so that they would read:

> (1) Subject to subsection (2), any order, judgment or other decision of the Crown Court may be questioned by any party to the proceedings, on the ground that it is wrong in law or is in excess of jurisdiction, by applying to the Crown Court to have a case stated by that court for the opinion of the High Court.
>
> (2) Subsection (1) shall not apply to—
>
> > (a)   an order, judgment or other decision of the Crown Court in any criminal cause or matter; or
> >
> > (b)   any decision of that court under . . . the Local Government (Miscellaneous Provisions) Act 1982 which, by any provision of any of those Acts, is to be final.

7.31   Subsection (3) would be unaffected. Subsection (4) would be amended so that it would read:

> (4) In subsection (2)(a) the reference to a decision of the Crown Court in any criminal cause or matter does not include a decision relating to an order under section 17 of the Access to Justice Act 1999.

7.32   The effect of subsection (4) is that Recovery of Defence Costs Orders can be challenged by way of appeal by case stated, and our recommendation does not change this.

"Order"

7.33 There is a difference between the wording of section 28(1) and section 28(2)(a) of the SCA 1981. Section 28(1) of the SCA 1981 refers to "any order, judgment or other decision of the Crown Court", but section 28(2)(a) disapplies section 28(1) to "a judgment or other decision of the Crown Court relating to trial on indictment". We have tried to discover why this is, but have not succeeded. Section 28(1) creates a right of appeal which we wish to remove wholly in relation to criminal causes or matters by virtue of section 28(2)(a), and we have therefore included "order" in the amended section 28(2)(a).

"In any criminal cause or matter"

7.34 The recommendation refers to "in any criminal cause or matter". It does not thus extend to civil proceedings. See clause 1 in the Bill.

7.35 Orders *in* a criminal cause or matter are not the same as orders collateral to a criminal cause or matter.[17] Proceedings for forfeiture of a recognizance from a surety for bail might also be described as collateral to a criminal cause or matter.[18]

Extent

7.36 Section 28 of the SCA 1981 extends to England and Wales.[19] The extent of any amendment is the same.[20]

Consequential amendments

7.37 In considering the need for consequential amendments we have taken the view that, because case stated will persist as a mechanism of appeal in relation to civil cases and also in relation to criminal cases stated by a magistrates' court, in many places where legislation deals with appeals by way of case stated, no consequential amendment is needed. We now discuss two cases where consequential amendments are needed.

---

[17] *Re O (Restraint order: disclosure of assets)* [1991] 2 QB 520 (CA) by Donaldson MR. Restraint orders derived from ss 76 to 82 of the Criminal Justice Act 1988 are civil in character and collateral to the criminal regime. Therefore an appeal from the disclosure order in the restraint proceedings lay to the Court of Appeal (Civil Division). This was approved in *Government of the United States v Montgomery* [2001] UKHL 3, [2001] 1 WLR 196.

[18] *R v Southampton JJ ex parte Green* [1976] QB 11.

[19] SCA 1981, s 153(4).

[20] See cl 15(8) of the Bill.

Section 40(4) of the Road Traffic Offenders Act 1988

7.38   Section 40 of the Road Traffic Offenders Act 1988 falls within Part II of the Act, which is headed "Sentence". Section 40 is headed: "Power of appellate courts in England and Wales to suspend disqualification". Where D is convicted in England and Wales and disqualified from driving, subsection (2) allows the Crown Court to suspend the disqualification where D appeals to the Crown Court. Similarly, if D seeks to appeal to the Supreme Court, the Divisional Court or the Court of Appeal may suspend the disqualification.[21] Subsection (4) states:

> Where a person ordered to be disqualified makes an application in respect of the decision of the court in question under section 111 of the Magistrates' Courts Act 1980 (statement of case by magistrates' court) or section 28 of the Senior Courts Act 1981 (statement of case by Crown Court) the High Court may, if it thinks fit, suspend the disqualification.

7.39   Section 40 can only come into play in a criminal matter. The effect of our principal recommendation – to remove appeal by way of case stated against decisions and rulings and orders of the Crown Court in criminal matters – is that the defendant would not be able to apply to the Crown Court for a case to be stated in a criminal matter. The words "or section 28 of the Senior Courts Act 1981 (statement of case by Crown Court)" in section 40(4) will be without a purpose and paragraph 1(1) of Schedule 1 to the Bill repeals them by way of consequential amendment.

EXTENT

7.40   The provision in question clearly applies in relation to England and Wales only, though it extends to Scotland. Amendment to the Act has the same extent. See clause 15(9)(b) of the Bill.

Section 130(5) of the Licensing Act 2003

7.41   Part 6 of the Licensing Act 2003 concerns "Personal Licences". A personal licence is one granted to an individual by an authorised body to supply or authorise the supply of alcohol.[22] The individual may apply for a licence to a licensing authority. The authority is given powers to grant or reject the application for a licence. Such a licence is a valuable asset, and although the Act is concerned primarily with the licensing regime, it includes an additional sentencing power on conviction of a criminal offence, in section 129.

---

[21]   Road Traffic Offenders Act 1988, s 40(3).

[22]   Licensing Act 2003, s 111.

7.42   Section 129 gives the court which sentences a person for a "relevant offence"[23] an additional sentencing power: the court "may (a) order the forfeiture of the licence, or (b) order its suspension for a period not exceeding six months".[24] If the court makes such an order, it may suspend the order pending an appeal against the order.[25] The aim clearly is for a criminal court to take action to prevent a person from retaining a licence where he or she is not suitable to hold one by virtue of a criminal conviction.

7.43   Section 130 is headed "Powers of appellate court to suspend order under section 129". In the same way as the court making the section 129 order may suspend it pending an appeal, other courts are given the power to suspend it pending appeals. Section 130(5) gives the High Court the power to suspend the section 129 order where "the offender" appeals by way of case stated against a decision of the Crown Court under section 28 of the SCA 1981.

7.44   The removal of appeal by way of case stated which we seek to effect will mean that an offender cannot make an application for a case to be stated as described in section 130(5) of the Licensing Act 2003 and the words "or section 28 of the Senior Courts Act 1981 (c. 54) (statement of case by Crown Court)" in section 130(5) will be without a purpose. Paragraph 1(2) of Schedule 1 to the Bill therefore repeals those words by way of consequential amendment.

EXTENT

7.45   The Licensing Act 2003 extends to England and Wales only (with the exception of section 155(1) and the amendments and repeals it contained, which do not concern us).[26] Therefore amendment to the Act has the same extent.

Section 37(1)(b) of the Criminal Justice Act 1948 and section 81(1)(d) of the SCA 1981

7.46   It might appear at first sight that these provisions require consequential amendment because they concern powers of the High Court to grant bail in relation to case stated, but in fact the High Court may still seek to use those powers even once case stated is abolished for criminal causes and matters in the Crown Court, as we now explain.

7.47   Section 37(1)(b)(i) of the Criminal Justice Act 1948 allows the High Court to grant bail where a person has applied to have a case stated by the Crown Court or for judicial review of the Crown Court, and section 81(1)(d) of the SCA 1981 allows the Crown Court to grant bail where a person has applied to the Crown Court to state a case for the High Court.

---

[23]   Defined in Licensing Act, Sch 4.

[24]   Licensing Act 2003, s 129(2).

[25]   Licensing Act 2003, s 129(4).

[26]   Licensing Act 2003, s 201.

7.48   We have considered whether these provisions might have any application if case stated were removed in relation to criminal proceedings before the Crown Court. We have concluded that they could apply where civil proceedings are appealed from the magistrates to the Crown Court, and then there is a further appeal by way of case stated. This might occur where a person is bound over by the magistrates' courts to keep the peace,[27] and appeals to the Crown Court.[28]

7.49   Where the person has given notice of appeal to the Crown Court, the magistrates may grant bail under section 113 of the Magistrates' Courts Act 1980, but the Bail Act 1976 does not apply.[29] If they refuse bail then the individual may appeal against that refusal to the Crown Court which may grant bail under section 81(1)(c) of the SCA 1981.

7.50   If the appeal at the Crown Court fails, the individual may appeal by way of case stated. At this point the individual might still wish to appeal against a refusal of bail and would seek to rely on section 81(1)(d) of the SCA 1981 if applying to the Crown Court for bail, or on section 37(1)(b) of the Criminal Justice Act 1948 if applying to the High Court for bail.

7.51   These provisions could therefore serve a purpose even if appeal by way of case stated from the Crown Court is removed in any criminal cause or matter, and we have concluded therefore that no consequential amendment is appropriate.

Commencement

7.52   We anticipate that all the provisions relating to removal of appeal by case stated should come into effect at the same time, but that they could be implemented independently of other reforms in this report.

7.53   The reform would apply only to decisions made after the date the Bill is brought into force.

7.54   If an application to state a case has already been made but then the reform comes into effect before it has been determined, our view is that it is best for it to proceed. There is a time limit for applying for a case to be stated after all, which is relatively short, and no power to extend it.

---

[27]   There are common law powers and various statutory powers for a court to bind a person over to keep the peace. One such, s 115 of the Magistrates' Courts Act 1980, provides for a complaint to be made to a magistrates' court, and proceedings started by complaint are normally civil proceedings. In *Percy v DPP* [1995] 1 WLR 1382, the High Court did not determine whether such proceedings are civil or criminal. Ordinarily they would be considered civil – and there was no criminal charge nor allegation that a criminal offence had been committed – but where there was an attendant threat of imprisonment, the court was inclined to think they are criminal.

[28]   Under the Magistrates' Courts (Appeal from Binding Over Orders) Act 1956, s 1(1).

[29]   *Blackstone's* (2010) D28.13.

PART 8
JUDICIAL REVIEW OF THE CROWN COURT IN CRIMINAL PROCEEDINGS

8.1 In Part 2 above we described how the interpretation in the case law of the exclusionary bar in section 29(3) of the SCA 1981 has not been consistent. The imprecision of the expression "relating to trial on indictment" has given rise to frequent and costly litigation, and continues to do so.[1] The boundaries of the bar are still unclear, and there is no one rationale underpinning the conclusions in the cases. The problem is, in part, one of definition. We aim to recast section 29(3) in clearer terms.

8.2 In Part 6 above we discussed the policy reasons behind the exclusion of judicial review of the Crown Court in trial on indictment. We concluded that, because the risk of delay and interruption to proceedings is less significant once the trial has ended, the boundary needs to be redrawn to permit judicial review of rulings made after the end of a trial.

8.3 We think that both these aims can be achieved by amending section 29(3) of the SCA 1981. Thus section 29(3) would grant jurisdiction over the Crown Court to the High Court (as it does now) but exclude it in relation to the exercise of its trial on indictment jurisdiction up to the end of the trial, and this Part explains how that would work.

8.4 As we state at paragraphs 6.58 to 6.60 above, we think there should be an exception to the prohibition on judicial review for refusals of bail. That exception is described in Part 9 below.

OVERVIEW OF THE REFORMED PROVISION

8.5 As is stands, section 29(3) simultaneously grants and prohibits jurisdiction of the High Court over the Crown Court. We follow that model, but we would change the scope of the excluded jurisdiction. In addition, we define an exclusion period with beginning and end points: any decision within that exclusion period is not to be susceptible of judicial review unless it falls within an exception. Exceptions relate to bail, as described in Part 9, and to hospital orders, as described at paragraphs 8.62 to 8.64 below.

8.6 **We recommend that the High Court should not have supervisory jurisdiction over decisions in proceedings on indictment in the Crown Court which are within the exclusion period (which we define below) or which we specify in paragraphs 8.59 to 8.61 below, and that section 29(3) of the Senior Courts Act 1981 be amended accordingly.** See clause 2 of the Bill and the proposed new section 29A(1) to (3) of the SCA 1981. We describe the exclusion period below. Decisions specifically stated to be within the excluded jurisdiction are described at paragraphs 8.59 to 8.61 below.

---

[1] In 2009 the question came before the High Court whether s 29(3) barred judicial review of a refusal by a judge of the Crown Court to recuse himself when hearing a wasted costs application: *R (AB) v X Crown Court* [2009] EWHC 1149 (Admin), [2009] All ER (D) 230.

Limits of the excluded jurisdiction

8.7 It follows that if the Crown Court is exercising a jurisdiction *other* than its jurisdiction in proceedings on indictment, then the High Court's jurisdiction over it is not barred. This will be the case where the Crown Court is acting as an appellate court, is dealing with a person who has been committed to the Crown Court by the magistrates for sentence, is dealing with a person who has been found unfit to plead or be tried, or is exercising some other statutory jurisdiction.[2] It will also be the case where the Crown Court is exercising its civil jurisdiction.

8.8 An example of this last jurisdiction would be an application for judicial review by a surety who stands to lose money.[3] In *R v Southampton Justices ex parte Green*,[4] which was decided in the Civil Division of the CA, it was held that a recognizance is a "civil debt upon a bond" and an application to estreat a recognizance is a civil application.

THE EXCLUSION PERIOD

Defining the bar in terms of the stage of proceedings

8.9 The exclusion period is based on a chronological approach: cases move through different stages, and the bar on judicial review is effective for part of the time-line of a case. The High Court should not have jurisdiction over the Crown Court from the moment the latter is seised of a trial on indictment[5] up to the end of the trial.

8.10 The exclusion period begins when the case goes from the magistrates' court to the Crown Court for trial, or when an indictment is preferred[6] at the Crown Court via some other route.

---

[2] Such as the power to bind over a person to be of good behaviour. This power is derived from the Justices of the Peace Act 1361 and is exercised according to s 1(7) of the Justices of the Peace Act 1968.

[3] A surety is a person who offers a sum of money to the court which he or she will forfeit in the event of the accused not surrendering to the court at the appointed time. The sum of money is called the recognizance. The procedure by which the surety is ordered to forfeit the money is referred to as forfeiture of a recognizance or estreating the recognizance.

[4] [1976] QB 11. Comments in subsequent cases indicate that if the issue of what is a criminal cause or matter came before the Supreme Court it could be decided differently. Even if, however, proceedings for forfeiture of a recognizance were held to be criminal, rather than civil, the court would not be exercising its trial on indictment jurisdiction, and so the bar on judicial review that we recommend would not bite.

[5] The phrase "trial on indictment" encompasses cases where the defendant pleads not guilty to some or all charges and evidence is then heard, and cases where the defendant pleads guilty and there is no "trial": *Re Smalley* [1985] AC 622, 642 by Lord Bridge.

[6] "Preferred" is the term used in the primary legislation. It means that the indictment is served on the court officer or is laid before the court.

The beginning point: how a case reaches the Crown Court for trial

Cases sent, transferred or committed for trial by the magistrates' courts

8.11   Most trials on indictment originate in the magistrates' courts. A case may be sent, transferred or committed to the Crown Court from the magistrates' court for trial. In the future, all committal and transfer proceedings will be abolished, and all cases which go to the Crown Court from the magistrates will be "sent for trial" to the Crown Court under new "allocation" procedures.[7]

Cases coming from the Court of Appeal

8.12   A case can reach the Crown Court for trial on indictment other than via the magistrates' courts where a retrial is ordered by the Court of Appeal following a quashed conviction[8] or a quashed acquittal.[9] In those circumstances a fresh indictment is preferred.

The voluntary bill procedure

8.13   An alternative way for an indictment to be laid before the Crown Court is where the prosecution uses the "voluntary bill" procedure. The prosecution may present a draft indictment, with the consent of a High Court judge.[10] Such an indictment is called a voluntary bill of indictment.

8.14   This procedure might be needed where, for example, some defendants have been committed for trial and the prosecutor wishes other defendants to be tried in the same proceedings (and therefore does not wish to lose a trial date by waiting for committal proceedings to take place in respect of the second group of defendants); or where a charge was dismissed by magistrates at committal but the prosecution wishes to proceed on it.

8.15   The procedure might be needed where the prosecution wishes to proceed on a different indictment from the one before the court. Instead of amending the existing indictment the prosecutor might seek the court's leave to prefer a fresh indictment and for the first indictment to be quashed.

---

[7]   Sections 51 and 51A to 51E of the Crime and Disorder Act 1998 as substituted by the CJA 2003, s 41 and Sch 3, para 18, not all of which are yet in force or fully in force.

[8]   Under s 8 of the CAA 1968.

[9]   Under s 77(1) and (3) of the CJA 2003.

[10]   Administration of Justice (Miscellaneous Provisions) Act 1933, s 2(2)(b). See *Blackstone's* (2010) D10.48 and following.

Cases where a bill of indictment is preferred under section 22B(3)(a) of the Prosecution of Offences Act 1985

8.16 Particular parts of the passage of a case through the criminal justice system need to happen within a specified time limit. If the relevant stage of proceedings has not been completed in time, the appropriate court "shall stay the proceedings".[11] If such a stay is ordered, and the prosecution wishes to re-ignite the proceedings, section 22B of the Prosecution of Offences Act 1985 applies. It states that, if there is authorisation by a person in the prosecuting body of a specified status, then proceedings may be re-instituted within three months of the stay, or within a longer period if the court permits. In the case of proceedings which were stayed in the Crown Court, re-institution of the proceedings is "by preferring a bill of indictment" under section 22B(3)(a).

The beginning point is itself to be within the exclusion period

8.17 The exclusion period has the effect that the act of committal, transfer or sending, or the preferring of an indictment may not itself be challenged by judicial review.

8.18 In the majority of cases, it will be evident that the case has been sent, transferred or committed for trial, and it will be obvious that judicial review is not possible.

8.19 We have considered what might happen if a party raises the question of whether a case was in fact sent (or transferred or committed) from the magistrates' court to the Crown Court, due to error. If there was an error such that the case had not been validly sent, a party might argue that the exclusion, which only applied from the point when a case was sent to the Crown Court, did not bite. Similarly, if the verdict was allegedly invalid for some reason, there could then be argument about whether the point had been reached when the exclusion no longer applied. We believe that, in the light of recent case law, the High Court would agree that the exclusion period was nevertheless effective.[12]

8.20 **We therefore recommend that the exclusion period should begin with, and include, the earliest to happen of the following:**

> **the defendant is committed, transferred or sent for trial to the Crown Court,**
>
> **or a bill of indictment is preferred.**

See subsection (1) of the proposed new section 29B of the SCA 1981.

---

[11] Section 22(4) of the Prosecution of Offences Act 1985 and, in relation to time limits applicable in the case of a person under the age of 18 at the time of arrest, s 22A(5).

[12] See, eg, *Salubi* which concerned joined appeals about the then new procedure under s 51 of the Crime and Disorder Act 1998 for sending cases for the magistrates to the Crown Court without any committal proceedings. The defendants' cases straddled the implementation of s 51 and thus mistakes were made, and some defendants were "committed" when they should have been "sent". The High Court (Auld LJ and Gage J) held it had no jurisdiction to entertain applications for judicial review: [2002] EWHC 919 (Admin), [2002] 1 WLR 3073 at [49] by Auld LJ.

The end point of the exclusion period

8.21 Our view is that judicial review should be possible as regards rulings made after the end of the trial where no alternative remedy exists, for the reasons given in Part 6 above. The exclusion period therefore ends when the trial ends. In most cases it will be evident when a trial is over as regards each defendant, but we think that the statutory provision needs to specify when this is. It will be in one of the following ways.

A charge is dismissed

8.22 Before the defendant has been arraigned[13] (and whether or not an indictment has been preferred), if charges have been "sent" to the Crown Court under section 51 of the Crime and Disorder Act 1998, an application may be made to the Crown Court for the charges to be dismissed, under paragraph 2 of Schedule 3 to that Act.

8.23 The test for dismissal of a charge is whether it appears to the judge that "the evidence against the applicant would not be sufficient for him to be properly convicted". If the judge is so satisfied then he or she will dismiss the charge and, if an indictment has been preferred, quash the count. If the prosecution nevertheless wishes to proceed with the charge, its only option is to seek consent to a voluntary bill of indictment.

8.24 If the prospective changes to the ways in which cases move from the magistrates to the Crown Court for trial (see paragraph 8.11 above) are brought into force, then far more cases will be sent for trial, and the opportunity to apply for dismissal of the charges will assume greater importance.

A finding of unfitness to plead or to be tried

8.25 A defendant who appears before the Crown Court in its trial on indictment jurisdiction may suffer from such a disability such that it would be unfair for him or her to be tried in the usual way. When there is a question whether the defendant is fit to plead, the judge determines the issue. This may occur at any stage of the proceedings. After such a finding, the proceedings cease to be a trial on indictment.

After the indictment has been preferred

8.26 Once an indictment has been preferred, something has to happen to it, as described by Lord Goddard CJ:

---

[13] Arraignment is "a word meaning no more than reading the counts in an indictment to a defendant or defendants, and asking them to plead to those counts": Glidewell LJ in *R v Maidstone Crown Court, ex p Clark* [1995] 1 WLR 831, at 837. It takes place at the beginning of a preparatory hearing if there is one. This is not the point at which a jury is sworn. Custody time limits cease to run once arraignment has taken place.

Once an indictment is before the court the accused must be arraigned and tried thereon unless (a) on motion to quash or demurrer pleaded it is held defective in substance or form and not amended; (b) matter in bar is pleaded and the plea is tried or confirmed in favour of the accused; (c) a *nolle prosequi* is entered by the Attorney-General, which cannot be done before the indictment is found; or (d) if the indictment disclosed an offence which a particular court has no jurisdiction to try, for example, an indictment at sessions for an offence punishable with imprisonment for life in the first instance.[14]

8.27   An indictment may be amended but only with leave of the court, by virtue of section 5 of the Indictments Act 1915.[15] If the indictment is so defective as to be a nullity, it has to be quashed, not amended.

8.28   A verdict is given in respect of each count and each defendant joined in a count (unless the jury has been discharged entirely or from giving a verdict on a specific count).

Each count in an indictment is the equivalent of a separate indictment and falls to be dealt with as though it were a separate indictment...[16]

8.29   An indictment is not indivisible.[17] There are a number of possible permutations of defendants, counts (charges), and indictments. There may be more than one defendant on a single indictment.[18] While there may be more than one indictment in existence for a single defendant, there may not be more than one indictment in a single trial.[19] Thus if the prosecution has more than one indictment against D for the same offence – which may occur for good reason[20] – it will have to choose which one it wishes to pursue.

---

[14]   See *County of London Quarter Sessions ex parte Downes* [1954] 1 QB 1, 6 and *Blackstone's* (2010) D3.54. The terms "demurrer", "plea in bar" and "nolle prosequi" are explained in paragraphs 8.38 to 8.39 and 8.48 below.

[15]   Section 5(1): "Where, before trial, or at any stage of a trial, it appears to the court that the indictment is defective, the court shall make such order for the amendment of the indictment as the court thinks necessary to meet the circumstances of the case, unless, having regard to the merits of the case, the required amendments cannot be made without injustice."

[16]   *Plain* [1967] 1 All ER 614, 617 by Winn LJ.

[17]   "The law focuses not on the physical document, but on information contained in it. And all defendants, and all counts, cannot always be tried at the same time. In our judgment, a court undoubtedly has an inherent jurisdiction to stay an indictment in part where there are a number of defendants or a number of counts": *Munro* (1993) 97 Cr App R 183, 186 by Steyn LJ.

[18]   See *Assim* [1966] 2 QB 249 in which two defendants were jointly tried on separate counts on the one indictment, there was no joint charge on the indictment, but it was held proper for them to be tried together.

[19]   Consolidated Criminal Practice Direction, IV.34.2. *Crane v DPP* [1921] AC 299 in which two defendants were jointly tried on separate indictments, on connected facts.

[20]   See, eg *Groom* [1977] QB 6.

8.30   Conversely, an indictment may be severed, meaning that one or more counts are separated off and heard in a separate trial. A different situation again is that more than one defendant may be jointly charged in a single count, but they may be tried separately.

GUILTY/NOT GUILTY

8.31   The defendant should enter a plea or give an indication of plea at the first hearing in the Crown Court, if not before.[21] Putting the charge to the defendant and taking the plea is the arraignment. The arraignment does not necessarily happen at the same time as the empanelling of the jury. If a new count is added to an indictment after arraignment, then a plea will still need to be taken to it. A defendant's plea may thus be taken before or after the jury is sworn.

8.32   When the plea is taken, if the defendant pleads guilty, then he or she is convicted, but this is not a verdict.

8.33   If the defendant pleads guilty, but the facts on which he or she is to be sentenced are not agreed between the prosecution and defence then, if there is a material dispute, the court may hold a *Newton* hearing[22] at which evidence is called, and the judge will make findings of fact which will be the basis of sentence.[23]

8.34   A defendant may change a guilty plea up to the moment sentence is passed.[24] There may even be a change of plea after the jury's verdict has been entered, in unusual circumstances.

8.35   If the defendant pleads not guilty, there may be a jury trial, or a non-jury trial. If a trial takes place, there will be a verdict, which may be not guilty, guilty or a special verdict.[25]

Quashing of the indictment

8.36   A count may be quashed at any stage of the trial, on application by either the prosecution or the defence. A whole indictment may also be quashed. A quashed count or indictment is not equivalent to an acquittal and the prosecution may start fresh proceedings for the offences charged in the quashed indictment.

Staying the indictment/staying proceedings

8.37   An indictment may be stayed, in whole or in part, for example, as an abuse of process. Where the court adopts this course of action, it may not direct a verdict of not guilty.[26] A stay may be imposed at any stage of the proceedings. If a stay is subsequently lifted, then the proceedings may continue.

---

[21]   Criminal Procedure Rules, r 3.8(2)(b).

[22]   Named after *Newton* (1982) 77 Cr App R 13.

[23]   See Consolidated Criminal Practice Direction IV.45.13.

[24]   See *Drew* [1985] 1 WLR 914, 918 in which Lord Lane CJ said this is "well established on abundant authority".

[25]   "Special verdict" means "not guilty by reason of insanity": Criminal Procedure (Insanity) Act 1964, s 5(1).

[26]   *Griffiths* (1981) 72 Cr App R 307, 310.

Nolle prosequi[27]

8.38 A *nolle prosequi* may be entered on the initiative of the Attorney General after the indictment has been preferred and before the verdict. It prevents the prosecution proceeding.

8.39 Although the use of Latin is generally discouraged, this particular phrase has been used in a statute less than a decade ago[28] as well as in the Contempt of Court Act 1981; it is still used, without explicit translation, in the latest editions of practitioners' books *Blackstone's* and *Archbold*. As the phrase is still embedded in practitioner terminology (though it arises rarely in practice) it appears in the Bill.

Acquittal

8.40 An acquittal may result after the jury has heard the whole case. There may also be an acquittal in the following circumstances.

PROSECUTION OFFERS NO EVIDENCE

8.41 The prosecution may offer no evidence on individual counts or on the whole indictment, and it may do so before or after the jury has been sworn. The judge may consent or may not, but cannot prevent the prosecution taking this course. If the prosecution offers no evidence, the judge will either order a verdict of not guilty to be entered under section 17 of the Criminal Justice Act 1967 or, if a jury has been sworn, direct the jury to deliver a verdict of not guilty.

SUCCESSFUL SUBMISSION OF NO CASE TO ANSWER

8.42 If a case comes to an end because the judge rules there is no case to answer, a verdict must be taken from the jury under section 17 of the Criminal Justice Act 1967.[29]

Charges ordered to be left on the file

8.43 Charges may also be ordered to be "left on the file" and not to be pursued without the leave of the court. This step is rarely taken without the consent of the accused. The effect is often to terminate the proceedings in relation to those charges. It is usually a course of action taken because the defendant has pleaded guilty to (or been found guilty of) counts sufficiently serious that there is no public interest in proceeding on the other counts. To put it another way, if the Crown were compelled to proceed to trial, it would expect a guilty verdict but there is no public interest in proceeding to that point.

---

[27] *Nolle prosequi* translates as "unwilling to pursue", but the phrase is used as a noun, as described in Black's Law Dictionary (5th edition): "A formal entry upon the record...by the prosecuting officer in a criminal action, by which he declares that he 'will no further prosecute' the case, either as to some of the defendants, or altogether."

[28] Section 41(3) of the Justice (Northern Ireland) Act 2002 (not yet in force) transfers the power to enter a nolle prosequi from the Attorney General for Northern Ireland to the Director of Public Prosecutions for Northern Ireland.

[29] Unless the effect of the judge's ruling is of no effect because the prosecution exercises its right of appeal under section 58 of the CJA 2003.

Sentence

8.44 Following conviction, a defendant will be sentenced. We refer to the definition of "sentence" in section 50(1) of the CAA 1968, but exclude orders deferring sentence[30] (see the proposed new section 29A(6)). Section 50(1) reads:

> (1) In this Act "sentence", in relation to an offence, includes any order made by a court when dealing with an offender including, in particular—
>
> (a) a hospital order under Part III of the Mental Health Act 1983, with or without a restriction order;
>
> (b) an interim hospital order under that Part;
>
> (bb) a hospital direction and a limitation direction under that Part;
>
> (c) a recommendation for deportation;
>
> (ca) a confiscation order under Part 2 of the Proceeds of Crime Act 2002;
>
> (cb) an order which varies a confiscation order made under Part 2 of the Proceeds of Crime Act 2002 if the varying order is made under section 21, 22 or 29 of that Act (but not otherwise);
>
> (cc) a direction under section 20(3) or 21(3) of the Crime (Sentences) Act 1997 (extended supervision for sexual or violent offenders);
>
> (d) a confiscation order under the Drug Trafficking Act 1994 other than one made by the High Court;
>
> (e) a confiscation order under Part VI of the Criminal Justice Act 1988;
>
> (f) an order varying a confiscation order of a kind which is included by virtue of paragraph (d) or (e) above;
>
> (g) an order made by the Crown Court varying a confiscation order which was made by the High Court by virtue of section 19 of the Act of 1994; and
>
> (h) a declaration of relevance, within the meaning of section 23 of … under the Football Spectators Act 1989; and
>
> (i) an order under section 129(2) of the Licensing Act 2003 (forfeiture or suspension of personal licence).

---

[30] A sentence may be deferred under s 1 of the Powers of Criminal Courts (Sentencing) Act 2000. The order deferring sentence counts as a sentence for the purposes of s 50(1) of the CAA 1968, being an "order made by a court when dealing with an offender". Section 50(1) is not confined to final orders: *AG's Ref (No 22 of 1992)* (1993) 97 Cr App R 275. The effect of the new s 29A(6) is that the exclusion period continues if sentence is deferred and ends after the imposition of the deferred sentence.

8.45 Case law shows that a sentence within section 50(1) of the CAA 1968 also includes: an order to pay costs,[31] an order to pay compensation, a restitution order under the Theft Act 1968,[32] a bindover on conviction,[33] the revocation of a parole licence,[34] and financial reporting orders made under section 76 of the Serious Organised Crime Prevention Act 2005.[35]

8.46 There is a range of orders which may be made in addition to sentences which may be passed under the Powers of the Criminal Courts (Sentencing) Act 2000, such as anti-social behaviour orders on conviction.[36] If made by a court when dealing with an offender, they fall within the definition of "sentence" in section 50(1) of the CAA 1968.

The trial ends by virtue of some other order or decision

8.47 The most usual pleas are guilty or not guilty, as discussed above. There is, however, a variety of pleas which may be entered at or before arraignment: the most common of which are pleas of *autrefois convict* or *autrefois acquit*. The meaning of either of these pleas is that the defendant has been prosecuted before on the charges and a further prosecution should not proceed. If the prosecution agrees with either of these pleas, the defendant is discharged. If the prosecution does not agree, it becomes a matter for the judge. If the judge upholds the plea, the defendant is discharged. If the judge does not uphold the plea, the matter proceeds.

8.48 The plea of pardon is a plea in bar, but described as obsolete.[37] There are also the highly unusual pleas of demurrer[38] and plea to the jurisdiction.[39] As with the pleas of *autrefois convict* and *autrefois acquit*, ultimately the plea will either succeed (leading to discharge of the jury) or fail, in which case the matter proceeds.

8.49 If the judge accepts one of these pleas, then proceedings on the relevant count may not be pursued.

---

[31] *Hayden* [1975] 1 WLR 852.

[32] *Blackstone's* (2010) D25.36.

[33] This is a common law power, exercisable only by the Crown Court. It is exercisable in respect of any offence except where the penalty is fixed by law. (*Blackstone's* (2010) E13.1) Such an order counts as a "sentence" for the purpose of appeals: *Williams* [1982] 1 WLR 1398, though Professor Di Birch queried this: [1987] Criminal Law Review 417.

[34] *Welch* [1982] 1 WLR 976.

[35] *Adams* [2008] EWCA Crim 914, [2009] 1 WLR 310 and *Wright* [2008] EWCA Crim 3207, [2009] 2 Cr App R (S) 313.

[36] Made under s 1C of the Crime and Disorder Act 1998.

[37] *Blackstone's* (2010) D12.45.

[38] According to Cantley J this is "an objection to the form or substance of the indictment apparent on the face of the indictment…": *Inner London Quarter Sessions, ex parte Metropolitan Police Commissioner* [1970] 2 QB 80, 83G and *Blackstone's* (2010) D12.43.

[39] This asserts that the Crown Court has no jurisdiction to try the offence charged. This may be because the offence is a summary offence or because it has been committed abroad and there is no jurisdiction to try it. See *Blackstone's* (2010) D12.44.

Multiple counts

8.50 A verdict is given on a count, not on an indictment, and so a single indictment may have multiple endings (guilty verdict on count A, not guilty verdict on count B, no evidence offered on count C, guilty plea on count D, counts E and F to lie on file).

8.51 If judicial review were possible in relation to a ruling made after proceedings had concluded on one count but when they were continuing on a different count, there would be a risk of delay and interruption to the trial. It follows that, if there is more than one charge then the exclusion period should end after the last of the charges has been dealt with at the trial.

8.52 **We recommend that the exclusion period should end immediately after one (or the earliest) of the following happens or, if there is more than one charge, happens in relation to the last of the charges to be dealt with at the trial:**

(1) **the charge is dismissed;**

(2) **a *nolle prosequi* is entered;**

(3) **the indictment, or the relevant count, is quashed;**

(4) **the defendant is found to be unfit to plead or to be tried;**

(5) **the defendant is acquitted or sentenced;**

(6) **the charge is ordered to lie on the file;**

(7) **the proceedings, or the proceedings on the relevant count, are stayed;**

(8) **any other order or decision is made which puts an end to the proceedings.**

See subsection (2) of the proposed new section 29B of the SCA 1981.

Retrials ordered by the Crown Court

8.53 Once a jury has been sworn, it must be discharged, either after it has delivered its verdict or without delivering a verdict. A jury may be discharged at any time between being sworn and delivering its verdict. For example, a judge might give leave for an indictment to be amended, but decide to discharge the jury and order a retrial on the amended indictment.[40]

8.54 A jury may be discharged during the ordinary course of the trial, or as a result of a failure to agree (by the necessary majority) on a verdict.[41]

---

[40] Indictments Act 1915, s 5(5), *Blackstone's* (2010) D11.94.

[41] For example, where the judge decides to discharge the jury due to jury tampering, he or she may order that the trial shall continue without a jury, or that a new trial shall be held (without a jury).

8.55　Where the jury is discharged and a retrial ordered then no verdict is given.[42] The discharge of the jury without a verdict brings the trial to a halt, but is not equivalent to a verdict of not guilty.[43] The defendant can be tried again, without the need for any further formalities.

8.56　None of the events listed at paragraph 8.52 above will have happened. The exclusion period would, therefore, continue to apply where the jury was discharged without delivering a verdict.

The exclusion period ends immediately after the end point
8.57　The exclusion period should end immediately after the end point. Thus the end point should itself be within the exclusion period, with one exception which we now describe.

Re-starting proceedings
8.58　Following a stay of proceedings the stay may be lifted. Similarly, following an order that a charge shall not be proceeded with unless the leave of the court is given, leave may be obtained. In either of these situations judicial review should be barred in respect of the rejuvenated proceedings, and **we recommend that a new exclusion period should begin if either leave is given for further proceedings in relation to a charge which has been ordered to lie on the file or if a stay of proceedings in relation to a particular count is lifted**. This is effected by subsections (3) and (4) of the new section 29B of the SCA 1981. The new exclusion period would continue until the end of the exclusion period in any of the ways identified in paragraph 8.52 above.

Re-sentencing
8.59　A defendant may return to court for re-sentencing in relation to an offence where the sentence is reviewed,[44] varied or rescinded under section 155 of the Powers of Criminal Courts (Sentencing) Act 2000,[45] corrected,[46] imposed after being suspended,[47] or following breach of the first sentence.[48]

---

[42]　*Robinson* [1975] QB 508.

[43]　*Davison* (1860) 2 F & F 250.

[44]　Under s 74 of the Serious Organised Crime and Police Act 2005. The defendant already has a statutory right of appeal under s 74(8).

[45]　Section 155 of the Powers of Criminal Courts (Sentencing) Act 2000 allows the Crown Court to vary or rescind a sentence or other order it has made when dealing with an offender within 56 days of making it. The steps taken by the Crown Court under s 155 need not all be taken on the same occasion, though they must all be taken within the time limit: eg, the court may rescind the sentence on one day and resentence on another day: *Dunham* [1996] 1 Cr App R (S) 438. And compare to *Stillwell* (1991) 94 Cr App R 65.

[46]　Variation under section 155 is distinguished from correction of minor mistakes, which may take place outside the time limit in s 155. Such corrections are made pursuant to the Crown Court's inherent jurisdiction: *Michael* [1976] QB 414; *Saville* [1981] QB 12.

[47]　CJA 2003, s 189.

[48]　For breach of a conditional discharge see s 13(6) of the Powers of Criminal Courts (Sentencing) Act 2000. For breach of a community order see Sch 8 to the CJA 2003.

8.60   The defendant has a right of appeal in relation to all such sentences, and so judicial review would not be available in respect of them for the defendant in any event. In some cases, the prosecution may bring an Attorney General's reference, in the usual way, on the grounds that the varied sentence is unduly lenient. However, we do not wish to create the possibility of judicial review by the defendant in respect of any ruling during the re-sentencing process, nor for a third party, nor by the prosecution where a statutory right of appeal does not exist. Nor do we wish to create the possibility of judicial review in respect of a refusal to make a ruling.

8.61   **We therefore recommend that any decision made in connection with the consideration of any of the following should also not be subject to the supervisory jurisdiction of the High Court:**

    correction of a minor mistake in sentencing;

    amendment or activation of a suspended sentence;

    amendment or revocation of a community order;

    re-sentencing for the offence in respect of which a community order or conditional discharge was imposed or where a sentence is reviewed under section 74 of the Serious Organised Crime and Police Act 2005; or

    variation or rescission of a sentence under section 155 of the Powers of Criminal Courts (Sentencing) Act 2000.

    Subsection (3) of the proposed new section 29A states that decisions made in connection with any of the above are within the excluded jurisdiction.

    A matter not falling within the excluded jurisdiction: hospital orders under section 51(5) of the Mental Health Act 1983

8.62   There is one specific order which does not fall within the excluded jurisdiction and for which we make specific provision. A hospital order under section 51(5) of the Mental Health Act 1983 is made without there being a conviction. It may arise as follows. If a defendant is remanded into custody pending trial, and then becomes mentally ill, he or she may be transferred to a suitable hospital by a transfer direction made under section 48(2)(a) of the Mental Health Act 1983. The Crown Court may subsequently hold a hearing about whether he or she is fit to plead. If there is a finding of unfitness then the trial on indictment has come to an end.

8.63   If, however, there is no finding of unfitness because, for example, the defendant is too ill to be brought before the court, then the trial on indictment has not been brought to an end by such a finding. The court may nevertheless make a hospital order in respect of the defendant under section 51(5) of the Mental Health Act 1983, which provides as follows:

    (5) If … it appears to the court having jurisdiction to try or otherwise deal with the detainee—

    (a) that it is impracticable or inappropriate to bring the detainee before the court; and

(b) that the conditions set out in subsection (6) below are satisfied,

the court may make a hospital order (with or without a restriction order) in his case in his absence and, in the case of a person awaiting trial, without convicting him.

The conditions in subsection (6) relate to evidence of mental illness from medical practitioners.

8.64 Under the current law, this kind of hospital order may be challenged by way of judicial review. The appeal routes provided for by the CAA 1968 are not applicable, and although an appeal to the Mental Health Review Tribunal is available, our view is that it is not sufficient, and we wish to preserve the position under the current law. Therefore **we recommend that a decision by the Crown Court to make a hospital order under section 51(5) of the Mental Health Act 1983 should not fall within the excluded jurisdiction of the Crown Court.** See subsection (5) of the proposed new section 29A of the SCA 1981.

RULINGS WHICH WOULD BE SUSCEPTIBLE TO JUDICIAL REVIEW

8.65 It is an accepted principle that judicial review is only permitted in respect of rulings for which no alternative remedy, such as a statutory right of appeal, is available. The effect of the end of the exclusion period would be that any decision made by the Crown Court after the end of the exclusion period would be susceptible of judicial review, subject to that general principle. Bearing that in mind, the following are examples of rulings which would be susceptible of judicial review:

(1)   Recovery of Defence Costs Orders (RDCOs);

(2)   a refusal to make a costs order, in particular a refusal to make a costs order out of central funds in favour of an acquitted defendant;

(3)   an order that one party pay the costs of another where they have been "unnecessarily and improperly incurred";

(4)   bindover of an acquitted defendant;

(5)   bindover of a witness after the end of the trial;

(6)   refusal to vary a restraining order made on acquittal; and

(7)   where the judge refuses a defendant a representation order after the end of the trial.

We now describe each of these kinds of order.

Recovery of Defence Costs Orders

8.66 A Recovery of Defence Costs Order[49] is a way for the state to recoup public money paid for a defendant's representation. If the defendant has been convicted at the Crown Court, then it is likely that he or she will be expected to contribute to the costs of representation by way of an RDCO. Exceptionally, an RDCO will be made against an acquitted defendant.

8.67 RDCOs are made at the conclusion of the proceedings in the Crown Court.[50] It is clear that an RDCO is not part of the sentence despite the fact that it can only be made at the conclusion of the proceedings and only in exceptional circumstances if the defendant is acquitted.[51] The exclusion period ends immediately after one of the events in subsection (2) of the proposed section 29B, and an RDCO will therefore fall outside the exclusion period.

8.68 It follows from the above that section 29(6) of the SCA 1981, which takes RDCOs outside the exclusionary bar in section 29(3), is not needed, and **we recommend that section 29(6) of the SCA 1981 is omitted**. The effect would be to preserve the current position: that judicial review is possible in respect of RDCOs. See clause 2(1)(b) of the Bill.

Refusal to make a defence costs order in favour of an acquitted defendant

8.69 When a defendant is acquitted at the Crown Court, the court has power to make a defendant's costs order pursuant to section 16 of the Prosecution of Offences Act 1985. The court is required to follow the *Practice Direction (Costs: Criminal Proceedings)*.[52]

8.70 Evidently, a defendant who is acquitted cannot appeal any order made against him or her as if it were a sentence. A defendant who is acquitted at the Crown Court but refused an order of costs in his or her favour is precluded under the current law from challenging that decision by section 29(3) of the SCA 1981. The situation is as described by Lord Justice Waller in *R v Canterbury Crown Court ex parte Regentford*.[53] He said:

---

[49] Made under s 17 of the Access to Justice Act 1999.

[50] Regulations 4 and 11 of the Criminal Defence Service (Recovery of Defence Costs Orders) Regulations 2001 (SI 2001 No 856) as amended by regulations 2 and 3 of the Criminal Defence Service (Recovery of Defence Costs Orders) (Amendment) Regulations 2004 (SI 2004 No 1195).

[51] Section 50(3) of the CAA 1968, as amended, provides:
    An order under section 17 of the Access to Justice Act 1999 is not a sentence for the purposes of this Act.

[52] [2004] 1 WLR 2657. Rule 76.4 of the Criminal Procedure Rules is applicable to defence costs orders. Rule 76.4(5) states that the general rule is that the court will make an order but it may decline to make a defence costs order, and it then gives two instances when the court might refuse.

[53] [2000] All ER 2415. See CP 184, paras 3.17 to 3.19.

…it is not as it seems to me altogether satisfactory that a defendant who obtains no order for costs or for that matter had an order for costs made against him after an acquittal has no remedy even if the judge was "plainly wrong". Furthermore, if one imagines for a moment that a judge has clearly impugned the innocence of a defendant after acquittal by a jury, the order made by the judge would have infringed a Convention right (see *Sekanina v Austria* (1994) 17 EHRR 221 in particular paragraph 30), and there would apparently be no remedy.[54]

8.71 The result is that an acquitted defendant may not challenge a refusal to make a defence costs order under the current law. The reform would allow him or her to do so by way of judicial review.

An order for one party to pay costs which need not have been incurred

8.72 A court may make an order for payment of costs incurred as a result of an unnecessary or improper act or omission by, or on behalf of, another party to the proceedings. Such an order is made under section 19(1) of the Prosecution of Offences Act 1985 and under regulations in Part II of the Costs in Criminal Cases (General) Regulations 1986. Regulation 3 is headed "Unnecessary or improper acts or omissions". It reads:

> (1) Subject to the provisions of this regulation, where at any time during criminal proceedings—
>
> (a) a magistrates' court,
>
> (b) the Crown Court, or
>
> (c) the Court of Appeal
>
> is satisfied that costs have been incurred in respect of the proceedings by one of the parties as a result of an unnecessary or improper act or omission by, or on behalf of, another party to the proceedings, the court may, after hearing the parties, order that all or part of the costs so incurred by that party shall be paid to him by the other party.
>
> (2) When making an order under paragraph (1), the court may take into account any other order as to costs which has been made in respect of the proceedings.
>
> (3) An order made under paragraph (1) shall specify the amount of costs to be paid in pursuance of the order.
>
> (4) Where an order under paragraph (1) has been made, the court may take that order into account when making any other order as to costs in respect of the proceedings.
>
> (5)….

---

[54] [2000] All ER 2415 at [19].

8.73   Unlike the provisions in those regulations which deal with wasted costs orders against representatives and third party costs orders, there is no route of appeal to the Court of Appeal against an order made under regulation 3 in Part II. The reform which we recommend would permit both the prosecution[55] and the defence to challenge an order made, and a refusal to make an order, pursuant to section 19(1) and regulation 3.

An order committing an acquitted defendant to prison unless he agrees to be bound over[56]

8.74   The court has the statutory power to make an order binding over a defendant to keep the peace.[57] In *Ex parte Benjamin*,[58] the court held that a bindover of a defendant who had been acquitted was not an order "which affected the course of the trial" and therefore judicial review was not precluded.

8.75   A bindover in these circumstances may thus be the subject of judicial review and we do not seek to change that: as there is no other means of appeal, it is right that judicial review should be available. As a ruling following an acquittal, it would be outside the exclusion period.

Bindover of a witness

8.76   The power of bindover may also be used in respect of a witness.[59] As with the bindover of a defendant, the witness is committed to keeping the peace and at risk of forfeiting a sum of money if he or she breaches the bindover. If a witness is bound over after the end of the trial, then the exclusion period would not apply, and the individual could apply for judicial review under our reform.

Refusal to vary or discharge a restraining order following an acquittal

8.77   If a restraining order is made following acquittal in the Crown Court, the person against whom it is made may appeal it to the CACD as if it were a sentence. There is, therefore, no question of creating a right of judicial review for the defendant in respect of such an order.

---

[55]   The prosecution does have a right of appeal against a wasted costs order, as in *R v CPS (London) (Wasted Costs)* [2005] EWCA Crim 2982, [2005] All ER (D) 288, but this is a different kind of order.

[56]   Such an order is possible under s 115 of the Magistrates' Courts Act 1980, the Justices of the Peace Act 1361, or s 1(7) of the Justices of the Peace Act 1968.

[57]   Under s 1(7) of the Justices of the Peace Act 1968. If the defendant fails to keep the peace, he or she may forfeit a sum of money. If the defendant fails to pay that sum of money, the court has power to order imprisonment.

[58]   (1987) 85 Cr App R 267.

[59]   *Sheldon v Bromfield JJ* [1964] 2 QB 573, [1964] 2 All ER 131, and see for example *R (Harlow-Hayes) v Cambridge Crown Court* [2008] EWHC 1023 (Admin) in which there had long been a dispute between the complainants and the defendant which the judge sought to resolve by binding them all over to keep the peace.

8.78   If a court refuses to make a restraining order following acquittal, the question might arise of whether the complainant could obtain judicial review of the refusal. The courts would probably refuse judicial review on the basis that an alternative remedy existed (namely a civil injunction).[60]

8.79   A person for whose protection a restraining order is made has the right to apply for it to be varied or discharged, as does the person against whom it is made. The application is made to the Crown Court. The next question is what the position would be in respect of a refusal to vary or discharge such an order, for the complainant and for the person against whom the order is made. Our view is that the person for whose protection the order is made would not obtain permission to apply for judicial review on the basis that an alternative remedy would be available.

8.80   The person against whom the order is made could, under our recommendations, seek judicial review of a refusal to vary or discharge a restraining order following acquittal, and our view is that it is right that a person should have some way of challenging the lawfulness of a decision which restricts his or her liberty. This is consistent with our recommendation that there should be an exception to the prohibition on judicial review in respect of refusals of bail.

Refusal of a representation order

8.81   A representation order is authorisation for a defendant's representation in criminal proceedings to be paid for from public funds. Under our reform, a refusal, after the end of the exclusion period, to make a representation order could be challenged by way of judicial review, but in practice this would be rare.

Deprivation or forfeiture order against a non-defendant

8.82   There are various statutory provisions which permit the court to order forfeiture of an item which belongs to someone other than the defendant, following conviction. There is a general power in section 143 of the Powers of the Criminal Courts (Sentencing) Act 2000 to make a deprivation order, and there is a variety of specific powers to make forfeiture orders following conviction.

8.83   Where a forfeiture order is made against someone other than a defendant, the appeal provisions under the CAA 1968 will not be relevant. Under the current law, the High Court is able to accept an application for judicial review made by the owner of the property to be forfeited where that person is not the defendant.[61] The policy is to preserve the current position.

8.84   Any such order may be made after the end of the exclusion period, in which case judicial review will be possible. In any event, the owner could apply for the return of the property under the Police (Property) Act 1897 or by way of judicial review of the body retaining it.

---

[60]   On the same basis as judicial review was refused to a victim who had, through error, been denied a compensation order: *R (Faithfull) v Ipswich Crown Court* [2007] EWHC 2763 (Admin), [2008] 1 WLR 1636.

[61]   In *R v Maidstone Crown Court ex parte Gill* [1986] 1 WLR 1405 the High Court accepted jurisdiction for judicial review over an order made under s 27 of the Misuse of Drugs Act 1971.

RULINGS WHICH WOULD NOT BE SUSCEPTIBLE TO JUDICIAL REVIEW

8.85   As noted above, judicial review will not be available in relation to a ruling if it may be appealed by virtue of an existing statutory provision. There are, for example, statutory routes of appeal:

(1)   for the defendant against conviction and/or sentence (which includes an order to pay costs);[62]

(2)   for a third party against a costs order made against him or her;[63]

(3)   against a wasted costs order;[64]

(4)   against punishment for contempt of court;[65]

(5)   in respect of a sentence that has been reviewed under section 74 of the Serious Organised Crime and Police Act 2005;[66]

(6)   against a restraining order made following an acquittal;[67]

(7)   in respect of reporting restrictions;[68]

(8)   for the prosecution on a point of law following an acquittal;[69]

(9)   for the prosecution against an acquittal under Part 10 of the CJA 2003;

(10)   for the prosecution against a refusal to make a football banning order;[70] and

(11)   for the prosecution where it considers that a sentence was unduly lenient.[71]

Therefore, even if one of the above orders is made outside the exclusion period, judicial review would not be possible in respect of it.

---

[62]   CAA 1968, s 9.

[63]   Costs in Criminal Cases (General) Regulations 1986 (SI 1968 No 1335), reg 3H and Part 68 of Criminal Procedure Rules.

[64]   Costs in Criminal Cases (General) Regulations 1986 (SI 1968 No 1335), reg 3C and Part 68 of the Criminal Procedure Rules. As regards orders made against solicitors, see s 50(3) of the Solicitors Act 1974 , s 50(3) (inserted by the SCA 1981, ss 147, 152(4) and Sch 7).

[65]   Administration of Justice Act 1960, s 13(2(bb).

[66]   Serious Organised Crime and Police Act 2005, s 74(8)

[67]   A restraining order made following an acquittal may be appealed as if it were a sentence: s 5A(5) of the Protection from Harassment Act 1997.

[68]   Reporting restrictions may be appealed by any person aggrieved under s 159 of the Criminal Justice Act 1988. See also the appeal we recommend in Part 10 below.

[69]   Criminal Justice Act 1972, s 36.

[70]   Football Spectators Act 1989, s 14A(5A).

[71]   Criminal Justice Act 1988, s 36.

CONSEQUENTIAL AMENDMENT

8.86   Section 22 of the Prosecution of Offences Act 1985 enables the Secretary of State to set time limits for the completion of preliminary stages of proceedings and an appropriate court may extend the time limit or stay the proceedings. By virtue of section 22(13), where the court does so, its decision is susceptible of judicial review, despite section 29(3) of the SCA 1981. A consequential amendment would be needed to section 22(13) of the Prosecution of Offences Act 1985 in light of the amendment to section 29(3) of the SCA 1981 we recommend. The end result would be to preserve the position as it is now, namely, that the jurisdiction conferred on the Crown Court by section 22 is susceptible of judicial review. This is effected by paragraph 2 of Schedule 1 to the Bill.

PART 9
JUDICIAL REVIEW OF A REFUSAL OF BAIL

9.1   In the previous Part we recommended that judicial review should not be possible for trials on indictment up to the end of the trial, with one exception. This Part is about that exception: refusals of bail.

9.2   The position under the current law is described in detail below but can be summarised by saying that a defendant who is remanded in custody by a Crown Court will usually have, at most, one opportunity to have that denial of bail reconsidered by the Crown Court unless there is a change of circumstances. The position of defendants is not the only consideration here. Witnesses are rarely remanded into custody in the course of a trial at the Crown Court, but when they are, they have no right to challenge that denial of bail.

9.3   Under the current law, judicial review of refusals of bail by the Crown Court is permitted in some circumstances, despite section 29(3) of the SCA 1981. If we did not provide an exception to the prohibition on judicial review during the exclusion period that we recommend, then judicial review would no longer be available in respect of refusals of bail. We think that the exception ought to be available to witnesses as well as defendants. We also believe that the exception ought to be available to defendants throughout the exclusion period. Our recommendations thus go further than the current law in making judicial review of refusals of bail possible in those two respects.

9.4   We begin by explaining why we believe judicial review should be available to defendants and witnesses in trials on indictment. We then describe the rights of challenge to a remand in custody under the current law. From paragraph 9.43 onwards, we describe our recommendations.

WHY JUDICIAL REVIEW OF REFUSALS OF BAIL IN TRIALS ON INDICTMENT IS DESIRABLE

9.5   In Part 6 above we refer to the values at stake in the criminal system, and in particular to the need to avoid interruption to trials, but also to the need to give effect to Convention rights. Where a person is remanded in custody during a trial, those values clash.

9.6   While we note the views of Lord Justice Auld in his "Criminal Courts Review" that opportunities to challenge remands in custody should be limited, and the legislative amendment in 2003 designed to restrict those opportunities, we still think there is weight in the argument we put forward in CP 184:

it is understandable why, despite the relevant provisions of the Criminal Justice Act 2003 and section 29(3) of the Supreme Court Act 1981, the High Court should be anxious to retain some control over bail decisions of the Crown Court against which there is no statutory appeal. The liberty of the citizen is at stake and a seriously flawed refusal of bail could well constitute a breach of article 5 of the ECHR.[1]

9.7 We also said, at paragraph 5.47 of CP 184, "deprivation of liberty is a serious matter irrespective of whatever stage in the proceedings it occurs", and the European Court of Human Rights speaks of "the dramatic impact of deprivation of liberty on the fundamental rights of the person concerned".[2]

9.8 The case of *Cordingley*[3] illustrates the issue. The defendant claimed that the judge withdrew bail and remanded the accused in custody peremptorily. The judge stated at the end of the first day's hearing that he had formed the view that the defendant was "beginning to realise for the first time the peril in which he stands in relation to evidence and sentence" and that it was likely he would not attend the next day.[4] The Court of Appeal commented that in this case the withdrawal of bail "was at least questionable".[5] Other examples may be taken from those decisions of the High Court where the withdrawal of bail was quashed on judicial review because it was outside the range of reasonable decisions.[6]

9.9 We noted in Part 6 above that a post-conviction right of appeal may be treated as an adequate remedy in many situations. This situation is, however, one where that right of appeal is of no help. An appeal against conviction will be irrelevant to a witness or acquitted defendant, and even for a defendant who is convicted, an appeal at that stage can have no bearing on time spent in custody before the trial is concluded: a defendant cannot be given back the time spent incarcerated if the appeal succeeds. A claim for damages is only partially relevant. Habeas corpus may not be available. In our view, it must be right that there is an opportunity to challenge an unlawful remand in custody even though that might mean delay and interruption to the trial. As one consultee put it: irrational remands in custody, involving as they do the liberty of the subject, require immediate review.

THE CURRENT LAW

Defendants and bail

9.10 The following paragraphs (up to 9.35) concern refusal of bail to defendants. The position of witnesses is discussed at paragraphs 9.33 to 9.40 below.

---

[1] Para 2.111.

[2] In *Garcia Alva v Germany* [2001] ECHR 2541/94 para 39, recalled at para 46 of *Allen v UK* [2010] ECHR 18837/06.

[3] [2007] EWCA Crim 2174, [2008] Criminal Law Review 299.

[4] *Cordingley* [2007] EWCA Crim 2174, [2008] Criminal Law Review 299, [9].

[5] *Cordingley* [2007] EWCA Crim 2174, [2008] Criminal Law Review 299, [13].

[6] See, for example, *R (Prifti) v Lewes Crown Court* [2008] EWHC 2769 (Admin) in which the High Court said, in the course of granting the application for judicial review, it thought that "the positive reasons for refusing bail are best described as very slight". See also *R (Fergus) v Southampton Crown Court* [2008] EWHC 3273 (Admin), *R (Lynch) v Lincoln Crown Court* [2008] EWHC 3358 (Admin). In some cases, the consequences may be so serious that Article 2 of the ECHR is engaged: see *Renolde v France* (2009) 48 EHRR 42.

9.11   Once the case has been committed or sent or transferred from the magistrates to the Crown Court for trial (or for sentence), section 81(1)(a) of the SCA 1981 allows him or her to apply to the Crown Court for bail.[7] There is also a general provision in section 81(1)(c) which allows the Crown Court to grant bail to any person "who is in the custody of the Crown Court pending the disposal of his case by that court".

After the trial has started

9.12   Section 81(1)(c) of the SCA 1981 again provides power to the court to grant bail. An application for bail by the accused during the trial is governed, subject to the Bail Act 1976, by the Consolidated Practice Direction paragraph III.25:

> III.25.2   Once a trial has begun, the further grant of bail, whether during the short adjournment or overnight, is in the discretion of the trial judge. It may be a proper exercise of this discretion to refuse bail during the short adjournment if the accused cannot otherwise be segregated from witnesses and jurors.

> III.25.3   An accused who was on bail while on remand should not be refused overnight bail during the trial, unless in the opinion of the judge there are positive reasons to justify this refusal. Such reasons are likely to be:

> > (a)   that a point has been reached where there is a real danger that the accused will abscond, either because the case is going badly for him or for any other reason;

> > (b)   that there is a real danger that he may interfere with witnesses or jurors.

> III.25.4   There is no universal rule of practice that bail shall not be renewed when the summing-up has begun. Each case must be decided in the light of its own circumstances and having regard to the judge's assessment from time to time of the risks involved.[8]

The right to bail

9.13   Section 4(1) of the Bail Act 1976 provides a right to bail, but bail need not be granted if the court is satisfied that there are substantial grounds to believe that the defendant will fail to surrender to custody, commit an offence while on bail, or interfere with witnesses. The court may also withhold bail if it is satisfied the accused should be kept in custody for his or her own protection: this is a less common ground for refusing bail. There are statutory exceptions to this presumption in favour of bail, but they are not discussed here. If a Crown Court refuses bail it will often be required to give its reasons. Once a person has been convicted the right to bail in section 4(1) is not applicable, and different provisions govern the grant or refusal of bail.

---

[7]   From the prospective amendment of s 81(1)(a), it seems that the Crown Court will retain this power under this provision once the procedures for moving cases from the magistrates' courts to the Crown Court have changed. See para 8.11 above.

[8]   Practice Direction (Criminal Proceedings: Consolidation) para III.25 [2002] 1 WLR 2870.

Provision in the current law for challenges to a refusal of bail at the Crown Court for a defendant on trial on indictment

9.14   Section 4(1) of the Bail Act 1976 imposes the duty on the court to consider bail: it states that "a person to whom this section applies shall be granted bail except as provided in Schedule 1 to this Act." If bail has been refused at a previous hearing, paragraph 1 of Part 2A of Schedule 1 applies:

> If the court decides not to grant the defendant bail, it is the court's duty to consider, at each subsequent hearing while the defendant is a person to whom section 4 above applies and remains in custody, whether he ought to be granted bail.

9.15   Thus *Blackstone's* writes that "in theory the court is obliged to consider bail each time an accused who is entitled to the benefit of the BA 1976, s 4(1), appears before it in custody".[9] Section 4 applies to an accused who has been remanded in custody and makes an application to the Crown Court for bail.

9.16   The defendant has a right at common law to make a bail application at any stage. This right may be an empty right if the defendant is not allowed to repeat arguments advanced previously, but it still exists in principle.[10]

9.17   Part 2A of Schedule 1 to the Bail Act 1976 (inserted by section 154 of the Criminal Justice Act 1988) neither removed the common law right to make an application nor altered the court's duty under section 4. Instead it made provision concerning the arguments a court is required to entertain and those provisions reflected, in part, recent developments in the common law. Paragraphs 2 and 3 read:

> 2.   At the first hearing after that at which the court decided not to grant the defendant bail he may support an application for bail with any argument as to fact or law that he desires (whether or not he has advanced that argument previously).
>
> 3.   At subsequent hearings the court need not hear arguments as to fact or law which it has heard previously.

9.18   Paragraphs 2 and 3 of Part 2A of Schedule 1 thus put limits on what arguments of fact or law a court is required to hear: the court "need not" hear arguments it has heard previously, so evidently it may do so in the exercise of its discretion.

9.19   If, however, the defendant is able to marshal fresh arguments (popularly called a change of circumstances)[11] then paragraph 3 of Part 2A will not stand in his or her way, and D will be able to renew the application for bail.

9.20   Where a defendant applies to the Crown Court for bail, he or she must inform the court of any previous application for bail, to the Crown Court or to the High Court, in the same proceedings.[12]

---

[9]   *Blackstone's* (2010) D7.49.

[10]   N Corre and D Wolchover, *Bail in Criminal Proceedings* (3rd ed 2004) para 5.6.2.8.

[11]   See *R (Mongan) v Isleworth Crown Court* [2007] EWHC 1087 (Admin) at [6] to [8].

Summary of when a defendant may re-apply for bail before or during trial

9.21 While in theory the court has a duty to consider bail for any defendant remanded in custody who applies to the Crown Court for bail, in practice there might need to be a change of circumstances in order for the court to entertain an application. This is partly the effect of Part 2A of Schedule 1 to the Bail Act 1976, but also because, if there is no change in circumstances, the court would follow its previous decision.

After conviction

9.22 A person may have been convicted but not yet sentenced. The court may adjourn for the purpose of enabling inquiries or reports to be made to assist the court in deciding upon sentence. It may remand the convicted defendant on bail or in custody for that period, and section 81(1)(c) gives the Crown Court power to grant bail in that circumstance.

9.23 The Crown Court has power to grant bail to a convicted defendant pending appeal under section 81(1)(f) of the SCA 1981, namely where the Crown Court has issued a certificate that the case is fit for appeal (conviction/sentence or both).

No appeal to the CA

9.24 There is no appeal to the CA against a refusal of bail for a defendant committed or sent or transferred to the Crown Court for trial on indictment. (Once a defendant has been convicted it is a different matter.)

Judicial review of a refusal of bail[13]

9.25 It used to be the case that a person refused bail at the Crown Court could apply for bail to the High Court.[14] Section 17 of the CJA 2003 removed that right.[15] By

---

[12] Criminal Procedure Rules, r 19.18(9).

[13] In addition to any power that it might have over bail decisions of the Crown Court by way of judicial review, the High Court has some statutory powers in relation to bail in criminal proceedings, but they are not relevant here.

[14] As described by Maurice Kay LJ in *R (M) v Isleworth Crown Court* [2005] EWHC 363 (Admin), [2002] All ER 42 (D) at [6].

> Until April of [2004] a person in the position of M would have applied to a High Court judge for bail. However, that form of access to the High Court was abolished by s 17(3) of the Criminal Justice Act 2003, which came into force on 5 April 2004. Clearly the intention and effect of that abolition is generally to confine decisions on bail to judges in the Crown Court. Its origin is to be found in Auld LJ's report which expressed concern about the wasteful duplication of bail applications.

> The application to a High Court judge for bail referred to was pursuant to its inherent jurisdiction. Judicial review was held to be unavailable in the light of that remedy: *R v Croydon Crown Court ex p Cox* [1997] 1 Cr App R 20.

[15] Section 17 is in Part 2 of the CJA 2003. The Explanatory Note to that Act states, at para 18, that Part 2 of that Act:

> also gives effect to recommendations of Lord Justice Auld in his *Review of the Criminal Courts of England and Wales* for simplifying the bail appeals system, including removing the High Court's bail jurisdiction where it is concurrent with that of the Crown Court.

section 17(3)(b), the High Court's inherent power "to entertain an application in relation to bail where the Crown Court has determined" an application under section 81(1)(a), (b), (c) or (g) of the SCA 1981 was abolished. Section 17(6), however, provided that

> (6) Nothing in this section affects-
>
> > (a) any other power of the High Court to grant or withhold bail or to vary the conditions of bail, or
> >
> > (b) any right of a person to apply for a writ of habeas corpus or any other prerogative remedy.

9.26　Within a year of section 17(6) of the CJA 2003 coming into effect, Mr Justice Gray commented:

> Interesting questions may arise as to quite what powers that subsection is intended to retain for the High Court. In particular, a question could arise as to whether the reference in the subsection to "any other prerogative remedy" is a reference to judicial review or whether it is a reference to the prerogative remedies which were conventionally invoked prior to the arrival of judicial review as a remedy.[16]

9.27　The effect of section 17(6) was considered in *Isleworth*.[17] (The court also had to consider whether section 29(3) of the SCA 1981 ousted its jurisdiction.) Lord Justice Maurice Kay said:

> I have no doubt that prerogative remedies in that context embrace those set out in section 29(1) of the Supreme Court Act 1981 – mandamus, prohibition and certiorari – which are now of course respectively called a mandatory order, a prohibiting order and a quashing order in Part 54 of the Civil Procedure Rules. That means that this court now has jurisdiction to review a bail decision by the Crown Court. In the recent case of *Serumaga* [2005] EWCA Crim 370, when sitting in the Court of Appeal Criminal Division, and when specifically considering the exceptional position of a person facing summary proceedings for contempt of court, I may have implied otherwise. However, the matter having arisen more generally and directly in the present case, I can now say that such an implication would be erroneous.[18]

The point was not fully argued before the court.

9.28　It appears from the judgment of Lord Justice Maurice Kay in *Isleworth*, and from subsequent judgments by Mr Justice Collins, that the High Court has no power to hear a bail application but it does have power to entertain an application for permission for judicial review of a bail decision.

---

[16]　*R (Rozo) v Snaresbrook Crown Court* [2005] EWHC 75 (Admin) at [15].

[17]　[2005] EWHC 363 (Admin), [2002] All ER (D) 42.

[18]　*R (M) v Isleworth Crown Court* [2005] EWHC 363 (Admin), [2005] All ER (D) 42 at [10].

9.29   In the initial cases before it, the High Court accepted jurisdiction partly on the basis that the application was being made at an "early stage" of proceedings, without defining what that meant.[19] The court clearly had in mind the undesirability of interrupting a trial that had begun. In more recent cases, the High Court has also accepted jurisdiction in post-conviction cases, as in *R (F) v Southampton Crown Court*[20] where Mr Justice Collins said:

> This of course is not an early stage of the criminal proceedings, it is a very late stage because it is after conviction and before sentence, so the trial on indictment is clearly still in being. ... On one view, the questions as to bail are always going to be truly collateral to the indictment, and thus it may be that the jurisdiction of this court exists.

> In all the circumstances of this case, I am prepared to assume that there is jurisdiction, although I am bound to say I have considerable doubts as to whether in reality there is when one is dealing with bail at this late stage of a trial. Having said that, I have to consider whether the decision in question is one which could be said to be unreasonable in the *Wednesbury* sense, because that is the test. Was it within the bounds of a reasonable decision?[21]

9.30   The result is that the courts continue to assume that they have jurisdiction, but it is not clear at what point in a trial it ceases to be possible to apply for judicial review. In their assumption that they have jurisdiction, the courts have interpreted section 29(3) of the SCA 1981, which prohibits judicial review of "matters relating to trial on indictment", as not applying to a refusal of bail to a person facing trial on indictment. In addition, the underlying rationale for permitting challenge by judicial review to a refusal of bail – that loss of liberty should only be the consequence of a lawful decision – should apply at all stages of a trial, but this rationale is not reflected in the current law.

HOW THE HIGH COURT APPROACHES APPLICATIONS

9.31   Applications to the High Court for judicial review of bail decisions will only rarely be entertained.[22] There have in fact, following *Isleworth*, been a number of

---

[19]   "Early stage" has subsequently been interpreted to include following arraignment, as in *R (Fergus) v Southampton Crown Court* [2008] EWHC 3273 (Admin).

[20]   [2009] EWHC 2206 (Admin).

[21]   *R (F) v Southampton Crown Court* [2009] EWHC 2206 (Admin) at [5] and [6]. Collins J did not quash the order but remitted it to the Crown Court and directed it to reconsider the question of bail on the correct basis. Cases where judicial review of a refusal of bail post-conviction was granted include: *R (Groves) v Newcastle Crown Court* [2008] EWHC 3123 (Admin), *R (JN) v Inner London Crown Court* [2008] EWHC 468 (Admin).

[22]   *R (M) v Isleworth Crown Court* [2005] EWHC 363 (Admin), [2005] All ER (D) 42 and *Allwin* [2005] EWHC 742 (Admin), [2005] All ER (D) 40. Mr Justice Collins has held that the High Court should decide whether the Crown Court's decision was one which fell within the "bounds of reasonableness", and that it should adopt "a strict review approach": *R (Wiggins) v Harrow Crown Court* [2005] EWHC 882 (Admin) at [35].

judicial reviews of bail decisions,[23] although the High Court is, on occasion, "assuming" it has jurisdiction rather than being sure that it does.[24]

9.32 In some of those cases judicial review is granted because the refusal was thought, by the High Court, to be irrational. In others, because the judge misdirected him or herself in law.[25] Procedural failings have also justified the grant of judicial review.[26]

Witnesses

9.33 With regard to witnesses, remanding a witness in custody is a means by which the Crown Court may enforce its own order requiring the witness to attend and give evidence.

9.34 The governing provisions are to be found in the Criminal Procedure (Attendance of Witnesses) Act 1965.[27] The procedure only applies in the context of a trial.[28] Section 2 allows a court to issue a summons on application by a party. Section 2D allows the court to issue a summons of its own motion. The summons requires a person to attend court as stated in the summons and to give the evidence or produce the document or thing specified in the summons. A witness may seek to have the summons set aside.[29]

9.35 Once a summons is in existence, section 4 gives the court power to take steps to make the summons effective. Subsection (1) allows the court to act where it can anticipate that the witness will not obey the summons. If a summons is in force, it need not have been served for the court to issue a warrant if satisfied that the witness is: "'unlikely to comply with it' and would be able to give and/or produce material evidence".[30] Subsection (2) allows the court to act where the witness does not obey the summons. In either event, the court may issue a warrant for the witness to be arrested and brought before the court.

9.36 Once the warrant has been executed, subsection (3) of section 4 allows the court to remand the witness. It reads:

---

[23] Eg, *R (Allwin) v Snaresbrook Crown Court*) [2005] EWHC 342 (Admin), [2005] All ER (D) 40, *R (Thompson) v Central Criminal Court* [2005] EWHC 2345 (Admin), [2006] ACD 9, *R (Fergus) v Southampton Crown Court* [2008] EWHC 3273 (Admin), *R (Lynch) v Lincoln Crown Court* [2008] EWHC 3358 (Admin), *R (Prifti) v Lewes Crown Court* [2008] EWHC 2769 (Admin), *R (Longhirst) v Newcastle Crown Court* [2007] EWHC 3520 (Admin) at [16], *R (Hoskin) v Northampton Crown Court* [2009] EWHC 2265 (Admin), [2009] All ER (D) 76.

[24] See, for example, the comments of Gray J in *R (Rozo) v Snaresbrook Crown Court* [2005] EWHC 75 (Admin) at [18].

[25] *R (JN) v Inner London Crown Court* [2008] EWHC 468 (Admin).

[26] *R (Khan) v Leicester Crown Court* [2008] EWHC 1000 (Admin).

[27] Amendments pending as a result of the prospective changes to the ways in which cases move from the magistrates' courts to the Crown Court – see para 8.11 above.

[28] *R v Manchester Crown Court ex parte Cunningham* [1992] COD 23.

[29] Criminal Procedure (Attendance of Witnesses) Act 1965, ss 2C(1) and 2E.

[30] *Doyle* [2005] EWCA Crim 3461 at [9] by Auld LJ.

(3) A witness brought before a court in pursuance of a warrant under this section may be remanded by that court in custody or on bail (with or without sureties) until such time as the court may appoint for receiving his evidence or dealing with him under section 3 of this Act;[31] and where a witness attends a court in pursuance of a notice under this section the court may direct that the notice shall have effect as if it required him to attend at any later time appointed by the court for receiving his evidence or dealing with him as aforesaid.

Our understanding is that this power of remand is not frequently used.

9.37 The power to remand was considered by the High Court in *R (TH) v Wood Green Crown Court*.[32] The court held that the power continued while the witness remained a potential witness: even though he had given his evidence, the Crown Court had lawfully remanded him.[33] The court also considered the effect of section 29(3) of the SCA 1981. It held:

> …the ordinary meaning of section 29(3) as applied to this case is that the decision taken in the course of the trial by the trial judge to detain the claimant as a witness pending receipt of further evidence was a matter relating to a trial on indictment. There is no need for section 29(3) to be read in any other way.[34]

9.38 Thus the High Court held it had no jurisdiction to entertain judicial review of the remand.

Distinct from contempt of court

9.39 If a witness disobeys a summons without "just excuse", section 3 of the Criminal Procedure (Attendance of Witnesses) Act 1965 provides that the witness is guilty of contempt of court. If a witness is remanded in custody as punishment for contempt of court, then there is already a means of appeal,[35] and our recommendations would not affect it.

9.40 We are concerned solely with the position of a witness who is remanded in custody pursuant to section 4(3) of the Criminal Procedure (Attendance of Witnesses) Act 1965.

---

[31] Footnote added. Section 3 is about powers of punishment for disobeying a witness summons or witness order.

[32] [2006] EWHC 2683 (Admin), [2007] 1 WLR 1670.

[33] *R (TH) v Wood Green Crown Court* [2006] EWHC 2683 (Admin), [2007] 1 WLR 1670 at [29] by Wilkie J: "That power does not expire until such time as [the witness] is released from further attendance at court."

[34] *R (TH) v Wood Green Crown Court* [2006] EWHC 2683 (Admin), [2007] 1 WLR 1670 at [23] by Wilkie J with whom Auld LJ agreed.

[35] Administration of Justice Act 1960, s 13.

Summary of the rights of challenge to a remand in custody under the current law

Defendants

9.41   A remand in custody will have been revisited once at the very least by the time the case approaches trial in the Crown Court unless a person is remanded for the first time by the judge at the Crown Court, pre-trial or during trial.[36] At the first hearing after which bail is refused, the defendant may advance any argument in support of an application for bail. The court need not subsequently entertain any arguments it has heard before, unless there is a change of circumstances. If the remand is at an "early stage of proceedings", or sometimes post-conviction, then judicial review of a refusal of bail may be sought.

Witnesses

9.42   If the person remanded in custody is a witness and the remand is by virtue of section 4(3) of the Criminal Procedure (Attendance of Witnesses) Act 1965, there is no mode of challenge.

THE RECOMMENDATIONS

9.43   We make two recommendations: one in respect of defendants and one in respect of witnesses.

Features common to both recommendations

9.44   Judicial review should be available to a defendant or witness who has been denied bail by the Crown Court acting in its trial on indictment jurisdiction. It should be available where that person is not able otherwise to renew the application for bail.

9.45   It is not to be available where a person has been granted conditional bail – only where bail has been denied. We acknowledge that restrictive conditions attached to bail that fall short of the deprivation of liberty involved in a remand in custody may, nonetheless, deny a person a significant amount or kind of liberty. However, the extent to which such conditions restrict liberty is a matter of degree, and the decision to impose restrictions is highly fact-sensitive. The benefits of permitting judicial review of such conditions in this context must be weighed against the uncertainty that would be generated over the kinds of cases that might and might not be amenable to judicial review. Further, while in theory the cumulative effect of conditions on bail could amount to a deprivation of liberty within Article 5 of the ECHR,[37] this seems to be extremely unlikely.[38] In our view, the promotion of certainty that is achieved by confining cases fit for review to those in which a person has been remanded in custody is the value clearly to be preferred in this context.

---

[36]   *R (Wiggins) v Harrow Crown Court* [2005] EWHC 882 (Admin) is an example of how bail may be refused for the first time at the Crown Court, bail having been granted up until then by the Crown Court and by the magistrates.

[37]   See *Guzzardi v Italy* 3 EHRR 333, para [93].

[38]   See *McDonald v Procurator Fiscal, Elgin* 2003 Scots Law Times 467 [17], [19], and *Davis v Secretary of State for the Home Department* [2004] EWHC 3113 (Admin).

9.46 In neither case (defendant or witness) is the availability of judicial review to be limited by the stage that the trial has reached.

9.47 The review may be determined by a single judge and not necessarily by a Divisional Court. Under the new arrangements for the Administrative Court (and the Divisional Court) to sit in the regions, this kind of challenge would, it seems to us, be suitable for hearing at the Administrative Court centre closest to the claimant.[39]

Defendants

9.48 We recommend that a decision during the exclusion period by the Crown Court to refuse bail to a defendant should be an exception to the bar on judicial review if the only arguments which would be available to the defendant to support an application for bail are ones which the court would not be obliged to hear.

9.49 The relevant provision in the Bill, subsection (4)(b) of the proposed new section 29A, reads:

> A decision during the exclusion period by the Crown Court not to grant bail does not fall within the excluded jurisdiction of the Crown Court if... the decision relates to a defendant, and the only arguments which would be available to the defendant in support of an application for bail are ones which (by virtue of paragraph 3 of Part 2A of Schedule 1 to the Bail Act 1976) the court would not be obliged to hear.

9.50 Thus, a defendant who is refused bail but who is entitled (by virtue of paragraph 2 of Part 2A of Schedule 1 to the Bail Act 1976) to make another application to the Crown Court would not fall within subsection (4), and a defendant who can make an application because the court accepts there has been a change of circumstances would not fall within subsection (4), but a defendant who is precluded from advancing arguments in support of a bail application by paragraph 3 of Part 2A and by there being no change of circumstances, would fall within the subsection (4) exception.

Witnesses

9.51 We recommend that a decision by the Crown Court during the exclusion period to refuse bail to a witness who is brought to the court pursuant to a warrant under section 4 of the Criminal Procedure (Attendance of Witnesses) Act 1965 should be an exception to the bar on judicial review. Our view is that this exception is justified, despite the potential for delay, by the fact that there is otherwise no way for a witness to challenge a remand in custody. This exception is provided by paragraph (a) of subsection (4) of the proposed new section 29A of the SCA 1981.

---

[39] See, eg, *KSS v Northampton Crown Court* [2010] EWHC 723 (Admin) where judicial review of the refusal of bail was heard by the Administrative Court sitting in Manchester. In discussion, one consultee said that when the High Court, exercising its inherent jurisdiction, used to entertain an application for bail on the merits, the application was frequently heard by a High Court judge on circuit.

9.52   This recommendation will partially reverse *R (TH) v Wood Green Crown Court.*[40] The extent of the power to remand (until the witness is released from further attendance) is unaffected. The non-availability of judicial review in respect of witness summonses is also unaffected. It is only with regard to the availability of judicial review of a remand in custody that the effect of the decision would be changed.

Effect on the proceedings at the Crown Court

9.53   It may be that in practice, a challenge to a remand in custody would not delay the trial at all. This might be the case where an application for permission for judicial review was made in writing and considered on the papers (without an oral hearing). The defendant's advocate might not, therefore, need to ask for an adjournment to pursue the application. In any event, the Crown Court has the power to adjourn the trial if necessary.

9.54   Our view is that where the trial is delayed by an application for judicial review in the terms we recommend, that delay is justified by the nature of the right at issue.

Extent and commencement

9.55   Extent and commencement provisions match those for the judicial review provisions in Part 8.

---

[40] On which, see para 9.37 above.

PART 10
A NEW STATUTORY APPEAL FOR CHILDREN AND YOUNG PERSONS

THE OBJECTIVE

10.1 We concluded in Part 6 above that the consequences of some rulings demand an opportunity to challenge them, even if a trial is interrupted or delayed as a result. This Part is about challenges to rulings in a trial on indictment which result in the identification of a child or young person.

10.2 Once a person's identity has been made public, it cannot be re-hidden, and any harm done by identification cannot be undone. When such harm may be done to a child or young person, Parliament has long taken the view that it is especially important to guard against its occurrence. The Crown Court has the power to make an order restricting the reporting of matters which will lead to the identification of a child or young person concerned in the proceedings. This power is provided by section 39 of the Children and Young Persons Act 1933. If a judge refuses to make such an order, or discharges an existing order, then the child might be identified.

10.3 In making an order prohibiting or permitting publication, a court must weigh the conflicting rights in Articles 8 and 10 of the ECHR. Article 10 contains a right to free expression, while Article 8(1) provides that "everyone has the right to respect for his private and family life, his home and his correspondence". Interference by a public authority may be justified where it is "in accordance with law", its aim is legitimate, and the restriction is "necessary in a democratic society in the interests of national security, public safety or the economic well-being of the country, for the prevention of disorder or crime, for the protection of health or morals, or for the protection of the rights and freedoms of others". An order which prohibits the identification of a child or young person will restrict Article 10 rights, but may be justified in the terms of his or her rights under Article 8. Conversely, there will be occasions when the trial judge will be right to permit identification.

10.4   It is very unlikely that a court would discharge, or refuse to make, a section 39 order while the criminal proceedings were continuing,[1] and we are conscious of the need to allow Crown Court judges to conduct trials unimpeded, but our view is that the protection of the Article 8 rights of children and young people is sufficiently important for there to be a right of appeal against a ruling which allows a child or young person in a trial on indictment to be identified. The rationale for restricting reporting of criminal proceedings in relation to child defendants is, we believe, their immaturity and the expectation that they will change. If their names are made public for crimes committed when children, their chances of rehabilitation may well be damaged. The European Court of Human Rights has commented on what it called, "the special position of minors in the criminal-justice sphere" and has noted "in particular the need for the protection of their privacy at criminal trials".[2]

10.5   We conclude, therefore, that there should be the possibility of challenge to the lawfulness of (a) a refusal to make a direction under section 39, and (b) a decision to discharge an existing direction under section 39, or (c) the terms of a direction, at any stage of the trial on indictment.

10.6   We have considered whether this challenge should be by way of judicial review or by way of appeal to the CACD. We have concluded, first, that new, specific rights of challenge should be part of the work of the CACD in line with other rights of challenge in recent years,[3] especially where, as in this case, challenges will be rare; and secondly, that this kind of case is likely to require a review of the merits in order for the child's welfare to be fully considered. In one sense this new right would mirror the right of any person aggrieved to challenge the making of a reporting restriction. An appeal against such a restriction is made to the CACD under section 159 of the Criminal Justice Act 1988. Accordingly, it is appropriate for the child or young person's appeal to go to the same court. For all those reasons, we consider that there should be a right of appeal to the CACD.

10.7   **We therefore recommend that where the Crown Court, in proceedings relating to a trial on indictment, discharges or refuses to make a direction prohibiting publication of material which will identify a child or young person concerned in the proceedings as a defendant or as a witness, that child or young person may appeal to the CACD against that discharge or refusal, or against the terms of a direction, subject to obtaining leave from the Crown Court or, if leave is refused by the Crown Court, from a single judge of the Court of Appeal.** See clause 3(1) of the Bill which inserts a new section 159A in the Criminal Justice Act 1988.

10.8   The rest of this Part describes the background (paragraphs 10.9 to 10.27) in the current law and then, from paragraph 10.28 onwards, the detail of the new appeal.

---

[1]   Young people are occasionally named as defendants in the course of a trial, as in http://news.bbc.co.uk/1/hi/england/manchester/8233964.stm. We do not know whether the younger defendant sought a section 39 order in this case.

[2]   *S v United Kingdom* (2009) 48 EHRR 50 at [124], referring to *V v United Kingdom* (2000) 30 EHRR 121.

[3]   Eg, s 159(1) of the Criminal Justice Act 1988, the prosecution appeal under s 58 of the CJA 2003, and appeals arising under the preparatory hearing regimes.

BACKGROUND

Section 39 of the CYPA 1933

10.9 Section 39 of the Children and Young Persons Act 1933 ("the CYPA 1933") allows a court to prohibit publication of material which will identify a child or young person "concerned in the proceedings". This power is exercised to protect the child or young person.[4] Section 39 reads:

> 39 Power to prohibit publication of certain matter in newspapers
>
> (1)   In relation to any proceedings in any court . . . the court may direct that—
>
> (a)   no newspaper report of the proceedings shall reveal the name, address, or school, or include any particulars calculated to lead to the identification, of any child or young person concerned in the proceedings, either as being the person [by or against] or in respect of whom the proceedings are taken, or as being a witness therein;
>
> (b)   no picture shall be published in any newspaper as being or including a picture of any child or young person so concerned in the proceedings as aforesaid;
>
> except in so far (if at all) as may be permitted by the direction of the court.
>
> (2)   Any person who publishes any matter in contravention of any such direction shall on summary conviction be liable in respect of each offence to a fine not exceeding level 5 on the standard scale.[5]

Thus, the court may make a direction prohibiting publication, but the court may specify an exception to the direction. Section 39(2) creates a summary offence for breach of section 39(1).

10.10 Child and "young person" are defined at section 107(1) of the CYPA 1933. "Child" means a person under the age of 14 years, and young person is one who has attained the age of 14 years and is under the age of 18.

10.11 Section 39 only allows for the protection of a child concerned in the proceedings as a defendant or witness, not as a relative of someone concerned in the proceedings.[6]

---

[4]   *Re Times Newspapers Ltd* [2007] EWCA Crim 1925, [2008] 1 WLR 234, [3].

[5]   By virtue of s 57(4) of the Children and Young Persons Act 1963, s 39 applies "with the necessary modifications", "in relation to sound and television broadcasts as they apply in relation to newspapers". Section 39 applies "with the necessary modifications" "in relation to reports or matters included in a cable programme service as they apply in relation to newspapers": para 4(3) of Sch 5 to the Cable and Broadcasting Act 1984. In addition, s 39 applies "with the necessary modifications" "in relation to reports or matters included in a programmed service, and in relation to including any such reports or matters in such a service, as they apply in relation to reports or matters published in newspapers and to publishing any matter in a newspaper": s 203 and para 3(2) of Sch 20 to the Broadcasting Act 1990. This paragraph is repealed (by Sch 2, para 1 to the Defamation Act 1996) but the repeal is not yet in force.

10.12 Section 39 applies to any proceedings in any court.[7] We are concerned only with criminal proceedings in the Crown Court.[8] A direction under section 39 may be made at any time.[9] If there is a change of circumstances, a further application may be made to the Crown Court.[10]

10.13 Making this kind of direction is such a common practice under the 1933 Act that the court may very well raise the matter of its own motion rather than expecting any formal application. An example is provided by *Ex parte Godwin* in which Lord Justice Glidewell said that "when counsel invites the judge to consider making an order under section 39 it is by way of reminder."[11]

10.14 By paragraph III.30.8 of the *Practice Direction (Criminal Proceedings: Consolidation)*, the court is reminded to make a reporting restriction "where relevant" before trial, sentencing or appeal.

10.15 On application for an order under section 39, the judge may hear representations from all parties with a legitimate interest.[12] *Ex parte Crook* gives guidance on the procedure for the court to follow.[13]

10.16 As is stated in *Archbold*:

> The various statutory provisions in respect of the reporting of information relating to juveniles are now to be read against the background of international law and practice that draws attention to the need carefully to protect the privacy of juveniles in legal proceedings, with great weight being given to their welfare; those interests of the juvenile come into collision with, and fall to be balanced against, the right to freedom of expression and the hallowed principle that justice is administered in public, open to full and fair reporting so that the public might be informed about the justice administered in their name...[14]

---

[6] *Re S (A Child) (Identification: Restriction on Publication)* [2004] UKHL 47, [2005] 1 AC 593; *Crawford v CPS* [2008] EWHC 854 (Admin), [2008] All ER 112.

[7] Section 39(1) and (2) extend to Scotland, but references to a court in ss 39 and 49 do not include a court in Scotland: s 57(3) of the Children and Young Persons Act 1963.

[8] In the youth court and appeals from the youth court, s 49 of the CYPA 1933 applies. The effect is that publication is restricted and the onus falls on the party seeking to have the restriction lifted. Section 39, by contrast, gives the court a power to restrict publication, with the onus falling on the party which wants the restriction.

[9] *R v Harrow Crown Court ex p Perkins* (1998) 162 Justice of the Peace 527.

[10] *Archbold* (2010) 4-27.

[11] *R v Crown Court at Southwark, ex p Godwin* [1992] QB 190, 193.

[12] *R v Central Criminal Court ex p Godwin and Crook* [1995] 1 WLR 139, an appeal under s 159(1) of the Criminal Justice Act 1988.

[13] [1995] 1 WLR 139.

[14] *Archbold* (2010) 4-29.

10.17 One statutory provision is particularly relevant: section 44 of the CYPA 1933 imposes a duty on all courts to have regard to the welfare of a child or young person.[15] Lord Justice Rose has said that "section 39...provides one possible mechanism to that end".[16]

Relationship to section 49 of the CYPA 1933

10.18 Section 49 of the CYPA 1933 imposes reporting restrictions in criminal proceedings in respect of a child or young person who is a defendant or witness. The court has power to dispense with any part of the restriction, if it is "in the public interest to do so" (section 49(4A)). The section applies in youth courts, in the Crown Court in the case of an appeal from a youth court, and in other courts which are not relevant here.

10.19 When a child or young person appears on a criminal charge before the Crown Court, other than on appeal from the youth court, section 49 does not apply, and section 39 CYPA 1933 is relied upon instead.

10.20 The position is, therefore, that in those courts where section 49 automatically comes into play, the court has power to dispense with it. In those courts where it does not apply, the court has power to make reporting restrictions under section 39. The end result might be the same, but the onus falls differently.

Challenges to an order under section 39

10.21 Section 39 does not itself afford a free-standing right to appeal the decision to make or not make a direction under section 39.[17]

The relationship with section 159 of the Criminal Justice Act 1988

10.22 Section 159(1) of the Criminal Justice Act 1988 gives a right of appeal to a "person aggrieved" against various orders restricting publication, but does not give a right of appeal to the child or young person against a refusal to make such an order or against a discharge of an order that has been made.

---

[15] Section 44 of the CYPA 1933 is prospectively amended. Subsections (1A) and (1B) have been inserted by s 9(3) of the Criminal Justice and Immigration Act 2008 but the insertion is not yet in force.

[16] *R v Manchester Crown Court, ex p H and D* [2000] 1 WLR 760, 769.

[17] *Littlewood* [2002] All ER 328. D had asked the court to order a restriction on the publication of his name and address. The judge refused. The Court of Appeal held that it had no jurisdiction to entertain an appeal against the refusal. See also *Lee* [1993] 1 WLR 103, in which the defendant, whose identity had been revealed, argued that s 39 gave the Court of Appeal jurisdiction to reimpose an order restricting publication because of its wide wording: "in relation to any proceedings in any court...". The Court of Appeal was not persuaded: it held that "any proceedings" meant "any proceedings in the court that is making the order". Judicial review, however, *was* available. Thus, if the Court of Appeal is seised of an appeal, s 39 accords it jurisdiction to make an order restricting publication, but s 39 does not give the Court of Appeal free-standing jurisdiction.

The relationship with section 29(3) of the SCA 1981

10.23   Judicial review of an order pursuant to section 39 of the CYPA 1933 made after the verdict and sentence is possible (see the next paragraph), but there is no decided authority on the availability of judicial review in relation to a ruling before the verdict.

10.24   The Divisional Court considered the interaction between section 29(3) of the SCA 1981 and section 39 of the CYPA 1933 in *R v Manchester Crown Court, ex parte H and D*.[18] The court concluded that it did have jurisdiction to consider the application in relation to the discharge of the section 39 order. It noted that it had been recognised in an earlier case that if it did not have jurisdiction by way of judicial review, then there would be "no means at all" of challenging the decision to lift the reporting restriction.[19]

10.25   In *ex parte H and D*, the juvenile defendants had been convicted of murder (in the adult court). Lord Justice Rose relied on the pointers given by Lord Bridge in *Smalley*,[20] noting that the trial could not be delayed by the application, and that a section 39 order is not an "integral part of the trial process", nor an order which arises in the issue between the Crown and the defendant formulated by the indictment. It is a separate child protection power. He also placed great emphasis, when considering the jurisdictional issue, on the fact that the trial had been concluded. He contrasted the position before him with that in *ex parte Crook*[21] where the trial judge had made the restriction order at the beginning of the trial, "intending…to 'influence the conduct of the trial' by affording protection to the witness outside the court".[22]

10.26   Although the authority has been followed,[23] the point has not been definitively decided.

Prospective changes

10.27   From a day yet to be appointed, section 39 of the CYPA 1933 will not apply to criminal proceedings, and section 45 of the Youth Justice and Criminal Evidence Act 1999 ("the 1999 Act") will apply to criminal proceedings instead.

---

[18]   [2000] 1 WLR 760. The court considered itself bound by *Lee* [1993] 1 WLR 103. *R v Winchester Crown Court, ex p B (a minor)* [1999] 1 WLR 788 in which judicial review was said not to be available, was not followed in *ex p H and D*.

[19]   See *R v Winchester Crown Court ex p B* [1999] 1 WLR 788.

[20]   [1985] AC 622. See para 2.48 above.

[21]   *R v Central Criminal Court ex p Godwin and Crook* [1995] 1 WLR 139.

[22]   *R v Manchester Crown Court, ex parte H and D* [2000] 1 WLR 760, 767

[23]   Eg *R v Central Criminal Court, ex p W, B and C* [2001] 1 Cr App Rep 7.

THE NEW APPEAL

Scope of the new appeal

10.28   Section 39 applies to any court. Our remit extends only to the Crown Court, and then only to criminal proceedings. Our recommendation extends only to trials on indictment. Therefore the proposed appeal does not relate to *any* refusal or discharge of a direction under section 39 but only those made in proceedings relating to a trial on indictment. See subsection (1) of the proposed new section 159A of the Criminal Justice Act 1988.

Effect of creating the new appeal

10.29   As noted above,[24] it is probably the case that a refusal to make, or an order discharging, a direction under section 39 may be challenged by way of judicial review post-conviction, but not pre-conviction. The effect of the new appeal would be to remove the need for judicial review proceedings in either case.

Detail of the new appeal

10.30   Clause 3(1) of the draft Bill appended to this report inserts a new section 159A into the Criminal Justice Act 1988. It does not precisely mirror section 159 of that Act (which provides a right for a "person aggrieved" to appeal against the making of reporting restrictions) but it covers some of the same ground.

10.31   A child or young person concerned in the proceedings (as defendant or witness) may appeal against the refusal to make a direction pursuant to section 39 of the CYPA 1933, against the terms of a direction, or against the revocation of a direction made pursuant to section 39 of the CYPA 1933 made by the Crown Court in its trial on indictment jurisdiction. This right of appeal is contained in subsection (1) of the proposed section 159A (see clause 3).

10.32   The ruling in question might be made at any stage of the proceedings before the Crown Court.

10.33   The appeal lies to the CACD.[25]

Proceedings before the Crown Court

10.34   Parties may make representations at the Crown Court on the exercise of the power.

10.35   The trial may continue while the appeal is brought, but the Crown Court may adjourn the trial pending the determination of the appeal.

Automatic reporting restriction pending the determination of the appeal

10.36   It would defeat the purpose of the appeal if the disputed matters could be published before the determination of the appeal. Accordingly, there needs to be a holding ban: a restriction on the reporting of the disputed matters which applies from notification by a party of an intention to appeal until the appeal is determined or abandoned.

---

[24]   See paras 10.23 to 10.26 above.

[25]   This is provided for in s 159(2) of the Criminal Justice Act 1988, which would apply to the proposed s 159A by virtue of s 159A(8).

10.37   A party wishing to appeal would have to indicate to the court, immediately after the ruling has been made, that it intends to appeal, and that indication then acts as the trigger for the holding ban. That indication may be oral or in writing.

10.38   If leave is granted by the Crown Court, the holding ban would remain in effect until the appeal is determined or abandoned.

10.39   If leave is refused by the Crown Court, the child or young person may seek leave from the Court of Appeal. So that the holding ban does not continue in effect for longer than is necessary, there should be a time limit on the period that may elapse between leave being refused by the Crown Court and leave being sought from the Court of Appeal. The precise length of that period is best specified in secondary legislation, but we anticipate it would be short, possibly 48 hours.

10.40   The holding ban would be in the standard terms of a prohibition under section 39, without any exception to it.[26] There would therefore be a broad prohibition for a temporary period, and the CA would have full scope, on appeal, to decide what may or may not be published.

10.41   **We therefore recommend that, if a person indicates an intention to ask for leave to appeal, the Crown Court is to be treated as having made a direction prohibiting reporting under section 39 of the CYPA 1933.** See subsections (1) and (2) of the proposed new section 159B of the Criminal Justice Act 1988.

10.42   **We also recommend that that direction should remain in force:**

> **if leave to appeal is granted, until the appeal has been determined or abandoned; or**
>
> **if leave is refused by the Crown Court, until the specified period of time expires without leave being sought from the CA, or the appellant indicates within that period that he or she will not seek leave from the CA, or the CA grants or refuses leave.**
>
> See subsections (3) and (4) of the proposed new section 159B of the Criminal Justice Act 1988.

Leave required[27]

10.43   The appellant must obtain leave to appeal and that leave may be granted by the Crown Court or, if leave is refused by the Crown Court, on appeal to a single judge of the Court of Appeal.[28]

10.44   If leave is refused by the single judge, the application for leave can be renewed before the full CA. If the full court confirms the refusal of leave, that is the end of matter.

---

[26]   The court's power under s 39 is set out at para 10.9 above.

[27]   "Leave to appeal" is used in the CAA 1968, and "permission to appeal" is used in the Criminal Procedure Rules.

[28]   Subsection (2) of the proposed section 159A. A single judge means any judge of the CA or of the High Court: s 45(2) of the CAA 1968.

Proceedings before the Court of Appeal

The power to give directions

10.45 The single judge and the registrar will have the power to give such directions as appear to the judge or the registrar to be appropriate.

The power to adjourn proceedings

10.46 Although the Crown Court would very likely adjourn the proceedings before it, pending the outcome of the appeal, **we recommend that the Court of Appeal should also have the power to adjourn any proceedings in any other court until after the appeal is disposed of**. See subsection (5)(a) of the proposed section 159A.

Powers of CA on hearing the appeal

10.47 If the Crown Court has decided to discharge an order under section 39, it may stay the implementation of that decision pending the determination of the appeal. An order may therefore be in existence. If, on the other hand, there has been a refusal to make an order, there may not be an order in existence. The principal power which the CA needs, therefore, is the power to make an order as it thinks fit, and this is provided by subsection (5)(b) to (d) of the proposed section 159A. **We recommend that the Court of Appeal should have power to confirm the refusal, to confirm or reverse the revocation, or, if the appeal is against the terms of a direction, to confirm or reverse the direction and, in all cases, to make any direction which the Crown Court could have made.**

Costs

10.48 **We recommend that the CA should have the power to make such order as to costs as it thinks fit** (see subsection (6) of the proposed section 159A).

Penalty for breach of the order made on appeal

10.49 **We recommend that breach of a reporting restriction made on determination of an appeal should constitute an offence, punishable by the same penalty as for a breach of an order made by the Crown Court.** This is the effect of subsection (8)(a) of the new section 159A of the Criminal Justice Act 1988.

No further appeal

10.50 The right of appeal we have in mind is similar in nature to that provided by section 159 of the Criminal Justice Act 1988. **We recommend, therefore, that the decision of the Court of Appeal should be final**, as with section 159 of the Criminal Justice Act 1988, and this is stated in subsection (4) of the proposed section 159A.

Interaction with other statutory provisions

10.51 Any prohibition or restriction on a publication imposed by virtue of any other enactment is unaffected.

Effect if the child or young person attains the age of 18

10.52 A reporting restriction imposed because the person whose identity is protected is a child or young person ceases when the young person becomes an adult.[29] A court would, therefore, have no power to make an order restricting reporting under section 39 of the CYPA 1933 and it would therefore be misguided for the appeal to be pursued on or after the appellant's 18th birthday.

Extent

10.53 An order made on determination of an appeal under the proposed section 159A, and a holding ban under the proposed section 159B, would have the same extent as an order made under section 39 of the CYPA 1933, both in terms of geographical extent and in terms of the kinds of media affected.[30]

Extent: service courts

10.54 Our remit does not extend to making recommendations as regards service courts. Therefore, the new appeal does not extend to service courts, even though the provision setting out the order at the heart of the appeal does so. On the implications for Court Martial of the reform recommended in this Part, see paragraphs 13.61 to 13.65 below.

Related proceedings

10.55 Post-conviction proceedings would be "proceedings relating to a trial on indictment" within subsection (1) of the new section 159A, and therefore the new appeal would be applicable. We now describe two instances of post-conviction proceedings where the question of whether to make reporting restrictions to protect children or young people might arise.

Anti-social behaviour orders following conviction

10.56 Section 1C of the Crime and Disorder Act 1998 makes it possible for a court to make an anti-social behaviour order where a person has been convicted of a "relevant offence",[31] provided that certain conditions are satisfied.[32] It may be made at the conclusion of a trial on indictment of a child or young person.

10.57 The new appeal would be available in respect of all appeals against a refusal to make a direction, or to discharge a direction, under section 39 of the CYPA 1933 if made by the Crown Court in its trial on indictment jurisdiction. If a convicted child or young person is facing an anti-social behaviour order on conviction pursuant to section 1C of the Crime and Disorder Act 1998, and asks the court to restrict reporting under section 39 but the court refuses, then the new appeal would be available.

---

[29] *T v DPP* [2003] EWHC Admin 240, (2004) 168 JR 194.

[30] See cl 3(2) of the Bill and subsection (2) of the proposed s 159B.

[31] Meaning, "an offence committed after the coming into force of section 64 of the Police Reform Act 2002": s 1C(10) of the Crime and Disorder Act 1998.

[32] Crime and Disorder Act, s 1C(1) and (2).

Drinking banning orders following conviction

10.58 Section 6 of the Violent Crime Reduction Act 2006 provides that a court shall consider making a drinking banning order against a defendant on conviction if specified conditions are satisfied. It can only do so in respect of a defendant who is 16 or over. Thus, it could apply to a "young person" within the definition of the CYPA 1933. The court can also make an interim order.[33]

10.59 If the court decides not to make a drinking banning order, because the conditions are not satisfied or for some other reason, it must state its reasons in open court. In the case of a young person, the question of reporting restrictions would arise. and the onus is on the party seeking to shield the defendant from publicity.

10.60 As with anti-social behaviour orders on conviction, the appeal we recommend in this Part would be available against a refusal to make an order restricting reporting of proceedings relating to drinking banning orders, including proceedings for breach of a drinking banning order, where a child or young person is concerned in the proceedings.

Prospective changes and transitory provisions

Section 45 of the Youth Justice and Criminal Evidence Act 1999

10.61 By virtue of section 39(3) of the CYPA 1933,[34] section 39 will not apply to criminal proceedings from a day yet to be appointed. Section 45 of the 1999 Act will apply to criminal proceedings instead. The new provision allows a court, on appeal, to dispense with any direction restricting reporting, but there is no specific provision for an appeal against a refusal to make an order.

10.62 Paragraph 4 of Schedule 1 to the Bill makes provision for the replacement of orders under section 39 of the CYPA 1933 with the new provisions in the 1999 Act by stating that, when the 1999 Act provisions come into force, section 159A is amended as stated. As a direction made under section 45 of the 1999 Act would extend to the United Kingdom, so a holding direction made under the proposed section 159B of the Criminal Justice Act 1988 would extend to the United Kingdom too (see paragraph 5 of Schedule 1 to the Bill).

Commencement

10.63 The provisions about the new statutory appeal relating to reporting restrictions could be brought into effect independently of any other reforms recommended. Commencement of these provisions is to be made by order and not tied to commencement of any other provisions.

10.64 The new appeal would be available from a date to be appointed, and it could be exercised in relation to any refusal or discharge made on or after that date.

---

[33] Violent Crime Reduction Act 2006, s 9.

[34] Inserted by s 48, Sch 2, para 2 to the Youth Justice and Criminal Evidence Act 1999.

PART 11
A NEW STATUTORY APPEAL WHERE THERE IS A REAL AND IMMEDIATE RISK TO LIFE

11.1   We established in Part 6 above that a right of challenge to a court ruling can be justified, even though it will cause delay and interrupt the trial, where a post-conviction appeal cannot undo the harm, where no alternative remedy is available, where a fundamental right is at issue and the consequences could be sufficiently serious. This Part is about providing a right of challenge where a ruling in a trial on indictment could lead to a real and immediate risk to life.

A RIGHT OF APPEAL

11.2   We have considered whether this route of challenge should be by way of judicial review or by appeal. In either case, in this instance, whichever court is reviewing a decision made by another which engages a person's right under Article 2 of the ECHR, it will "anxiously scrutinise" a decision where fundamental rights are concerned.[1]

11.3   We appreciate that any right of appeal which may be exercised before or during the course of a trial has the potential to cause delay, to the detriment of justice, not just to those in the instant case but also to those involved in other cases. The following factors argue in favour of a specific right of appeal, as opposed to one which may be part of a general right to apply for judicial review:

  (1)   The grounds could be tightly drawn.

  (2)   The appellate court would be able to substitute its own view for that of the Crown Court.

  (3)   It fits with the pattern in recent years for appeals on criminal matters to go to the CACD.

  (4)   If it were left to judicial review, the issue of who might have standing would have to be resolved by the Administrative Court, which would leave the law uncertain and invite litigation.

  (5)   There are precedents for the creation of third party rights in relation to criminal proceedings.[2]

11.4   We therefore conclude that the right of challenge should be in the form of a right of appeal to the CACD.

---

[1]   Se, eg *R v Lord Saville of Newdigate* [2000] 1 WLR 1855, [37] by Lord Woolf MR.

[2]   Section 9 of the Serious Crime Act 2007 gives a person the right to make representations in relation to a Serious Crime Prevention Order if the court "considers that the making of the order would be likely to have a significant adverse effect on that person". This right applies in relation to such orders before the High Court, before the Crown Court, and before the CA where it is hearing an appeal from the Crown Court (see s 24) or from the High Court (see s 23).

AVAILABLE TO A PERSON

11.5   We see no reason that this right should be confined to defendants: witnesses' Article 2 rights might be engaged, for example. The question does arise whether the person whose life is potentially threatened should be able to appeal against the ruling or should have to go through one of the parties to the proceedings.

11.6   It might be argued that the prosecution could represent a witness, but there is a question mark over the proper role of the prosecution in acting for a witness. Its role is to represent the state, and the interests of the public generally, and the complainant. However, the prosecution is neither the advocate for the complainant, nor is it the guardian of the jurors' interests. Its proper duties may well not extend to protecting the interests of any directly affected third party. Similarly, a defendant's interests might not coincide with those of a witness, so it might not be appropriate for the defence to bring an appeal on behalf of a third party.

11.7   It is also questionable whether a defendant's representation order (the authority by which his or her advice and representation is paid for by public funding) could or would extend to acting on behalf of a third party.

11.8   We therefore conclude that the right of appeal should be available to a person, not a party.

REPRESENTATIONS

11.9   The right to appeal a ruling is to be contingent on the right to make representations about it.[3]

11.10   A party to the proceedings will be in a position to make representations to the trial judge about a ruling that the judge proposes to make in any event. If a person is not a party to the proceedings, it will not be possible for him or her to make representations to the court without specific provision. That person may be a witness or potential witness in the case, or someone who is neither witness nor defendant, such as a juror. **We recommend that a person should have a right to make representations to the Crown Court in a trial on indictment about a ruling made or proposed to be made if it appears to the court that the ruling could result in a real and immediate risk to his or her life from the criminal act of another.** See clause 4 of the Bill.

11.11   The kind of ruling or proposed ruling which could be the subject of representations to the court by a person is the same as the kind of ruling or proposed ruling which is to be the subject of appeal – on which, see paragraphs 11.24 to 11.28 below.

---

[3]   Analogies for this approach may be found in the prosecution right of appeal against the grant of bail provided for by the Bail Amendment Act 1993 and in the Serious Crime Act 2007 in relation to Serious Crime Prevention Orders: s 24 of the Serious Crime Act 2007 contains a right of appeal to the Court of Appeal against a decision of the Crown Court to make, to vary or not to vary a Serious Crime Prevention Order for "any person who was given an opportunity to make representations in the proceedings concerned by virtue of s 9(4)".

11.12   If a third party applies to the Crown Court to be heard and is refused and that refusal falls within the exclusion period, then judicial review would not be possible.

THE APPEAL TO THE COURT OF APPEAL

11.13   **We recommend that an appeal may be made to the CACD,**

if leave is given by the Crown Court or, if the Crown Court refuses leave, the Court of Appeal,

against a ruling which is made in a trial on indictment and which could affect the conduct of proceedings in which the strict rules of evidence apply,

by a person who has made representations to the Crown Court about it or about the same issue,

on the grounds that the ruling could entail a real and immediate risk to the person's life from the criminal act of another, and that the ruling is wrong in law or one which it is not reasonable for the Crown Court to have made,

and that the CACD may confirm, reverse or vary the ruling as it thinks fit, make any ruling which the Crown Court could have made, or remit it to the Crown Court.

See clause 5 and subsection (2) of clause 7 of the Bill.

THE APPEAL IN DETAIL

Leave

11.14   Because the right of appeal may only be exercised by a person who has made representations to the Crown Court about the ruling in dispute, it follows that a person must have made representations about the ruling before seeking leave.

11.15   The appellant must obtain leave to appeal and that leave may be granted by the Crown Court or, if leave is refused by the Crown Court, on appeal to a single judge of the Court of Appeal. See subsection (2) of clause 5.

11.16   There is a standard assumption that leave is only granted for an appeal if there is a substantial chance of success. Therefore, in considering whether to grant leave, a court would take into account the basis on which an appeal might or might not succeed.

Appeal limited to rulings in a trial on indictment which could affect the conduct of proceedings in which the strict rules of evidence apply

11.17   The appeal is to be available in respect of rulings made by the Crown Court in its trial on indictment jurisdiction where the ruling could affect the conduct of proceedings in which the strict rules of evidence apply.

11.18 The recommendation applies only to rulings of the Crown Court made in the exercise of its jurisdiction concerning trial on indictment. It is to make no difference whether the trial on indictment is with or without a jury.

11.19 The concept of "criminal proceedings in relation to which the strict rules of evidence apply" is found in Part 11 of the CJA 2003, namely the Part which contains the rules on evidence.[4] We are concerned with a subset of such proceedings, namely trial on indictment.

11.20 The limitation to "rulings which could affect the conduct of proceedings in which the strict rules of evidence apply" serves to limit potential appeals to rulings which could affect: a trial for an offence, and a *Newton* hearing.[5] Bail hearings,[6] sentencing hearings, and confiscation proceedings following conviction[7] are not such hearings.

A refusal to make an order

11.21 A refusal to make an order is itself a ruling, and could be the subject of an appeal. This is not the same as an omission by the court.

The grounds of the appeal

11.22 The appeal is to be available where the ruling could entail a real and immediate risk to a person's life from the criminal act of another. The limitation that the risk arises from the criminal act of another excludes appeals where the risk to life is said to arise from, for example, ill-health brought on or exacerbated by the ruling.

11.23 It is irrelevant whether the ruling is or will be implemented: some rulings might not actually have the potential to create any risk unless implemented, but the court should not have to assess the likelihood of its ruling being implemented.

The nature of the risk posed by the ruling

11.24 In case law it has been said that for there to be a real and immediate risk to life, there must be a realistic likelihood of the risk occurring imminently, or a serious possibility or a real possibility.[8]

---

[4] Sections 112(1), 134 and 140 of the CJA 2003.

[5] This is a hearing following a plea of guilty to establish the facts on which the defendant is sentenced. It is resorted to when there is dispute between the prosecution and defence version of the facts and the dispute is significant enough to affect sentence. It is conducted like a trial.

[6] *Moles* [1981] Criminal Law Review 170, cited in *R (DPP) v Havering Magistrates' Court* [2001] 3 All ER 997.

[7] *Silcock* [2004] EWCA Crim 408, [2004] 2 Cr App R (S) 323.

[8] *R (Widgery Soldiers) v the Saville Inquiry* [2001] EWHC Admin 888, [2001] All ER 233 at [32] by Rose LJ.

11.25 In *Re Officer L*,[9] the House of Lords, considering witness anonymity in an inquiry, accepted that Article 2 of the ECHR would be engaged if there were a "real and immediate" risk to life.[10] Drawing on *Re Officer L* in *Re Times Newspapers Limited*,[11] the Court Martial Appeal Court was prepared to grant anonymity to some defendants as a "reasonable and proportionate precaution" in order to protect other defendants.[12]

11.26 The appeal arises where the risk to life follows from the court's own ruling. In this respect, the House of Lords' view in *Re Officer L*[13] is instructive. Lord Carswell, with whom Lords Mance, Hoffmann, Woolf and Brown agreed, held:

> The right to life is simply and briefly expressed in the first sentence of article 2 of the Convention: "Everyone's right to life shall be protected by law." As the Strasbourg jurisprudence has laid down, this covers not only the negative obligation, not to take the life of another person, but imposes on contracting states a positive obligation, to take certain steps towards the prevention of loss of life at the hands of others than the state. The locus classicus of this doctrine is *Osman v United Kingdom* (1998) 29 EHRR 245, paras 115 – 6... .
>
> Two matters have become clear in the subsequent development of the case law. First, this positive obligation arises only when the risk is "real and immediate". The wording of this test has been the subject of some critical discussion, but its meaning has been aptly summarised in Northern Ireland by Weatherup J in *In re W's Application* [2004] NIQB 67, at [17], where he said that "a real risk is one that is objectively verified and an immediate risk is one that is present and continuing". It is in my opinion clear that the criterion is and should be one that is not readily satisfied: in other words, the threshold is high. There was a suggestion in para 28 of the judgment of the court in *R (A) v Lord Saville of Newdigate* [2002] 1 WLR 1249, 1261 (also known as the Widgery Soldiers case, to distinguish it from the earlier case with a very similar title) that a lower degree would engage article 2 when the risk is attendant upon some action that an authority is

---

[9] [2007] UKHL 36, [2007] 1 WLR 2135. See also *R (on the application of Officer A) v HM Coroner for Inner South London* [2004] EWCA Civ 1439, [2004] All ER 27 at [24] by Gage LJ citing *R (on the application of A) v Lord Saville of Newdigate* [2001] EWCA Civ 2048, [2002] 1 WLR 1249.

[10] *Re Officer L* [2007] UKHL 36, [2007] 1 WLR 2135 at [20] by Lord Carswell. In commentary on *Re Times Newspapers* [2008] EWCA Crim 2559, [2009] 1 WLR 1015, N Taylor has written:

> This is a high threshold and was given further explanation in *Re W's Application* [2004] NIQB 67 at [17], where Weatherall J said that "a real risk is one that is objectively verified and an immediate risk is one that is present and continuing".:

in [2009] Criminal Law Review 114, 116.

[11] [2008] EWCA Crim 2559, [2009] 1 WLR 1015.

[12] *Re Times Newspapers Ltd* [2008] EWCA Crim 2559, [2009] 1 WLR 1015 at [18] by Latham LJ.

[13] [2007] UKHL 36, [2007] 1 WLR 2135.

contemplating putting into effect itself. I shall return to this case later, but I do not think that this suggestion is well-founded. In my opinion the standard is constant and not variable with the type of act in contemplation, and is not easily reached. Moreover, the requirement that the fear has to be real means that it must be objectively well-founded.... . That is not to say that the existence of a subjective fear is evidentially irrelevant, for it may be a pointer towards the existence of a real and immediate risk, but in the context of article 2 it is no more than evidence.

Secondly, there is a reflection of the principle of proportionality, striking a fair balance between the general rights of the community and the personal rights of the individual, to be found in the degree of stringency imposed upon the state authorities in the level of precautions which they have to take to avoid being in breach of article 2. As the European Court of Human Rights stated in *Osman v United Kingdom* 29 EHRR 245, para 116, the applicant has to show that the authorities failed to do all that was reasonably to be expected of them to avoid the risk to life. The standard accordingly is based on reasonableness, which brings in consideration of the circumstances of the case, the ease or difficulty of taking precautions and the resources available. In this way the state is not expected to undertake an unduly burdensome obligation: it is not obliged to satisfy an absolute standard requiring the risk to be averted, regardless of all other considerations... .[14]

11.27   We note that other Convention rights and rights under the common law may be engaged, such as a right to a fair trial of a co-defendant, as well as the need for the criminal law to be effective. The trial judge might need to take account of these also in arriving at his or her ruling. There is a range of conclusions which the Crown Court might reach in response to representations. Within that range, there will be a band of reasonable conclusions. Where a Convention right is engaged, that band may be narrower, and the decision-making court's approach more constrained, than where no Convention right is engaged.

11.28   The types of rulings which could be the subject of such an appeal might be rulings as to: disclosure of a person's identity (including a ruling on special measures,[15] reporting of a defendant's identity, and identification of jurors); disclosure of other information;[16] whether proceedings are to be held in private; or reporting of proceedings.

---

[14]   [2007] UKHL 36, [2007] 1 WLR 2135 at [19] to [21]. Lord Carswell expresses the same view in *Re E* [2008] UKHL 66, [2009] AC 536 at [44] to [48].

[15]   "Special measures" directions include: screening the witness from the accused; enabling a witness to give evidence by means of a live video link; providing for a witness to be examined through an intermediary; enabling the witness to provide evidence in private; enabling a video recording of an interview with a witness to be admitted as evidence in chief of the witness. See Criminal Procedure Rules, SI 2005 No 384, r 29.1, *Archbold* (2010) ch 8.

[16]   As in, for example, *R (D) v Central Criminal Court* [2003] EWHC 1212 (Admin), [2004] 1 Cr App R 532.

This is not a merits-based appeal

11.29 The second ground of appeal is that the ruling was wrong in law or that it was not reasonable for the Crown Court to have made it. If one of these grounds cannot be made out, then the appeal will not succeed. It is not, therefore, an appeal on the merits.

Determination of the appeal by the Court of Appeal

11.30 The CACD will have the power to confirm, reverse or vary the ruling as it thinks fit or remit the ruling to the Crown Court. See subsection (2) of clause 7 of the Bill.

11.31 The CACD would not decide the matter afresh, but would make its own assessment of how one right is weighed against another. The intensity of the review will increase if an absolute Convention right or an unqualified obligation is engaged.[17]

11.32 As leave will only be given where the appeal has a reasonable chance of success, would-be appellants who can neither point to some error of law, nor show that the ruling was outside the range of reasonable rulings, would not obtain leave. It is not an appeal on the merits.

FURTHER APPEAL TO THE SUPREME COURT

11.33 Just as the CACD's decision on an appeal by the prosecution under section 58 of the Criminal Justice Act 2003 may be appealed to the Supreme Court from the CACD,[18] so it seems to us appropriate that there should be a further right of appeal to the Supreme Court in respect of this new appeal.

11.34 **We recommend that any party to an appeal to the CACD under this Part may appeal to the Supreme Court, with the leave of the CACD or if the CACD refuses leave, with the leave of the Supreme Court, against the determination by the CACD.** See subsections (1) and (2) of clause 8 of the Bill.

11.35 **We also recommend that leave may be given if and only if the CACD certifies that a point of law of general public importance is involved in the determination and it appears to the court considering leave that the point is one which ought to be considered by the Supreme Court.**[19] See clause 8(3) of the Bill.

PROCEDURAL MATTERS

11.36 **We recommend that the appellant must seek leave to appeal immediately the ruling in question is made.** See subsection (3) of clause 5 of the Bill.

---

[17] See *Huang* [2007] UKHL 11, [2007] 2 AC 167, and *Re E* [2008] UKHL 66, [2009] AC 536.

[18] CJA 2003, s 61.

[19] This is the case in relation to criminal appeals to the Supreme Court under the CAA 1968: s 33(2). If no certificate is granted by the CACD, that is the end of the matter.

11.37   **We recommend that, if the Crown Court refuses leave, and the appellant intends to seek leave from the CA, he or she must do so within a time period to be specified in rules of court.** The length of time specified in secondary legislation should be short, so that delays and interruptions to proceedings are minimised. See subsection (4) of clause 5 of the Bill.

Protecting the position of the appellant

11.38   There is a need for the courts to be able to protect the appellant while the appeal is resolved, For example, where the judge rules that D shall disclose his defence statement to the co-defendants and D claims that would put his life at risk, if D had to obey the judge's ruling, the appeal would be pointless. **We therefore recommend that, once leave to appeal is sought, the ruling appealed against should be of no effect until, if leave is granted, the appeal has been determined or abandoned; or, if leave is refused by the Crown Court, until either the application is abandoned or leave is refused by the CA.** See subsections (1) and (2) of clause 9 of the Bill.

11.39   In cases where the ruling which is the subject of the appeal is a refusal to make an order sought – for example an order protecting the identity of a witness – then the appellant's position will not be protected simply by stating that the ruling shall be of no effect and the court may need to make an interim order specifically for the purpose of protecting the appellant. **We therefore recommend that if a person asks the Crown Court for leave to appeal, it may make such order as it thinks fit to protect the appellant pending conclusion of the appeal, and that it may vary or revoke any order that it makes for this purpose.** See subsections (1) to (4) of clause 10.

Power of the Crown Court to adjourn the proceedings

11.40   The trial may continue while the appeal is brought, but the Crown Court may adjourn the trial pending the determination of the appeal.

Expedited appeals

11.41   It might be necessary for the appeal to be expedited. Whether it is necessary should be for the judge who gives leave to decide in each case. (This may be the trial judge or the single judge of the CA.) **We recommend that the court granting leave must decide whether the appeal should be expedited.** See subsection (1) of clause 6 of the Bill.

11.42   **We recommend that if the Crown Court decides that the appeal should be expedited, then it or the CA may reverse that decision, and that if the CA decides that the appeal should be expedited, then the CA may reverse that decision.** See subsections (3) and (4) of clause 6 of the Bill.

11.43   **We recommend that if an appeal is not to be expedited, the court should have power to adjourn the proceedings in the Crown Court, discharge the jury or order that the jury be discharged.** See subsections (2) and (5) of clause 6 of the Bill.

A procedure enabling information to be withheld from another party

11.44 It is conceivable that in some circumstances, the appellant might wish to withhold information from another party for fear of compromising the safety of someone's life. In extreme cases, the appellant might even wish the other party not to know that the appeal is being made.

11.45 The starting position always is that all applications to the court are made on notice to other parties, that evidence in support of the application is supplied to the other parties, and that proceedings are held in public.[20] As the rationale for the appeal in this Part is that a post-conviction appeal will not be able to undo any harm caused by an unlawful ruling, it follows that, in appropriate cases, rules may allow a party and the court to proceed in a more restrictive way, but the restrictions must only be those which are strictly necessary to provide the protection that is needed.

11.46 There might be three categories of case:

(i) appeals made on notice, with copies of supporting documentation supplied to other parties and with all parties present at the hearing;

(ii) appeals made on notice but without full disclosure of the grounds and/or supporting evidence and with parties potentially excluded from all or part of the hearing; and

(iii) appeals made without notification to other parties and without their presence at the hearing.

11.47 We consider that the power to make rules of court to provide for such circumstances needs to be expressly given in the Bill, and **we therefore recommend that rules of court may prescribe circumstances in which applications for leave to appeal and an appeal may be made, from the Crown Court to the CACD and from the CACD to the Supreme Court, without notice or disclosure of relevant material to any other party, and without any other party being present at a hearing in the appeal, but that the circumstances must not be wider than the minimum reasonably required to protect the safety of any person concerned in the proceedings.** Clause 11 of the Bill gives effect to this recommendation.

Power of the Crown Court to restrict reporting of proceedings pending determination of the appeal

11.48 It is necessary for the Crown Court to be able to restrict reporting of proceedings, if it thinks it necessary to do so, pending the outcome of the appeal, as it may be the case that, if the appellant's fear is well-founded, publicity will make it more likely that his or her life will be at risk. If the appellant succeeds in due course in securing a reversal of the ruling, the protection afforded by being able to appeal against the ruling could be undermined by publication in the meantime. For example, if the ruling concerns the identification of a witness, and the witness's life is genuinely at risk, even reporting of the appeal against the ruling could result in the witness's identity being revealed or worked out.

---

[20] For a recent statement of the importance of these common law principles, see *R (Al Rawi)* [2010] EWCA Civ 482, [14] to [17].

11.49   The power should be to restrict the reporting of the ruling to be appealed against, and the fact that it is being appealed, including an application for leave to appeal against the ruling. **We accordingly recommend that the Crown Court should have the power to restrict the reporting of proceedings to the extent necessary in the interests of justice until the earliest of the following: the appeal is determined by the CA or abandoned; if the Crown Court refuses leave, the period of time specified for seeking leave expires without leave being sought; or the appellant indicates that leave will not be sought; or leave is refused by the CA.** See subsections (1) and (3) of clause 12 of the Bill. Publication after that date should be a matter dealt with by the CA (on which, see paragraph 11.59 below).

11.50   Thus, to take the example of a defendant who wishes a witness to be unidentified, D would initially ask the judge to rule that the witness should not be identified. D might make such an application in private, having previously alerted the judge to the problem.

If the judge rules against him, D may seek leave to appeal against that ruling from the judge. D would at the same time wish to secure a restriction on reporting of the ruling and of the defence application for leave.

If leave is granted, D would ask for the restriction to continue pending determination of the appeal.

If leave is refused, D may take the application to a single judge of the CA, and again seek a continuation of the reporting restriction pending either the refusal of leave or the determination of the appeal.

If leave is still refused, the reporting restriction would come to an end. If leave were granted by the CA, the reporting restriction would continue.

Breach of the reporting restriction

ATTORNEY GENERAL'S CONSENT

11.51   Returning to first principles, there should be a consent requirement "where it is very likely that a defendant will reasonably contend that the prosecution for a particular offence would violate his or her Convention rights". We stated this principle in our report "Consents to Prosecution".[21] We had in mind particularly prosecutions which might undermine a person's freedom of expression. Prosecution for breach of a reporting restriction should, therefore, require the Attorney General's consent.

11.52   **We recommend that breach of a reporting restriction made in connection with an appeal recommended in this Part should be an offence, but that the consent of the Attorney General must be obtained for a prosecution of the offence.** See clause 13 of the Bill.

---

[21]   "Consents to Prosecution" LC 255 (1998).

11.53   Publication in breach of the reporting restriction in Scotland and Northern Ireland would need to be an offence, as in England and Wales, but given our remit, we feel that this is a matter for those implementing our recommendations, rather than for us.

Proceedings before the Court of Appeal

Power of single judge and registrar to give directions

11.54   **We recommend that section 31B of the CAA 1968 should be amended so that the single judge and the registrar have the power to give such directions as appear to the judge or the registrar to be appropriate.** This is effected by paragraph 6(3) of Schedule 1 to the Bill.

The power to adjourn proceedings

11.55   Although the Crown Court would very likely adjourn the proceedings before it pending the outcome of the appeal, **we recommend that the CA should have the power to adjourn any proceedings in any other court until after the appeal is disposed of.** See subsection (1) of clause 7 of the Bill.

Incidental orders

11.56   **We recommend that the CA should have the power to make such incidental orders as it thinks fit.** This is effected by subsection (3) of clause 7 of the Bill.

Costs

11.57   **We recommend that the CA should have the power to make such order as to costs as it thinks fit.** This is effected by clause 7(4) of the Bill.

The power of the CACD to protect the appellant

11.58   In the same way as it may be necessary for the Crown Court to make an order protecting the appellant pending resolution of the appeal, it may be necessary for the CACD to make an order protecting the appellant for the duration of the appeal proceedings or to change or revoke such an order made by the Crown Court. **We therefore recommend that the CACD should be able to make such order as it thinks fit to protect the appellant pending conclusion of the appeal, and that it may vary or revoke any order made for this purpose, whether made by it or by the Crown Court.** See subsections (5)(a), (5)(b) and (6) of clause 10.

The power of the CA to restrict publication

11.59   **We recommend that, once the appeal is determined by the CA, the CA should have the power to vary or revoke a direction given by the Crown Court, and to make any new or further restriction on the reporting of the content or the fact of the appeal.** See subsections (4) to (6) of clause 12 of the Bill. As with breach of a reporting restriction made by the Crown Court, breach of the reporting restriction should be an offence, and prosecution for breach of a reporting restriction made by the CA should require the consent of the Attorney General (see clause 13).

11.60   If leave to appeal to the Supreme Court is sought, the reporting restriction may need to remain in place until the conclusion of those proceedings. Therefore, **we recommend that if leave to appeal to the Supreme Court is sought, a reporting restriction made by the CA should continue in effect, unless it is revoked, until the CA refuses to grant a certificate that the ruling involves a point of law of general public importance or, if it does grant such a certificate,**

> **if the CA refuses leave to appeal, until the period for applying to the Supreme Court for leave expires without an application for leave having been made or the person indicates that no application will be made, or**

> **until the Supreme Court refuses leave, or**

> **if the Supreme Court grants leave, until the appeal is determined or abandoned.** See subsection (7) of clause 12 of the Bill.

Proceedings before the Supreme Court

Expedited appeals

11.61   If a party seeks to appeal to the Supreme Court it may be that, as with the initial appeal to the CACD, the appeal will need to be expedited. The Rules of the Supreme Court permit requests for appeals to be expedited.[22]

Continued suspension of the ruling

11.62   In the same way as the ruling in question needs to be suspended while the appeal to the CACD is resolved, so, if an appeal to the Supreme Court is pursued, the ruling will need to continue to be suspended. **We therefore recommend that if leave to appeal to the Supreme Court is sought, the ruling in question should continue to be of no effect until the earliest of the following:**

> **the CA refuses to grant a certificate that the ruling involves a point of law of general public importance or,**

> **if the CA refuses leave to appeal, until the period for applying to the Supreme Court for leave expires without an application for leave having been made or (if sooner) the person indicates that no application will be made, or**

> **the Supreme Court refuses leave, or**

> **if leave is granted, by the CA or by the Supreme Court, until the appeal is determined or abandoned.**

> See subsections (4) and (5) of clause 9 of the Bill.

---

[22]   Supreme Court Rules 2009, SI 2009 No 1603, r 31.

Protection of the appellant pending appeal to the Supreme Court

11.63   If the appeal is pursued to the Supreme Court, it may be that an order protecting the position of the person who appealed to the CACD is needed pending resolution of the appeal to the Supreme Court, **We therefore recommend that if leave to appeal to the Supreme Court is sought, the CA should be able to make such order as it thinks fit to protect the person who appealed to it pending conclusion of the appeal, and that it may vary or revoke any order made for this purpose.** See subsections (5)(c), (5)(d) and (6) of clause 10.

The procedure enabling information to be withheld from another party

11.64   The powers to restrict notice and disclosure provided for in relation to an appeal to the CACD (see paragraphs 11.44 to 11.47 above) will need to apply to an application for a certificate and for permission to appeal to the Supreme Court and to any appeal following the grant of permission to appeal. See clause 11 of the Bill.

The power of the Supreme Court to restrict publication

11.65   Our recommendations at paragraphs 11.59 and 11.60 above cover the time from when the CACD determines the appeal, if a party seeks to appeal to the Supreme Court. When it hears an appeal, the Supreme Court may need to be able to alter or revoke the direction that has been made. When it determines the appeal before it, it may consider that justice requires it to restrict reporting of the proceedings, and **we therefore recommend that if the Supreme Court hears an appeal, it should be able to vary or revoke a direction given by the CA, and that when it determines an appeal, it should be able to make such direction restricting publication of any matter relating to the appeal proceedings as it thinks fit**. See subsections (8) and (9) of clause 12 of the Bill.

11.66   Once the appeal proceedings have been concluded, it may be necessary for the Crown Court to alter or revoke the reporting restriction that has been put in place by the Supreme Court, and **we therefore recommend that the Crown Court should be able to vary or revoke a direction given by the Supreme Court**. See subsection (10) of clause 12 of the Bill.

11.67   As with breach of a reporting restriction made by the Crown Court or the CACD, prosecution for breach of a reporting restriction made by the Supreme Court should require the consent of the Attorney General (see clause 13).

Powers of the Supreme Court

11.68 **We recommend that when an appeal is heard by the Supreme Court as described in this Part, it should have the same powers as the CA to deal with it.** It should be able to adjourn proceedings in another court if necessary, and it should be able to dispose of the appeal by confirming, reversing or varying the ruling, making any order which the Crown Court could have made, or remitting the case to the Crown Court to dispose of it in accordance with any directions that the Supreme Court might give. The Supreme Court would also need to be able to make such order as to costs as it thinks fit. Rules 29 and 46 of the Supreme Court Rules 2009 provide these powers.[23]

EFFECT OF CREATING THE NEW APPEAL

11.69 It is important to note that there have already been cases where a defendant has challenged a ruling which, he argued, was going to lead to a risk to his life. As judicial review of a court ruling made in a trial on indictment is barred by section 29(3) of the SCA 1981, the defendant has sought judicial review of the prosecution decision to continue with the prosecution instead.[24]

11.70 The recommended new appeal amounts to a partial reversal of *C*[25] in which the CACD held that appeals against witness anonymity orders ought not to be the subject of interlocutory appeals, "unless it is quite apparent that they are orders which should not have been made".[26] It may therefore be possible, even under the current law, for witness anonymity orders to be challenged on appeal. Our recommendation would permit challenge to such orders on judicial review-type grounds.

---

[23] SI 1603 of 2009.

[24] See, eg, *R (D) v Central Criminal Court* [2004] EWHC 1212, [2004] 1 Cr App R 41 in which the defendant and co-defendants were being prosecuted for serious drug offences. The defendant was an informant, and while the co-defendants suspected as much, disclosure of his defence statement would have made it clear to them that this had indeed been the case. There was a reasonable basis for thinking that they would seek revenge, even to the point of harming him or his family. In this case, it was the decision of Customs and Excise to continue with the prosecution, at risk to the life of D and D's family, in the light of an order on disclosure by the trial judge, which was at issue. The High Court noted that the application for judicial review was an indirect way of challenging the judge's decision which was not itself amenable to judicial review by virtue of s 29(3).

[25] [2008] EWCA Crim 3228, [2008] All ER 99.

[26] *C* [2008] EWCA Crim 3228, [2008] All ER 99 at [16] by Latham LJ. The trial judge made witness anonymity orders, pursuant to the Criminal Evidence (Anonymity of Witnesses) Act 2008. The defence sought to appeal against those orders pre-trial. There was discussion at the CACD whether the hearing at which the judge had made the orders really constituted a preparatory hearing, in which case, the defence had a right of interlocutory appeal under s 35 of the Criminal Procedure and Investigations Act 1996. The CACD accepted that it did, for the purposes of the appeal before them, and held at [16] by Latham LJ:

> The witness anonymity orders that are in place here are orders that may or may not, at the end of the day, produce the results which the prosecution hopes and the defence fears. The witness anonymity orders – unless it is quite apparent that they are orders which should not have been made – should not be the subject matter of interlocutory appeals. The problem is that until the trial is under way and it can be seen what the real issues are, and the way in which the defendants are affected in their ability to deal with evidence by the anonymity orders, there is no proper way in which that assessment can be made.

11.71   The new appeal would also amount to a partial reversal of *Littlewood*.[27]

Interaction with other forms of appeal

11.72   The new appeal would be available in addition to any other statutory interlocutory appeal. In practice, if an appeal was being brought in part on reliance on the new right of appeal described in this Part and another appeal, we would expect the Registrar to direct that they were processed and heard as one.

Commencement

11.73   We regard the recommendations in this Part as connected to the recommendations on judicial review: if the High Court's powers of judicial review over the Crown Court are to be clearly excluded in relation to trials on indictment, then the right of appeal envisaged in this Part needs to come into effect at the same time as judicial review is reformed.

11.74   Commencement will be by order.

Consequential amendment: effect on time limits for completion of stages of a criminal case

11.75   Statutory time limits for the completion by a case of stages of the criminal justice process are set pursuant to section 22 of the Prosecution of Offences Act 1985. **We recommend that time should cease to run for the purposes of those statutory time limits while the appeal to the CACD, and any further appeal to the Supreme Court, is pursued.**

11.76   The Bill gives effect to this recommendation by amendment of section 22(6B) of the Prosecution of Offences Act 1985.[28]

---

[27]   [2002] All ER (D) 328. See fn 17 in Part 10 above.

[28]   See Schedule 1, para 7.

PART 12
THE IMPLICATIONS FOR MAGISTRATES' COURTS

12.1 In CP 184 we envisaged High Court jurisdiction in criminal proceedings being reduced and transferred, in the main, to the CACD. In Part 6 of the CP we set out the implications of our provisional proposals for magistrates' courts. We received helpful comments on that Part in particular from the OCJR, the Justices' Clerks' Society, and the Council of HM District Judges (Magistrates' Courts) Legal Committee.

12.2 The OCJR thought the implications for magistrates' courts were well brought out and commented that "a point of interest here is that the Crown Court is not a court of precedent, no less presumably in its appellate jurisdiction than its first instance jurisdiction. If the High Court jurisdiction over the magistrates' court were abolished, one option might be to grant Crown Court rulings on appeal from the magistrates' court precedent status. But this would require further thought."

12.3 In the CP we noted that, if the idea is to streamline procedure, then, if the jurisdiction of the High Court over the Crown Court in criminal proceedings were transferred to the CACD, it would leave the jurisdiction of the High Court over criminal proceedings in the magistrates' courts as an anomaly. The Justices' Clerks' Society agreed.

12.4 Further, as we stated in the CP,[1] if the High Court's existing jurisdiction in relation to decisions made by magistrates' courts were replaced by a new statutory appeal to either the Crown Court or the Court of Appeal, the High Court would still retain a jurisdiction to review some decisions made in respect of criminal matters. For example, it is not uncommon for the Director of Public Prosecutions or the police to make decisions prior to or instead of criminal proceedings being instituted in magistrates' courts. It would still be possible to apply to the High Court for judicial review of such decisions.

IMPLICATIONS FOR MAGISTRATES' COURTS IF THE RECOMMENDATIONS IN THIS REPORT ARE ENACTED

12.5 It is obvious that our change in direction from the CP means that the implications for magistrates' courts are different from those stated in the CP.

12.6 To recap the position under the current law: a defendant who is convicted in the magistrates' courts may:

(1) appeal to the Crown Court by way of rehearing;

(2) appeal to the High Court by case stated;

(3) apply to the High Court for judicial review.

---

[1] CP 184, para 6.47.

12.7 The current law provides two means of challenging decisions made by the Crown Court when exercising its appellate jurisdiction: appeal to the High Court by case stated and judicial review in the High Court. Both the prosecution and the defence may make use of either avenue of appeal, but there are significant differences between the two:

(1) A claim for judicial review can only be made with permission whereas, once a case has been stated, the High Court must hear the appeal.

(2) The time limits on appealing by case stated are different from the time limit on seeking permission for judicial review.

(3) Evidence may be received, usually on affidavit, in applications for judicial review whereas evidence is not received in appeals by cases stated.[2]

(4) Both the prosecution and the defendant can appeal by way of case stated on the basis that the decision was wrong in law, or in excess of jurisdiction.[3]

(5) Judicial review is open to persons with sufficient interest. Case stated is available to the parties.

(6) Appeal by way of case stated is not available to challenge interlocutory decisions.[4]

12.8 Since the publication of the CP the length of time within which the Crown Court may vary a sentence has been extended. The "slip rule" now in section 155 of the Powers of Criminal Courts (Sentencing) Act 2000 provides that "a sentence imposed, or other order made, by the Crown Court when dealing with an offender may be varied or rescinded by the Crown Court" within 56 days.[5] This power is not limited to sentences or orders imposed following trial on indictment; it thus applies to sentences and orders following conviction after a rehearing or when a defendant has been committed to the Crown Court for sentence.

12.9 This means that whereas a party who was out of time to seek to have a sentence corrected would have proceeded by case stated, he or she might now return to the Crown Court under the amended slip rule.

The effect of our recommendation to remove case stated in relation to the Crown Court

12.10 Our recommendation in relation to appeal by way of case stated will remove one of the routes of appeal available to a defendant whose conviction is upheld by the Crown Court on appeal from the magistrates' court. The result would be that the defendant will only be able to challenge a ruling of the Crown Court in its appellate jurisdiction by way of judicial review.

---

[2] For further detail, see CP 184, para 1.37.

[3] SCA 1981, s 28(1).

[4] *Loade v DPP* [1990] 1 QB 1052,1064.

[5] Increasing the length of time from 28 days: para 28 of Sch 8 to the Criminal Justice and Immigration Act 2008.

AN ALTERNATIVE POSSIBILITY

12.11 The response of the Council of HM District Judges (Magistrates' Courts) Legal Committee suggested the following possibility: remove appeal by way of case stated and judicial review from the magistrates' court *and* from the Crown Court acting in its appellate jurisdiction so that all appeals from the magistrates' courts go to the Crown Court, whether law, fact, or both. There could then be an appeal from the Crown Court to the CACD solely on a point of law. This possibility entails reforming the jurisdiction of the High Court over the magistrates' court, which is outside our remit, but we nevertheless think it is worth discussing it in a little detail here.

12.12 Suppose we accept that the right of rehearing from the magistrates' court to the Crown Court is retained, and that it would be preferable for there to be a single appellate route from the Crown Court for cases originally tried in the magistrates' court. It then follows that taking the case to the High Court, whether by case stated or by judicial review, should be prohibited.

12.13 If that were the position, there would need to be a way for a point of law to be taken to the CACD from the rehearing – available to both the prosecution and the defence.[6] Whether that would then entail a quashing of the conviction/acquittal is a separate matter. There would need to be a filter mechanism of leave, but only to ensure that the appeal really did concern a point of law (an alleged error of law) and not some more demanding leave hurdle. There would have to be a means of challenging the refusal of leave – as there is for appeals against conviction from trial on indictment.

12.14 There would, however, be wasteful duplication if a case had to be reheard at the Crown Court in order to get a point of law before the CACD. Therefore, there should be in addition a "leapfrog" mechanism whereby, if an appeal was being pursued purely on a point of law and the Crown Court certified it as being a point of law of sufficient novelty and/or difficulty that the CACD should hear it, then the case could be passed straight to the CACD without a substantive hearing at the Crown Court.

12.15 We doubt that there would have to be a mechanism for challenging the Crown Court's refusal to certify that it was that kind of case, because the refusal would not deny a party a route of appeal, just prevent them short-circuiting part of the process.

12.16 This option removes the possibility of appeals before there has been a verdict in the magistrates' court. It also removes the possibility of a third party bringing an appeal on a point of law.

12.17 The impact would be to transfer work from the Administrative Court to the Crown Court. It is not for us to say which court is better placed to bear the burdens of work.

---

[6] Points of law need to be decided at a level other than the Crown Court because that court is not a court of precedent, and, as one consultee emphasised, the kinds of points of law which might be decided can affect all cases tried in the magistrates' courts.

12.18   The impact would also be to increase the workload on the CACD, because after a rehearing a defendant would be able to seek leave to appeal on the point of law, even if leave was not granted. In other words, although the number of appeals actually heard by the CACD might not increase hugely, the number of applications for leave would increase, although it is hard to say by how much. There would also be appeals against refusal of leave.

PROSECUTION RIGHTS TO CHALLENGE AN ACQUTTAL IN THE MAGISTRATES' COURT

12.19   In the CP we wrote, at paragraph 2.25,

> In contrast to a defendant who is challenging a conviction by a magistrates' court, the prosecution cannot seek to challenge an acquittal by appealing to the Crown Court. However, the prosecution can challenge the acquittal by:
>
> (1) appealing to the High Court by case stated;
>
> (2) applying to the High Court for judicial review.

12.20   Professor John Spencer mentioned to us that there were statutory exceptions to this statement, and that this project was an opportunity to abolish them. It is true that there are statutory exceptions to this statement,[7] but none which grant a jurisdiction to the High Court in criminal proceedings beyond the right to apply to have a case stated or to appeal by way of judicial review, and therefore such rights of appeal are outside our terms of reference.

12.21   It may be that, in the context of magistrates' courts, it would simplify criminal procedure if specific statutory provisions allowing the prosecution to appeal against an acquittal were abolished, but we have not consulted on the abolition of those rights of appeal, it being outside our remit to do so.

---

[7]   Such as s 147(3) of the Customs and Excise Management Act 1979 which provides: "In the case of proceedings in England or Wales, without prejudice to any right to require the statement of a case for the opinion of the High Court, the prosecutor may appeal to the Crown Court against any decision of a magistrates' court in proceedings for an offence under the customs and excise Acts."

PART 13
IMPLICATIONS FOR THE COURT MARTIAL

13.1 Our terms of reference require us to say what the implications of our recommendations for the civilian system are for service courts. We are not asked to make any recommendations for the service courts and we do not do so.

GENERAL POINTS ABOUT SERVICE LAW

13.2 The structure of criminal proceedings for military personnel and civilians attached to or residing with military personnel contained within the Armed Forces Act 2006 ("the AFA 2006") is described in Part 7 of CP 184.

13.3 Service law has recently undergone significant change. With the coming into force in October 2009 of the majority of the AFA 2006, the courts-martial were replaced by a single Court Martial and the Courts-Martial Appeal Court was renamed the Court Martial Appeal Court. New procedural rules made under the AFA 2006 aimed to reduce the differences in the procedure and practice of the Court Martial among the three Services.

13.4 We are grateful to those at the Office of the Judge Advocate General and the Ministry of Defence for their advice to us on how things work in practice in service courts.

Relationship to civilian law

13.5 The general approach is for service courts to mirror the civilian system, except where divergence is justified by the different circumstances of the services. For example, in the Armed Forces (Court Martial) Rules, in force on 31 October 2009, if something arises for which the rules have not provided, then rule 26 applies. It reads,

> *Circumstances not provided for*
>
> 26. Subject to any other enactment (including any other provision of these Rules), the judge advocate shall ensure that proceedings are conducted—
>
> (a) in such a way as appears to him most closely to resemble the way in which comparable proceedings of the Crown Court would be conducted in comparable circumstances; and
>
> (b) if he is unable to determine how comparable proceedings of the Crown Court would be conducted in comparable circumstances, in such a way as appears to him to be in the interests of justice.

13.6 We bear this general approach in mind in what we say below.

COMMENTS ON CP 184

13.7 In Part 7 of the CP we set out the implications of our provisional proposals for Court Martial. We received comments from three people, Master Venne and two lawyers at the Ministry of Defence ("MoD"). The two lawyers pointed out errors in Part 7.

13.8 We were mistaken at paragraph 7.27 when we wrote that "trials of military personnel before the Court Martial are the equivalent of Crown Court trials for non-military personnel." The Court Martial can try all service offences, including those which in the civilian system would be tried by a magistrates' court.

13.9 On a different point, we had written at paragraph 7.26 that

> there are certain statutory appeals which although available in respect of Crown Court decisions are not available in respect of the same decisions if made by the Court Martial. For example, statutory provisions which enable the prosecution to appeal in respect of "terminating" rulings and statutory provisions permitting appeals against reporting and public access restrictions do not apply to the Court Martial.[1]

13.10 This was not completely accurate. The MoD drew our attention to secondary legislation which provides for appeals. That secondary legislation has itself since changed, and the position is now as follows.

Interlocutory appeals

13.11 Statutory Instruments provide for interlocutory appeals against rulings at Court Martial (a) by the prosecution, (b) against reporting and public access restrictions, and (c) in sundry other circumstances. We take each of these in turn.

Prosecution appeals

13.12 There is an equivalent in service law of appeals by the prosecution under section 58 of the CJA 2003.[2] The situation is as described in *R v LSA* by Lord Justice Hughes:

---

[1] Part 9 of the CJA 2003 and s 159 of the Criminal Justice Act 1988. The provisions in respect of preparatory hearings under s 35 of the Criminal Procedure and Investigations Act 1996 and s 9 of the Criminal Justice Act 1987 have not been extended to the Court Martial. Therefore appeals from these hearings equally do not apply.

[2] Court Martial (Prosecution Appeals) Order 2009, SI 2009 No 2044. With regard to prosecution appeals against rulings under the equivalent of Part 9 of the CJA 2003, see *Arnold* [2008] EWCA Crim 1034, [2008] 1 WLR 2881 in which the Court Martial Appeal Court held that the prosecutor's right of appeal under the Courts-Martial (Prosecution Appeals) Order 2006 (the predecessor of SI 2009 No 2044) could not be exercised unless the prosecutor informed the court that it accepted that the defendant should be acquitted if leave to appeal was not granted.

The prosecution right of appeal under Article 4 is, just as is its civilian equivalent under s 58 Criminal Justice Act 2003, an interlocutory appeal. The assertion to the contrary made on behalf of the defendant in the course of argument was wrong. The scheme for these appeals is that the proceedings in the court below stand adjourned pending the hearing of the appeal: see Article 4(10), the mirror of s 58(10), under which the ruling is to have no effect pending the outcome of the appeal.

...

It is necessary also to consider the rules as to leave. Here there is a limited divergence between the rules applicable at Court-Martial and those applicable in the Crown Court. In both courts a Crown appeal may be brought only with the leave of either the lower court or this court. For Courts-Martial that is stipulated by article 3(4). The assertion made at the hearing on behalf of the defendant that no leave was required was wrong. The Courts-Martial (Prosecution Appeals) (Supplementary Provisions) Order 2006 then contains provisions specific to Courts-Martial for the making of application for leave. ...

As we have said, although the substantive provisions governing the right of appeal are the same for Courts-Martial as for Crown Courts, the procedural rules for making an application for leave are not the same. The procedural rules relating to Crown Court trials are to be found in the Criminal Procedure Rules 2005, as amended, part 67 (*Archbold 2008 paragraph 7.259a)*. For the Crown Court, those rules allow for the making of an application in writing for leave, and they do not command an oral hearing.

In this case it is the Courts-Martial rules which apply. They require an oral hearing.[3]

Appeals against reporting and public access restrictions

13.13   With regard to appeals against reporting and public access restrictions, section 29(3A) of the SCA 1981 precludes a challenge to a ruling in a Court Martial on reporting or public access, and section 159 of the Criminal Justice Act 1988 (which covers the situation in the civilian context) is not applicable. This is now covered by rule 154 of the Armed Forces (Court Martial) Rules 2009.[4] It provides that a person aggrieved may appeal to the Appeal Court (the CMAC), with leave of the CA, against orders restricting public access to proceedings or restricting publication.

[3]   [2008] EWCA Crim 1034, [2008] 1 ELR 2881 at [21] and [28] to [30] (emphasis in original).

[4]   SI 2009 No 2041.

13.14   At the hearing of the application for leave in *Times Newspapers Ltd v R*,[5] the CMAC ordered that in the absence of any rules of procedure, the procedure applicable to applications under section 159 was to be adopted.

Other interlocutory appeals from Court Martial

13.15   Pre-court-martial procedure used to be provided for by the Courts-Martial (Army) Rules 1997[6] and similar rules for the other services. There was no rule providing for an appeal against any order or ruling. New rules in 2007 (Courts-Martial (Army) Rules 2007,[7] and their equivalent for the other two services) introduced the possibility of an appeal in rule 90 which appeared to offer, in 90(1)(a), the possibility of either party appealing against any ruling in preliminary proceedings. Rule 90 has now been replaced by rule 50 of the Armed Forces (Court Martial) Rules 2009.[8] It comes in Part 8 of the Rules, which Part is headed, "Preliminary Proceedings". Preliminary proceedings are for the judge advocate "to give such directions as appear to him to be necessary to secure the proper and efficient management of the case", including rulings on joinder and severance, on the admissibility of evidence, and on "any other question of law, practice or procedure relating to the case".[9] Rulings given at preliminary proceedings continue in effect until varied or discharged.

13.16   Rule 50 says the following about interlocutory appeals:

> (1) The Appeal Court shall have jurisdiction to hear an appeal against any order or ruling made in preliminary proceedings.
>
> (2) An appeal under this rule may be brought only with leave of the Appeal Court.
>
> (3) A judge advocate may continue preliminary proceedings notwithstanding that leave to appeal has been granted under paragraph (2), but related proceedings (other than further preliminary proceedings) may not commence until the appeal has been determined or abandoned.

The "Appeal Court" means the Court Martial Appeal Court, by virtue of rule 3(2).

---

[5]   [2008] EWCA Crim 2559, [2009] 1 WLR 1015 (Court Martial Appeal Court).

[6]   SI 1997 No 169.

[7]   SI 2007 No 3442.

[8]   SI 2009 No 2041.

[9]   SI 2009 No 2041, rule 49.

13.17   It is interesting that in the service context, there appears to be this interlocutory right of appeal which is at large and yet little used.[10] In theory, a party could appeal a ruling, and could make repeated appeals on different points in the same proceedings, and cause considerable delay. In practice, that does not happen.

13.18   It is important to note that other statutory provisions or case law may bear on a particular issue, and rule 50 has to be read in light of them. For example, the general appeal in rule 50 would not be relied upon by the prosecution in relation to a ruling which had the effect of stopping the prosecution: the prosecution would rely instead upon the specific right of appeal provided in the Court Martial (Prosecution Appeals) Order 2009.

13.19   A second example might be special measures provisions. Chapter 6 of part 12 of the Armed Forces (Court Martial) Rules 2009 provides for special measures in the Court Martial. Rule 99 allows the judge advocate to vary or discharge a special measures direction, but there is no specific right of appeal in chapter 6 against a special measures direction (nor against the refusal to make one).

IMPLICATIONS FOR COURT MARTIAL OF THE POLICY IN THIS REPORT

13.20   In CP 184 we described the implications of our provisional proposals for proceedings before Court Martial and other military tribunals. As we have modified those proposals in the light of consultation responses, so it follows that the implications for the structure of appeals from the various military tribunals differ from the implications described in the CP.

Removal of case stated

13.21   If appeal by way of case stated from decisions of the Crown Court is removed, one could argue that case stated should also be removed in respect of rulings of the Summary Appeal Court.[11] It is a rarely-used procedure and where it has been used, the application could have been made as one for judicial review.[12] The Office of the Judge Advocate General (OJAG) tend to agree with this view, in contrast to the MoD who see case stated as an important means of appeal against rulings of the Summary Appeal Court.

13.22   We consider that this issue is a matter for the Government following appropriate consultation.

[10]   The predecessor of rule 50 was rule 90 of the Courts-Martial (Army) Rules 2007, SI 2007 No 3442. The 2007 Rules were only in force from 1 January 2008 to 30 October 2009, but we are not aware of any appeals made under them except for one appeal relying on rule 90(1)(b) in relation to reporting restrictions. There have been two reported appeals brought under the Prosecution Appeals Order of 2009, SI 2009 No 2044.

[11]   It is provided for by s 149(2) of the AFA 2006.

[12]   See *Khan v Royal Air Force Summary Appeal Court* [2004] EWHC 2230 (Admin), [2004] All ER 81.

Our recommendation for redefining the exclusionary bar in section 29(3), prohibiting judicial review of rulings in trial on indictment, and the jurisdictional bar in section 29(3A)

13.23 As we described in the CP, section 29(3A) – which states that the High Court has no jurisdiction to make prerogative orders "in relation to the jurisdiction of the Court Martial in matters relating to (a) trial by the Court Martial of an offence, or (b) appeals from the Service Civilian Court" – is not identical to section 29(3) of the SCA 1981.

13.24 Section 29(3A) was originally inserted in the SCA 1981 by section 23 of the Armed Forces Act 2001, but was subsequently substituted[13] and it now reads:

> (3A)   The High Court shall have no jurisdiction to make mandatory, prohibiting or quashing orders in relation to the jurisdiction of the Court Martial in matters relating to—
>
> (a)   trial by the Court Martial for an offence; or
>
> (b)   appeals from the Service Civilian Court.

13.25 In CP 184 we noted,

> The restriction of the High Court's jurisdiction over court-martial proceedings in subsection (3A) is broader than the equivalent restriction in subsection (3) relating to trials on indictment in the Crown Court. Subsection (3A) prevents review of all matters relating to trial by the Court Martial for an offence, whereas subsection (3) allows review of Crown Court matters, except those relating to trial on indictment. They are not, therefore, equivalent provisions. For the restriction in subsection (3) to be as broad as the restriction in subsection (3A), subsection (3) would have to prevent review of matters relating to trial by the Crown Court for an offence.
>
> However, subsection (3A) is not a blanket restriction on 'all decisions of the Court Martial', rather it is a restriction to matters relating to trial by the Court Martial. There is no reason why the boundaries of subsection (3A) should not be tested in the same way as those of subsection (3). However, it appears that since the commencement of subsection (3A), there have been no applications for judicial review of a decision by the Court Martial. This may be accounted for by the fact that there are significantly fewer cases in the Court Martial than in the Crown Court. Further, it would be unlikely that any application for judicial review would be made where a similar application had already been made and failed under subsection (3). It is also conceivable that subsection (3A) is perceived as precluding all applications for judicial review of a decision of the Court Martial.[14]

---

[13]   By s 378(1) and Sch 16, para 93 of the AFA 2006.

[14]   CP 184, paras 7.23 and 7.24.

13.26 Given that an authoritative text on service law states categorically that judicial review is not permissible in relation to Court Martial,[15] it is probably the case that subsection (3A) is perceived as we said.

13.27 We note that in discussion with the MoD before publication of CP 184, their view was that the same problems do not arise with regard to judicial review of rulings at Court Martial as are generated by section 29(3).

13.28 We note also that the less formal structure of the OJAG means that a defendant might be able to return to court to make an application more easily than in the civilian system and so there is less need to take the point elsewhere.

13.29 We are still not aware of any applications for judicial review of a decision by the Court Martial since the commencement of subsection (3A). We did not receive any responses to CP 184 which indicated that section 29(3A) is problematic, and we are not aware of any cases which show that there are any difficulties.

13.30 Although we said in CP 184 that the restriction in subsection (3A) is broader than that in subsection (3), this is debatable. Given that the Crown Court can only try matters on indictment, the difference between the two subsections does not seem to generate a different effect. Both subsections refer to "matters relating to", and this part of subsection (3) has been thought to be vague enough to make interpretation problematic.

Conclusion

13.31 Our conclusion is that the effect of the provision governing the High Court's jurisdiction over the Court Martial is, in law, the same as that of the provision governing the High Court's jurisdiction over the Crown Court, and the difference in results is explained by practical and cultural factors.

13.32 For these reasons, we do not see any amendment to section 29(3A) as being necessary.

Exceptions to the bar on judicial review

13.33 We are recommending two exceptions to the bar on judicial review of rulings in trial on indictment: one for rulings made after the verdict or after the jury has been discharged, such as costs orders, and one in relation to refusals of bail.

Costs orders

13.34 In relation to the civilian system, we have concluded that there is no right of appeal available in respect of orders made in the Crown Court pursuant to section 19(1) of the Prosecution of Offences Act 1985 and regulation 3 of the Costs in Criminal Cases (General) Regulations 1986, for the prosecution nor for the defence. We have also concluded that there is no right of appeal against a refusal to make costs orders, and in one particular situation this may produce an injustice (where an acquitted defendant is refused his or her costs). We now consider to what extent the same problems might exist in service law.

---

[15] J Rant and J Blackett, *Courts-Martial, Discipline, and the Criminal Process in the Armed Services* (2nd ed 2003) para 8.207.

13.35   The rules on costs orders are different in the service system from those in the civilian system. Regulation 3 of the Armed Forces (Proceedings) (Costs) Regulations 2009[16] allows service courts and the Court Martial Appeal Court to make an order that one party shall pay the costs of another where they have been incurred "as a result of an unnecessary or improper act or omission by, or on behalf of, another party".[17] It is in the same terms as the provision in the civilian system. Unlike the civilian system, however, there is a right of appeal against an order made under regulation 3, as provided by regulation 5.

13.36   With regard to wasted costs orders, such orders may be made under regulation 4 of the same regulations and, again, regulation 5 provides a right of appeal against such an order.

13.37   When it comes to appealing against conviction in the Court Martial, there is provision for both the accused and the prosecuting authority to be awarded costs on the appeal.

13.38   A convicted defendant cannot be ordered to make a contribution to the prosecution costs (apart from under regulation 3). The Practice Guide states that

> In practice, the effects on the defendant of the sentence plus the recommendation to contribute to defence costs are likely to soak up whatever amounts the defendant can reasonably be expected to pay in total

but allows that in some circumstances "there is scope to consider prosecution costs as well", referring back to regulation 3.[18]

13.39   We understand from OJAG that in practice it is unlikely that the Director of Service Prosecutions ("DSP") would seek a costs order at Court Martial, but not unthinkable. Most defendants are not people of means and, if convicted, they are likely to have even less means than before, so there is nothing to be gained by a costs order against them. However, if a prosecution is brought against an officer of means, then it might be worth the DSP seeking a costs order, depending on the penalty. It is, however, unlikely that the DSP would appeal against the refusal to make a costs order.

13.40   If a defendant pays for his or her own representation and is acquitted, he or she can ask the Judge Advocate to recommend reimbursement. Such applications tend to be successful. There is no specific statutory power for the Judge Advocate to order or recommend reimbursement. All such recommendations are made under the auspices of a Judge Advocate's general duty to conduct proceedings fairly. As there is no statutory basis for these recommendations, so there is no statutory basis for an appeal against them.

---

[16]   SI 2009 No 993.

[17]   The Office of the Judge Advocate *Practice in the Court Martial: Collected Memoranda* (Oct 2009) section 8.3.1 notes, "the very institution of proceedings is capable of being the subject of an order of this nature."

[18]   The Office of the Judge Advocate *Practice in the Court Martial: Collected Memoranda* (Oct 2009), section 9.10.

13.41   We note that in their evidence to the Select Committee on the Armed Forces Bill 2001, Liberty proposed that there should be a provision which would enable the court martial to make a "Defendants Costs Order" in favour of the defendant on being acquitted of all charges, on similar principles to those applicable in the civilian courts,[19] but no such provision has been enacted.

Publicly funded representation at Court Martial

13.42   The system for provision of public funds for representation in the service courts is different from that in the civilian system. The Armed Forces Criminal Legal Aid Authority ("AFCLAA") is the body which provides legal aid funding in the Services system. AFCLAA has no basis in primary or secondary legislation. Legal aid is thus provided on a contractual basis.

13.43   Means-testing is already in place for the funding of representation at Court Martial. Financial limits for eligibility are set out at paragraph 9.5 of the *Court Martial Collected Memoranda*.[20] All but the most junior members of the forces are required to make a contribution to their representation.

13.44   Legal aid might be refused on interests of justice grounds if a defendant is charged with a minor offence and wishes to take it to the Summary Appeal Court. The defendant can ask for an internal review of the decision (through the administration) and can also ask the Judge Advocate to reconsider it, but there is no further "right" of appeal.

13.45   The Judge Advocate has no power to order that a convicted defendant pay a contribution to his or her legal aid, but may make a recommendation to that effect. As this is a non-statutory step, there is no statutory right of appeal against such a recommendation.

13.46   One of the terms of the contract between the defendant and the AFCLAA is that, if convicted and the Judge Advocate makes a recommendation that the defendant will repay some or all of the legal aid received, he or she will comply. Similarly, it is the policy of AFCLAA to accept and implement recommendations of judges on other matters related to public funding.

13.47   There is generally no difficulty in recouping money paid out because the defendant is often in the employment of MoD. For the same reason, contributions do not need to be obtained from the defendant at the beginning of the case.

Conclusion

13.48   While public funding for defendants at Court Martial remains on a contractual, as opposed to a statutory, footing, legislative reform to provide, for example, a right of appeal against an order to contribute to the prosecutor's costs or to legal aid, seem to us to be inappropriate.

---

[19]   Liberty, *Armed Forces Bill – Evidence to Select Committee* (February 2001), para 22.

[20]   The Office of the Judge Advocate *Practice in the Court Martial: Collected Memoranda* (Oct 2009).

"Bail" and defendants

13.49   Chapter 2 of Part 4 of the AFA 2006 (sections 105 to 111) provides for custody after charge. It is modelled fairly closely on the civilian system in England and Wales. It is supplemented by the Armed Forces (Custody Proceedings) Rules 2009.[21] Sections 105 and 106 of the AFA 2006 provide what is in effect a presumption in favour of bail (though the Act does not call it bail). There are time limits on the period for which a person can be remanded in custody.

13.50   Under section 110 the accused can be taken into custody on the orders of his or her Commanding Officer (for example, if the Commanding Officer has reason to believe the accused may abscond), but he or she must then be brought before a judge advocate. Section 111 permits the Judge Advocate to direct the arrest of the accused following arraignment.[22]

13.51   If a defendant is serving in the forces or is a civilian subject to service discipline, then any remand prior to trial is to service detention at Colchester Military Corrective Training Centre (MCTC).[23] Such a remand differs from a remand into custody in the civilian system in that MCTC offers training, and spending time in MCTC does not have the stigma of going to prison. The incentive to challenge a remand in service detention is, therefore, less for someone in the forces than for a defendant making an analogous application in the civilian system.

13.52   A defendant who is remanded into service detention is entitled to reviews by the Judge Advocate as specified in the AFA 2006.[24] If there is a review of service custody between the arraignment and the conclusion of proceedings, then the Judge Advocate may authorise the keeping of the defendant in service custody, if one of the conditions in section 106 is met, for a maximum of eight days, but the order may then be renewed for subsequent periods of eight days.

13.53   It seems also that if the defendant has any new points to make, the Judge Advocate is likely to agree to hear an application, and also that the Judge Advocate has considerable discretion to hear applications for release even if there are no new points.

13.54   That said, there is no specific right of appeal to the CMAC against a remand in service detention and the only formal means of challenging a remand in service detention is by writ of habeas corpus (judicial review being precluded by section 29(3A) of the SCA 1981).

---

[21]   SI 2009 No 1098. The Court Martial Appeal Court (Bail) Order 2009 SI 2009 No 992 provides the Court Martial Appeal Court with power to grant bail pending an appeal.

[22]   The Court Martial Rules say that this also applies *before* arraignment.

[23]   See: Military Corrective Training Centre, http://www.army.mod.uk/agc/provost/2157.aspx (last visited 15 March 2010).

[24]   See ss 108 and 109 of the AFA 2006.

Bail and witnesses

13.55   There are provisions in the Armed Forces (Court Martial) Rules 2009[25] which deal expressly with the position of witnesses. The judge advocate may authorise a witness to be kept in service custody if he or she is satisfied "that there are substantial grounds for believing that, if released from service custody, the person would fail to attend the court as required" (rule 69(2)). The maximum period of the remand into custody is "8 days after the day on which the order is made" (rule 69(3)). The witness may be released on specified conditions as "appear necessary to secure his attendance before the court" (rule 69(5)), and the witness may ask the court to vary or discharge such a condition (rule 69(7)).

13.56   We understand that in practice witnesses are not remanded into service detention. A witness summons can be issued and when it is executed a witness can be brought to court but it does not seem they can be remanded into detention.

13.57   Many witnesses are themselves serving in the forces and so attendance at court is not a problem. If they are neither in the forces nor subject to service discipline, and if they are foreign nationals and the proceedings are taking place abroad, then it would not be appropriate to detain them in any event. If they are not in the forces, nor subject to service discipline, and if they are UK nationals and proceedings are taking place in the UK, it is not desirable for service courts to have jurisdiction over them, so again, arrest and detention would not be appropriate.

13.58   There is no provision in the rules for a witness to challenge the lawfulness of the remand. Section 29(3A) of the SCA 1981 precludes judicial review of an order that a person be kept in service custody.

Conclusion

13.59   If our recommendations for the civilian system were enacted, then it might be appropriate for there to be an exception to section 29(3A) of the SCA 1981 permitting judicial review of a remand in service detention. This is a matter for the Government and further consultation on all the circumstances.

Specific rights of appeal

13.60   We make recommendations for two specific rights of appeal in the civilian system: for children and young persons in relation to reporting restrictions, and where a court ruling gives rise to a real and immediate threat to life. We recommend in both cases that the appeal is heard by the CACD (after leave has been obtained), and in both cases the appeal could be made at any stage of the proceedings. We now consider how these rights of appeal could translate to the Court Martial system, if at all.

---

[25]   SI 2009 No 2041.

A right to appeal against a refusal to make reporting restrictions as they relate to children and young persons

13.61 Our recommendation for the civilian system is that if an order restricting reporting is refused, or has been made and is discharged by the court, then there should be a way in which that refusal or discharge may be appealed. A person under 18, whether employed by the forces or not, could be a witness or a defendant at a Court Martial.

13.62 In the civilian context, it is section 39 of the Children and Young Persons Act 1933 which provides the power to make an order restricting the identification of a child or young person in criminal proceedings.[26] Section 39 of the CYPA 1933 also applies to service courts. An application for reporting restrictions could be made under section 4 or section 11 of the Contempt of Court Act 1981, and automatic restrictions might apply as they do in the civilian system.

13.63 If sections 44 and 45 of the Youth Justice and Criminal Evidence Act 1999 are brought into force, then the situation will be different. Section 44, broadly speaking, provides for reporting restrictions in relation to alleged offences involving persons under 18 at the pre-proceedings stage, and section 45 provides for reporting restrictions once criminal proceedings have begun. Sections 44 and 45 are not yet in force. When they come into force, section 61(2) of the YJCEA 1999, will apply them to service courts and the relevant articles of the Youth Justice and Criminal Evidence Act 1999 (Application to Service Courts) Order 2009[27] will modify them.

13.64 Rule 154 of the Armed Forces (Court Martial) Rules 2009[28] allows any party aggrieved to appeal against the making of reporting restrictions (whether made under the Contempt of Court Act 1981 or otherwise).

Conclusion

13.65 Our recommendation for the civilian system is concerned to protect the young person who will be identified and who has no right of appeal against a refusal to make a reporting restriction. The same problem seems to exist in relation to Court Martial. This is a specific issue in respect of which it seems to us it is appropriate for the service courts to be aligned with the civilian system.

A right to appeal against a ruling which creates a real and immediate risk to life

13.66 On the face of it, the same problem could arise in proceedings before the Court Martial as in trial on indictment: the court could make a ruling which creates a real and immediate risk to life and the person whose life is at risk has no way of challenging the lawfulness of the ruling.

---

[26] "Child" and "young person" are defined at s 107(1) of the CYPA 1933: child is person under 14 and young person is someone who is 14, 15, 16 or 17.

[27] SI 2009 No 2083.

[28] SI 2009 No 2041.

13.67   There is no existing right of appeal against such a ruling by the Court Martial, although rule 50 of the Armed Forces (Court Martial) Rules 2009[29] might provide a means of appeal in preliminary proceedings.

Conclusion

13.68   The scope of rule 50 for appeal against a ruling in preliminary proceedings might not be sufficient to allow an appeal in these circumstances, and would not make an appeal possible in respect of an issue which arose after the preliminary proceedings. It therefore seems to us that specific provision ought to be made.

---

[29]   See para 13.16 above.

PART 14
RECOMMENDATIONS

APPEAL BY WAY OF CASE STATED

1   We recommend that section 28(2) of the Senior Courts Act 1981 be amended so as to preclude all orders, judgments or other decisions of the Crown Court made in any criminal cause or matter being challenged by way of appeal by case stated to the High Court.

(paragraph 7.28)

JUDICIAL REVIEW

2   We recommend that the High Court should not have supervisory jurisdiction over decisions in proceedings on indictment in the Crown Court which are within the exclusion period (which we define) or which we specify in recommendation 6 below, and that section 29(3) of the Senior Courts Act 1981 be amended accordingly.

(paragraph 8.6)

3   We recommend that the exclusion period should begin with, and include, the earliest to happen of the following:

the defendant is committed, transferred or sent for trial to the Crown Court,

or a bill of indictment is preferred.

(paragraph 8.20)

4   We recommend that the exclusion period should end immediately after one (or the earliest) of the following happens or, if there is more than one charge, happens in relation to the last of the charges to be dealt with at the trial:

the charge is dismissed;

a *nolle prosequi* is entered;

the indictment, or the relevant count, is quashed;

the defendant is found to be unfit to plead or to be tried;

the defendant is acquitted or sentenced;

the charge is ordered to lie on the file;

the proceedings, or the proceedings on the relevant count, are stayed;

any other order or decision is made which puts an end to the proceedings.

(paragraph 8.52)

5   We recommend that a new exclusion period should begin if either leave is given for further proceedings in relation to a charge which has been ordered to lie on the file or if a stay of proceedings in relation to a particular count is lifted.

(paragraph 8.58)

6   We recommend that any decision made in connection with the consideration of any of the following should also not be subject to the supervisory jurisdiction of the High Court:

correction of a minor mistake in sentencing;

amendment or activation of a suspended sentence;

amendment or revocation of a community order;

re-sentencing for the offence in respect of which a community order or conditional discharge was imposed or where a sentence is reviewed under section 74 of the Serious Organised Crime and Police Act 2005; or

variation or rescission of a sentence under section 155 of the Powers of Criminal Courts (Sentencing) Act 2000.

(paragraph 8.61)

7   We recommend that a decision by the Crown Court to make a hospital order under section 51(5) of the Mental Health Act 1983 should not fall within the excluded jurisdiction of the Crown Court.

(paragraph 8.64)

8   We recommend that section 29(6) of the Senior Courts Act 1981 is omitted.

(paragraph 8.68)

Exception: bail

Defendants

9   We recommend that a decision during the exclusion period by the Crown Court to refuse bail to a defendant should be an exception to the bar on judicial review if the only arguments which would be available to the defendant to support an application for bail are ones which the court would not be obliged to hear.

(paragraph 9.48)

Witnesses

10   We recommend that a decision by the Crown Court during the exclusion period to refuse bail to a witness who is brought to the court pursuant to a warrant under section 4 of the Criminal Procedure (Attendance of Witnesses) Act 1965 should be an exception to the bar on judicial review.

(paragraph 9.51)

APPEAL FOR CHILDREN AND YOUNG PERSONS

11   We recommend that where the Crown Court, in proceedings relating to a trial on indictment, discharges or refuses to make a direction prohibiting publication of material which will identify a child or young person concerned in the proceedings as a defendant or as a witness, that child or young person may appeal to the CACD against that discharge or refusal, or against the terms of a direction, subject to obtaining leave from the Crown Court or, if leave is refused by the Crown Court, from a single judge of the Court of Appeal.

(paragraph 10.7)

12   We recommend that, if a person indicates an intention to ask for leave to appeal, the Crown Court is to be treated as having made a direction prohibiting reporting under section 39 of the Children and Young Persons Act 1933.

(paragraph 10.41)

13   We also recommend that that direction should remain in force:

if leave to appeal is granted, until the appeal has been determined or abandoned; or

if leave is refused by the Crown Court, until the specified period of time expires without leave being sought from the Court of Appeal, or the appellant indicates within that period that he or she will not seek leave from the Court of Appeal, or the Court of Appeal grants or refuses leave.

(paragraph 10.42)

14   We recommend that the Court of Appeal should have the power to adjourn any proceedings in any other court until after the appeal is disposed of.

(paragraph 10.46)

15   We recommend that the Court of Appeal should have power to confirm the refusal, to confirm or reverse the revocation, or, if the appeal is against the terms of a direction, to confirm or reverse the direction and, in all cases, to make any direction which the Crown Court could have made.

(paragraph 10.47)

16   We recommend that the Court of Appeal should have the power to make such
      order as to costs as it thinks fit.

(paragraph 10.48)

17   We recommend that breach of a reporting restriction made on determination of
      an appeal should constitute an offence, punishable by the same penalty as for a
      breach of an order made by the Crown Court.

(paragraph 10.49)

18   We recommend that the decision of the Court of Appeal should be final.

(paragraph 10.50)

APPEAL IN RESPECT OF A THREAT TO LIFE

Representations

19   We recommend that a person should have a right to make representations to the
      Crown Court in a trial on indictment about a ruling made or proposed to be made
      if it appears to the court that the ruling could result in a real and immediate risk to
      his or her life from the criminal act of another.

(paragraph 11.10)

The appeal to the Court of Appeal

20   We recommend that an appeal may be made to the CACD,

> if leave is given by the Crown Court or, if the Crown Court refuses
> leave, the Court of Appeal,

> against a ruling which is made in a trial on indictment and which could
> affect the conduct of proceedings in which the strict rules of evidence
> apply,

> by a person who has made representations to the Crown Court about
> it or about the same issue,

> on the grounds that the ruling could entail a real and immediate risk to
> the person's life from the criminal act of another, and that the ruling is
> wrong in law or one which it is not reasonable for the Crown Court to
> have made,

> and that the CACD may confirm, reverse or vary the ruling as it thinks
> fit, make any ruling which the Crown Court could have made, or remit
> it to the Crown Court.

(paragraph 11.13)

Further appeal to the Supreme Court

21   We recommend that any party to an appeal to the CACD as described in recommendation 20 may appeal to the Supreme Court, with the leave of the CACD or if the CACD refuses leave, with the leave of the Supreme Court, against the determination by the CACD.

(paragraph 11.34)

22   We recommend that leave may be given if and only if the CACD certifies that a point of law of general public importance is involved in the determination and it appears to the court considering leave that the point is one which ought to be considered by the Supreme Court.

(paragraph 11.35)

Procedural matters

23   We recommend that the appellant must seek leave to appeal immediately the ruling in question is made.

(paragraph 11.36)

24   We recommend that, if the Crown Court refuses leave, and the appellant intends to seek leave from the Court of Appeal, he or she must do so within a time period to be specified in rules of court.

(paragraph 11.37)

Protecting the position of the appellant

25   We recommend that, once leave to appeal is sought, the ruling appealed against should be of no effect until, if leave is granted, the appeal has been determined or abandoned; or, if leave is refused by the Crown Court, until either the application is abandoned or leave is refused by the Court of Appeal.

(paragraph 11.38)

26   We recommend that if a person asks the Crown Court for leave to appeal, it may make such order as it thinks fit to protect the appellant pending conclusion of the appeal, and that it may vary or revoke any order that it makes for this purpose.

(paragraph 11.39)

Expedited appeals

27   We recommend that the court granting leave must decide whether the appeal should be expedited.

(paragraph 11.41)

28   We recommend that if the Crown Court decides that the appeal should be expedited, then it or the Court of Appeal may reverse that decision, and that if the Court of Appeal decides that the appeal should be expedited, then the Court of Appeal may reverse that decision.

(paragraph 11.42)

29   We recommend that if an appeal is not to be expedited, the court should have power to adjourn the proceedings in the Crown Court, discharge the jury or order that the jury be discharged.

(paragraph 11.43)

A procedure enabling information to be withheld from another party

30   We recommend that rules of court may prescribe circumstances in which applications for leave to appeal and an appeal may be made, from the Crown Court to the CACD and from the CACD to the Supreme Court, without notice or disclosure of relevant material to any other party, and without any other party being present at a hearing in the appeal, but that the circumstances must not be wider than the minimum reasonably required to protect the safety of any person concerned in the proceedings.

(paragraph 11.47)

Power of the Crown Court to restrict reporting of proceedings pending determination of the appeal

31   We recommend that the Crown Court should have the power to restrict the reporting of proceedings to the extent necessary in the interests of justice until the earliest of the following: the appeal is determined by the Court of Appeal or abandoned; if the Crown Court refuses leave, the period of time specified for seeking leave expires without leave being sought; or the appellant indicates that leave will not be sought; or leave is refused by the Court of Appeal.

(paragraph 11.49)

32   We recommend that breach of a reporting restriction made in connection with an appeal as described in recommendation 20 should be an offence, but that the consent of the Attorney General must be obtained for a prosecution of the offence.

(paragraph 11.52)

Proceedings before the Court of Appeal

33   We recommend that section 31B of the Criminal Appeal Act 1968 should be amended so that the single judge and the registrar have the power to give such directions as appear to the judge or the registrar to be appropriate.

(paragraph 11.54)

34   We recommend that the Court of Appeal should have the power to adjourn any proceedings in any other court until after the appeal is disposed of.

(paragraph 11.55)

35   We recommend that the Court of Appeal should have the power to make such incidental orders as it thinks fit.

(paragraph 11.56)

36   We recommend that the Court of Appeal should have the power to make such order as to costs as it thinks fit.

(paragraph 11.57)

THE POWER OF THE COURT OF APPEAL TO PROTECT THE APPELLANT

37   We recommend that the CACD should be able to make such order as it thinks fit to protect the appellant pending conclusion of the appeal, and that it may vary or revoke any order made for this purpose, whether made by it or by the Crown Court.

(paragraph 11.58)

THE POWER OF THE COURT OF APPEAL TO RESTRICT PUBLICATION

38   We recommend that, once the appeal is determined by the Court of Appeal, the Court of Appeal should have the power to vary or revoke a direction given by the Crown Court, and to make any new or further restriction on the reporting of the content or the fact of the appeal.

(paragraph 11.59)

39   We recommend that if leave to appeal to the Supreme Court is sought, a reporting restriction made by the CA should continue in effect, unless it is revoked, until the Court of Appeal refuses to grant a certificate that the ruling involves a point of law of general public importance or, if it does grant such a certificate,

> if the Court of Appeal refuses leave to appeal, until the period for applying to the Supreme Court for leave expires without an application for leave having been made or the person indicates that no application will be made, or

> until the Supreme Court refuses leave, or

> if the Supreme Court grants leave, until the appeal is determined or abandoned.

(paragraph 11.60)

Proceedings before the Supreme Court

CONTINUED SUSPENSION OF THE RULING

40 We recommend that if leave to appeal to the Supreme Court is sought, the ruling in question should continue to be of no effect until the earliest of the following:

> the Court of Appeal refuses to grant a certificate that the ruling involves a point of law of general public importance or,

> if the Court of Appeal refuses leave to appeal, until the period for applying to the Supreme Court for leave expires without an application for leave having been made or (if sooner) the person indicates that no application will be made, or

> the Supreme Court refuses leave, or

> if leave is granted, by the Court of Appeal or by the Supreme Court, until the appeal is determined or abandoned.

(paragraph 11.62)

PROTECTION OF THE APPELLANT PENDING APPEAL TO THE SUPREME COURT

41 We recommend that if leave to appeal to the Supreme Court is sought, the Court of Appeal should be able to make such order as it thinks fit to protect the person who appealed to it pending conclusion of the appeal, and that it may vary or revoke any order made for this purpose.

(paragraph 11.63)

THE POWER OF THE SUPREME COURT TO RESTRICT PUBLICATION

42 We recommend that if the Supreme Court hears an appeal, it should be able to vary or revoke a direction given by the Court of Appeal, and that when it determines an appeal, it should be able to make such direction restricting publication of any matter relating to the appeal proceedings as it thinks fit.

(paragraph 11.65)

43 We recommend that the Crown Court should be able to vary or revoke a direction given by the Supreme Court.

(paragraph 11.66)

Powers of the Supreme Court

44 We recommend that when an appeal is heard by the Supreme Court as described in recommendation 21, it should have the same powers as the CACD to deal with it.

(paragraph 11.68)

Consequential amendment: effect on time limits for completion of stages of a criminal case

45 We recommend that time should cease to run for the purposes of those statutory time limits while the appeal to the CACD, and any further appeal to the Supreme Court, is pursued.

(paragraph 11.75)

(*Signed*)   JAMES MUNBY, *Chairman*

ELIZABETH COOKE

DAVID HERTZELL

JEREMY HORDER

FRANCES PATTERSON

MARK ORMEROD, *Chief Executive*

25 June 2010

APPENDIX A: Criminal Justice (High Court Jurisdiction and Appeals) Bill

CONTENTS

DRAFT

OF A

BILL

TO

Make provision about case stated and judicial review in relation to the Crown Court; to provide for a right of appeal against certain decisions of the Crown Court in connection with directions restricting publication of matter relating to persons under 18; to provide for a right to make representations in relation to rulings or proposed rulings of the Crown Court which could result in a risk to life, and for a right to appeal in relation to such rulings; and for connected purposes.

B E IT ENACTED by the Queen's most Excellent Majesty, by and with the advice and consent of the Lords Spiritual and Temporal, and Commons, in this present Parliament assembled, and by the authority of the same, as follows: —

Case stated and judicial review

1   Restriction of criminal case stated from Crown Court

(1)   In section 28 of the Senior Courts Act 1981 (High Court jurisdiction in relation to appeals from Crown Court and inferior courts) —

    (a)   in subsection (2), for paragraph (a) substitute —   5

        "(a)   an order, judgment or other decision of the Crown Court in any criminal cause or matter;";

    (b)   in subsection (4), for "relating to trial on indictment" substitute "in any criminal cause or matter".

(2)   The amendments made by subsection (1) apply only in relation to orders,   10
judgments or other decisions of the Crown Court made or given after the coming into force of this section.

2   Crown Court: judicial review

(1)   In section 29 of the Senior Courts Act 1981 (mandatory, prohibiting and quashing orders) —   15

      (a)   in subsection (3), for "other than its jurisdiction in matters relating to trial on indictment," substitute "other than such of its jurisdiction as is excluded by virtue of section 29A,";

      (b)   omit subsection (6).

(2)   After section 29 of the Senior Courts Act 1981 insert—   *5*

"29A Exclusion of High Court jurisdiction: Crown Court

(1)   The excluded jurisdiction of the Crown Court mentioned in section 29(3) is its jurisdiction in proceedings on indictment, but only so far as provided in subsection (2).

(2)   That excluded jurisdiction, in its application to a particular trial of a   *10* defendant, extends only to—

      (a)   any decision falling within an exclusion period relating to that trial, other than a decision mentioned in subsection (4) or (5), and

      (b)   any decision mentioned in subsection (3).   *15*

(3)   A decision made in connection with the consideration of any of the following is also within the excluded jurisdiction of the Crown Court—

      (a)   the correction of a minor mistake in sentencing;

      (b)   an order that a suspended sentence is to take effect (with or without modifications), or the amendment of a suspended   *20* sentence order;

      (c)   the revocation or amendment of a community order (within the meaning of section 177 of the Criminal Justice Act 2003) or otherwise dealing with a defendant who is subject to one;

      (d)   the imposition under section 13 of the Powers of Criminal   *25* Courts (Sentencing) Act 2000 of a sentence for an offence for which an order for conditional discharge was made;

      (e)   the variation or rescission of a sentence under section 155 of that Act;

      (f)   a case referred back to the Crown Court under section 74 of the   *30* Serious Organised Crime and Police Act 2005.

(4)   A decision during an exclusion period by the Crown Court not to grant bail does not fall within the excluded jurisdiction of the Crown Court if—

      (a)   the decision relates to a witness, or   *35*

      (b)   the decision relates to a defendant, and the only arguments which would be available to the defendant in support of an application for bail are ones which (by virtue of paragraph 3 of Part 2A of Schedule 1 to the Bail Act 1976) the court would not be obliged to hear.   *40*

(5)   A decision during an exclusion period by the Crown Court to make a hospital order under section 51(5) of the Mental Health Act 1983 does not fall within the excluded jurisdiction of the Crown Court.

(6)   In this section and section 29B "sentence" is to be construed in accordance with section 50 of the Criminal Appeal Act 1968 (meaning   *45* of "sentence"), but does not include an order under section 1 of the Powers of Criminal Courts (Sentencing) Act 2000 deferring the passing of sentence; and related terms are to be construed accordingly.

(7)　Subsection (6) is subject to subsection (5).

29B　Section 29A — meaning of "exclusion period"

(1)　For the purposes of section 29A an exclusion period begins with (and includes) the earliest of the following to happen —

    (a)　the defendant is committed for trial under section 6 or 24 of the Magistrates' Courts Act 1980;

    (b)　a notice of transfer is given under section 4 of the Criminal Justice Act 1987 or section 53 of the Criminal Justice Act 1991;

    (c)　the defendant is sent to the Crown Court to be tried under section 51 or 51A of the Crime and Disorder Act 1998;

    (d)　a bill of indictment is preferred under section 2(2)(b) of the Administration of Justice (Miscellaneous Provisions) Act 1933;

    (e)　a bill of indictment is preferred under section 22B(3)(a) of the Prosecution of Offences Act 1985.

(2)　An exclusion period ends immediately after the earliest of the following to happen (or, if there is more than one charge, to happen in relation to the last of the charges to be dealt with at the trial) —

    (a)　the indictment, or the relevant count, is quashed;

    (b)　the defendant is found to be unfit to plead or to be tried;

    (c)　the defendant is acquitted or sentenced;

    (d)　the charge is ordered to lie on the file;

    (e)　a *nolle prosequi* is entered;

    (f)　the proceedings (or the proceedings on the relevant count) are stayed or discontinued;

    (g)　the charge is dismissed;

    (h)　any other order or decision is made which puts an end to the proceedings.

(3)　A new exclusion period begins if either of the following happens —

    (a)　leave is given for further proceedings in relation to a charge which has been ordered to lie on the file;

    (b)　a stay of proceedings in relation to a particular count is lifted.

(4)　Subsection (2) also applies to an exclusion period which begins by virtue of subsection (3)."

Reporting restrictions

3　Appeal relating to reporting restrictions directions concerning persons under 18

(1)　After section 159 of the Criminal Justice Act 1988 insert —

"159A　Crown Court proceedings — directions restricting publication of matter relating to persons under 18

(1)　A person under the age of 18 concerned in proceedings relating to a trial on indictment may, with leave, appeal to the Court of Appeal against —

    (a)　a refusal by the Crown Court to make a direction under section 39 of the Children and Young Persons Act 1933 ("the 1933 Act"),

  (b) the revocation by the Crown Court of such a direction, or

  (c) the terms of such a direction.

(2) In subsection (1), the leave referred to is—

  (a) that of the Crown Court, or

  (b) (if the Crown Court refuses leave) that of the Court of Appeal. 5

(3) If leave is sought from the Court of Appeal, it must be sought within a period to be specified in rules of court, beginning with the time when the Crown Court refuses leave.

(4) The decision of the Court of Appeal is final.

(5) On the hearing of an appeal under this section, the Court of Appeal has power— 10

  (a) to stay any proceedings in any other court until after the appeal is disposed of;

  (b) if the appeal is against the refusal by the Crown Court to make a direction under section 39 of the 1933 Act, to confirm the refusal or to make any direction which the Crown Court could have made; 15

  (c) if the appeal is against the revocation by the Crown Court of such a direction, to confirm or reverse the revocation, or to make any direction which the Crown Court could have made; 20

  (d) if the appeal is against the terms of such a direction, to confirm or revoke the direction, or to make any direction which the Crown Court could have made.

(6) The Court of Appeal may also make such order as to costs as it thinks fit. 25

(7) Subsections (2), (4) and (6) of section 159 apply for the purposes of this section as they apply for the purposes of that.

(8) A direction made or confirmed under this section is to be treated for the purposes of the following provisions as if it had been made under section 39 of the 1933 Act— 30

  (a) subsection (2) of that section;

  (b) section 57(4) of the Children and Young Persons Act 1963;

  (c) paragraph 3(2) of Schedule 20 to the Broadcasting Act 1990.

159B Appeal under section 159A: supplementary

(1) This section applies if a person mentioned in subsection (1) of section 159A indicates to the Crown Court that the person intends to ask for leave to appeal under that section. 35

(2) If that indication is given, the Crown Court is to be treated as having made a direction in relation to the proceedings under section 39 of the Children and Young Persons Act 1933, without exception. 40

(3) Such a direction is to remain in effect until leave is granted by the Crown Court, or, if leave is refused by the Crown Court, until—

  (a) the period referred to in section 159A(3) expires without leave being sought from the Court of Appeal, or (if sooner) the person indicates that leave will not be sought from the Court of Appeal, or 45

     (b)   if leave is sought within that period from the Court of Appeal, that court grants or refuses leave.

(4)   If leave is granted, whether by the Crown Court or the Court of Appeal, the direction continues to remain in effect until the appeal has been determined or abandoned."

(2)   For the purposes of a direction treated as made under section 39 of the Children and Young Persons Act 1933 by virtue of section 159A(8) or 159B(2) of the Criminal Justice Act 1988 (inserted by subsection (1)), sections 159A and 159B of that Act are to be treated as having the same extent as section 39 of the 1933 Act.

Rulings creating risk to life

4   Life-threatening rulings: right to make representations

(1)   If, in proceedings before the Crown Court in a trial on indictment, any person (whether or not concerned in the proceedings) applies to the court for an opportunity to make representations about a ruling which the court has made or is proposing to make, the court must give that person such an opportunity if the circumstances are as set out in subsection (2).

(2)   The circumstances are that it appears to the court that the ruling or proposed ruling could result in a real and immediate risk to the life of the person from the criminal act of another person.

(3)   In this section and in sections 5, 7, 9 and 12, "ruling" includes a decision, determination, direction, finding, notice, order, refusal, rejection or requirement.

5   Appeal to Court of Appeal

(1)   A person who has made representations to the Crown Court by virtue of section 4 may, with leave, appeal to the Court of Appeal against a ruling made by the Crown Court in the proceedings referred to in that section if—
    (a)   the conditions set out in subsections (5) and (6) are satisfied, and
    (b)   the grounds of appeal are as set out in subsection (7).

(2)   In subsection (1), the leave referred to is—
    (a)   that of the Crown Court, or
    (b)   (if the Crown Court refuses leave) that of the Court of Appeal.

(3)   If the leave of the Crown Court is sought, it must be sought immediately the ruling in question is made.

(4)   If the leave of the Court of Appeal is sought, it must be sought within a period to be specified in rules of court, beginning with the time when the Crown Court refuses leave.

(5)   The first condition is that the ruling appealed against and the ruling or proposed ruling which was the subject of the representations—
    (a)   are the same, or
    (b)   relate to the same issue.

(6)   The second condition is that the ruling could affect the conduct of proceedings in which the strict rules of evidence apply.

(7)   The grounds of appeal must be that—
   (a)   the ruling could result in a real and immediate risk to the life of the person from the criminal act of another person, and
   (b)   the ruling is wrong in law, or it was not reasonable for the Crown Court to have made it.

(8)   Subject to rules of court, the jurisdiction of the Court of Appeal under this section and sections 6 to 12 is to be exercised by the criminal division of that court, and references in all of those sections to the Court of Appeal are to be so construed.

6   Expedition of appeal to Court of Appeal

(1)   If leave for an appeal under section 5 is granted, the court granting leave must decide whether or not the appeal should be expedited.

(2)   If the court decides that the appeal should be expedited, it may order an adjournment of the proceedings in the Crown Court.

(3)   If the Crown Court decides that the appeal should be expedited, it or the Court of Appeal may subsequently reverse that decision.

(4)   If the Court of Appeal decides that the appeal should be expedited, it may subsequently reverse that decision.

(5)   If the court decides that the appeal should not be expedited, or reverses a decision that it should be expedited, it may—
   (a)   order an adjournment of the proceedings in the Crown Court, or
   (b)   if a jury has been sworn, discharge the jury there, or (if the decision or reversal is that of the Court of Appeal) order that it be discharged.

7   Powers of Court of Appeal

(1)   On the hearing of an appeal under section 5, the Court of Appeal has power to stay any proceedings in any other court until after the appeal is disposed of.

(2)   The Court of Appeal may dispose of the appeal by—
   (a)   confirming, reversing or varying the Crown Court's ruling,
   (b)   making any ruling which the Crown Court could have made, or
   (c)   remitting the matter to the Crown Court for the Crown Court to dispose of in accordance with any directions the Court of Appeal may give.

(3)   The Court of Appeal may also make such incidental or consequential orders as appear to it to be just.

(4)   The Court of Appeal may make such order as it thinks fit as to costs in relation to an appeal under section 5 and an application for leave to appeal.

8   Appeal to Supreme Court

(1)   Any party to proceedings before the Court of Appeal on an appeal to that court under section 5 may appeal to the Supreme Court against the Court of Appeal's decision in that appeal.

(2)   An appeal under subsection (1) lies only with the leave of the Court of Appeal or the Supreme Court.   *5*

(3)   Such leave must not be granted unless —
    (a)   the Court of Appeal certifies that a point of law of general public importance is involved in the decision, and
    (b)   it appears to the Court of Appeal or (as the case may be) the Supreme Court that the point is one which ought to be considered by the Supreme Court.   *10*

(4)   Section 33(3) of the Criminal Appeal Act 1968 (limitation on appeal from criminal division of Court of Appeal) does not prevent an appeal to the Supreme Court under subsection (1).   *15*

(5)   The Lord Chancellor may for the purposes of this section make an order containing provision corresponding to any provision in the Criminal Appeal Act 1968 relating to appeals to the Supreme Court from the Court of Appeal or any connected matter.

(6)   An order under subsection (5) is to be made by statutory instrument.   *20*

(7)   A statutory instrument made under subsection (5) is subject to annulment in pursuance of a resolution of either House of Parliament.

9   Effect of ruling pending appeal

(1)   If leave to appeal under section 5 is sought, the ruling in question is of no effect until leave is granted by the Crown Court, or, if leave is refused by the Crown Court, until —   *25*
    (a)   the period referred to in section 5(4) expires without leave being sought from the Court of Appeal, or (if sooner) the person indicates that leave will not be sought from the Court of Appeal, or
    (b)   if leave is sought within that period from the Court of Appeal, that court grants or refuses leave.   *30*

(2)   If leave is granted, whether by the Crown Court or the Court of Appeal, the ruling continues to be of no effect until the appeal has been determined or abandoned.

(3)   If the appeal is determined (rather than abandoned), the ruling still continues to be of no effect until the earliest of the following —   *35*
    (a)   leave to appeal under section 8 is sought from the Court of Appeal by any party to the appeal proceedings before the Court of Appeal;
    (b)   the period for applying for such leave expires;
    (c)   any party to the appeal before the Court of Appeal applies to that court for the ruling to have effect, and that court so directs.   *40*

(4)   If leave to appeal under section 8 is sought from the Court of Appeal, the ruling in question still continues to be of no effect until the Court of Appeal refuses to grant a certificate that a point of law of general public importance is involved in its decision, or, if it does grant such a certificate —   *45*

Criminal Justice (High Court Jurisdiction and Appeals) Bill

    (a) the Court of Appeal grants leave,

    (b) if the Court of Appeal refuses leave, the period for applying for leave to appeal to the Supreme Court expires without an application for such leave being made, or (if sooner) the party in question indicates that no such application will be made, or

    (c) the Supreme Court grants or refuses leave.

(5) If leave is granted, whether by the Court of Appeal or the Supreme Court, the ruling still continues to be of no effect until the appeal has been determined or abandoned.

10   Safeguarding of appellant pending appeal

(1) In this section—

    a "safeguarding order" means an order made for the purpose of safeguarding the appellant until any appeal proceedings have ended, whether they are in the Court of Appeal or in the Supreme Court, and

    the "appellant" means the person referred to in section 5(1).

(2) If leave to appeal is sought from the Crown Court under section 5, it may make a safeguarding order in such terms as it thinks fit.

(3) The Crown Court may make a safeguarding order—

    (a) whether or not it grants leave, and

    (b) when leave to appeal is sought or later (but before any proceedings in the Court of Appeal).

(4) The Crown Court may vary or revoke a safeguarding order which it has made.

(5) The Court of Appeal may also make a safeguarding order in such terms as it thinks fit in any of the following circumstances—

    (a) if leave to appeal to the Court of Appeal is sought from that court,

    (b) if that court grants leave, at any later stage of the proceedings before the Court of Appeal,

    (c) if leave to appeal to the Supreme Court is sought either from the Court of Appeal or from the Supreme Court under section 8,

    (d) if leave to appeal to the Supreme Court is granted, at any point before that appeal is determined or abandoned.

(6) The Court of Appeal may vary or revoke a safeguarding order made by it or by the Crown Court.

11   Notice and disclosure

(1) An application for leave to appeal under section 5 or 8, an application for a certificate mentioned in section 8(3)(a) and any appeal following the granting of leave to appeal, may in circumstances to be prescribed in rules of court be made—

    (a) without notice to any other party to the proceedings;

    (b) without disclosure of relevant material to any other party to the proceedings;

    (c) in the absence from any hearing of another party to the proceedings or of the party's legal representatives.

(2) In subsection (1), "relevant material" means any document or other material which would fall to be disclosed apart from this section and any rules of court.

(3) The circumstances prescribed in rules of court by virtue of subsection (1) must not be wider than the minimum reasonably required to protect the safety of any person concerned in the proceedings relating to the application for leave or for the certificate or to the appeal. 5

12 Reporting restrictions

(1) If leave to appeal under section 5 against a ruling is sought from the Crown Court, the court may give such direction as it thinks fit in the interests of justice restricting the publication of any matter relating to— 10
  (a) the ruling,
  (b) the leave and appeal proceedings, and
  (c) the person in question.

(2) The Crown Court may vary or revoke such a direction.

(3) A direction given by the Crown Court has effect, unless revoked, until the earliest of the following— 15
  (a) if the Crown Court refuses leave, the period referred to in section 5(4) expires without leave being sought from the Court of Appeal, or the person in question indicates that such leave will not be sought;
  (b) the Court of Appeal refuses leave; 20
  (c) the appeal is determined by the Court of Appeal or abandoned.

(4) If the Court of Appeal hears the appeal, it may vary or revoke a direction given by the Crown Court.

(5) On the determination of an appeal by the Court of Appeal, it may give such direction as it thinks fit in the interests of justice restricting the publication of 25 any matter relating to—
  (a) the ruling,
  (b) the leave and appeal proceedings, both for the appeal to the Court of Appeal and for any appeal to the Supreme Court, and
  (c) the person in question. 30

(6) The Court of Appeal may vary or revoke a direction given under subsection (5).

(7) If leave to appeal against the Court of Appeal's decision is sought under section 8, a direction given under subsection (5) has effect, unless revoked, until the earliest of the following— 35
  (a) the Court of Appeal refuses to grant a certificate that a point of law of general public importance is involved in its decision;
  (b) if the Court of Appeal refuses leave, the period for applying for leave to appeal to the Supreme Court expires without an application for such leave being made, or (if sooner) the party in question indicates that no 40 such application will be made;
  (c) leave is refused by the Supreme Court;
  (d) the appeal is determined by the Supreme Court or abandoned.

(8) If the Supreme Court hears the appeal, it may vary or revoke a direction given by the Court of Appeal. 45

(9)   On the determination of an appeal by the Supreme Court, it may give such direction as it thinks fit in the interests of justice restricting the publication of any matter relating to—

    (a)   the ruling,

    (b)   the leave and appeal proceedings, both for the appeal to the Court of   *5* Appeal and for the appeal to the Supreme Court, and

    (c)   the person in question.

(10) The Crown Court may vary or revoke a direction given by the Supreme Court.

(11) Nothing in this section affects any prohibition or restriction by virtue of any other enactment on the inclusion of any matter in a publication.   *10*

(12) In this section and section 13—

    "publication" includes any speech, writing, relevant programme, or other communication in whatever form, which is addressed to the public or a section of the public (and for this purpose every relevant programme is to be taken to be so addressed), and   *15*

    "relevant programme" means a programme included in a programme service (within the meaning of the Broadcasting Act 1990).

13   Reporting restrictions: offences

(1)   This section applies if a publication includes any matter in contravention of a direction under section 12.   *20*

(2)   If the publication is a newspaper or periodical, any proprietor, any editor and any publisher of the newspaper or periodical is guilty of an offence.

(3)   If the publication is a relevant programme, the following are guilty of an offence—

    (a)   any body corporate or Scottish partnership engaged in providing the   *25* programme service in which the programme is included, and

    (b)   any person having functions in relation to the programme corresponding to those of an editor of a newspaper.

(4)   In the case of any other publication, any person publishing it is guilty of an offence.   *30*

(5)   A person guilty of an offence under this section is liable on summary conviction to a fine not exceeding level 5 on the standard scale.

(6)   Proceedings for an offence under this section may not be instituted otherwise than by or with the consent of the Attorney General.

Final provisions   *35*

14   Minor and consequential amendments, and repeals

(1)   Schedule 1, which contains minor and consequential amendments, has effect.

(2)   Schedule 2, which contains repeals, has effect.

(3)   The repeals in Schedule 2 of words in section 40(4) of the Road Traffic Offenders Act 1988 and section 130(5) of the Licensing Act 2003 have effect in   *40* accordance with paragraph 1(3) of Schedule 1.

15 Citation, commencement, interpretation and extent

(1) This Act may be cited as the Criminal Justice (High Court Jurisdiction and Appeals) Act 2010.

(2) This section comes into force on the day on which this Act is passed.

(3) Otherwise, this Act comes into force on such day as the Lord Chancellor may by order appoint.

(4) Different days may be appointed for different purposes.

(5) An order under subsection (3) is to be made by statutory instrument.

(6) An order under subsection (3) may include such incidental, supplementary, consequential, transitional or saving provision as the Lord Chancellor considers appropriate in connection with the coming into force of any provision of this Act brought into force by the order.

(7) "Ruling", in sections 4, 5, 7, 9 and 12, has the meaning given by section 4(3).

(8) Except as mentioned in subsection (9), this Act extends to England and Wales only.

(9) The exceptions are—
  (a) section 3(2), and this section so far as it relates to it, extend also to Scotland;
  (b) paragraph 1(1) and (3) of Schedule 1 and the corresponding repeal in Schedule 2, and section 14 and this section so far as they relate to those provisions, extend also to Scotland;
  (c) paragraph 5 of Schedule 1, and section 14(1) and this section so far as they relate to it, extend also to Scotland and to Northern Ireland.

SCHEDULES

SCHEDULE 1   Section 14

MINOR AND CONSEQUENTIAL AMENDMENTS

Restriction of criminal case stated from Crown Court

1   (1) In section 40 of the Road Traffic Offenders Act 1988 (power of appellate   5
courts in England and Wales to suspend disqualification), in subsection (4),
omit the words from "or" to "Crown Court)".

      (2) In section 130 of the Licensing Act 2003 (powers of appellate court to
suspend order for forfeiture or suspension of a personal licence), in
subsection (5), omit the words from "or" to "Crown Court)".   10

      (3) The repeals made by this paragraph apply only in relation to decisions of the
Crown Court made or given after the coming into force of section 1.

Crown Court: judicial review

2   In section 22 of the Prosecution of Offences Act 1985 (power of Secretary of
State to set time limits in relation to preliminary stages of criminal   15
proceedings), for subsection (13) substitute—

      "(13)   For the purposes of sections 29(3) and 29A of the Senior Courts Act
1981 (High Court to have power to make prerogative orders in
relation to jurisdiction of Crown Court other than its jurisdiction in
proceedings on indictment), the jurisdiction conferred on the Crown   20
Court by this section shall be taken not to be part of its jurisdiction in
proceedings on indictment."

Appeal relating to reporting restrictions directions concerning persons under 18

3   The Criminal Appeal Act 1968 is amended as follows—
         (a) in section 31 (powers of court exercisable by single judge), in   25
subsection (2B), after "section 159" insert "or 159A";
         (b) in section 31B (procedural directions: powers of single judge and
registrar), in subsection (5), omit the "or" at the end of paragraph (b),
and after that paragraph insert—
             "(ba)   section 159A of the Criminal Justice Act 1988,".   30

4   (1) When section 45 of, and paragraph 2(1) of Schedule 2 to, the Youth Justice
and Criminal Evidence Act 1999 (which have the effect of transferring to
section 45 of that Act the power to restrict reporting of criminal proceedings
involving persons under 18) are brought into force, the amendments set out
in sub-paragraphs (2) and (3) are to be made to sections 159A and 159B of the   35
Criminal Justice Act 1988 (inserted by section 3).

(2) In section 159A of the Criminal Justice Act 1988 —

    (a)   in subsection (1), for paragraphs (a) to (c) substitute —

        "(a)   a refusal by the Crown Court to make a direction under section 45(3) of the Youth Justice and Criminal Evidence Act 1999 ("the 1999 Act"),

        (b)   the revocation by the Crown Court of such a direction, or

        (c)   the making or variation of an excepting direction under section 45(4) or (5) of the 1999 Act.";

    (b)   in subsection (5)(b), for "section 39 of the 1933 Act" substitute "section 45(3) of the 1999 Act";

    (c)   in subsection (5), for paragraph (d) substitute —

        "(d)   if the appeal is against the making or variation by the Crown Court of an excepting direction, to confirm or revoke the excepting direction or the variation, or to make any other excepting direction which the Crown Court could have made.";

    (d)   for subsection (8) substitute —

        "(8)   A direction made, confirmed or varied under this section is to be treated for the purposes of section 49 of the 1999 Act as if it had been made under section 45 of that Act."

(3) In section 159B of the Criminal Justice Act 1988, for subsection (2) substitute —

        "(2)   If that indication is given, the Crown Court is to be treated as having made a direction in relation to the proceedings under subsection (3) of section 45 of the Youth Justice and Criminal Evidence Act 1999, and no excepting direction under subsection (4) or (5) of that section."

(4) The amendments made by sub-paragraphs (2) and (3) do not apply in relation to any case in which section 39 of the Children and Young Persons Act 1933 continues to operate by virtue of paragraph 2(2) of Schedule 2 to the Youth Justice and Criminal Evidence Act 1999.

5   For the purposes of a direction treated as made under section 45 of the Youth Justice and Criminal Evidence Act 1999 by virtue of section 159A(8) or section 159B(2) of the Criminal Justice Act 1988 (inserted by section 3(1) and amended by paragraph 4), sections 159A and 159B of that Act are to be treated as having the same extent as section 45 of the 1999 Act.

Rulings creating risk to life

6   (1) The Criminal Appeal Act 1968 is amended as provided in sub-paragraphs (2) and (3).

    (2) In section 31 (powers of court exercisable by single judge), after subsection (2F) insert —

        "(2G) The power of the Court of Appeal to grant leave to appeal or a certificate under section 5 of the Criminal Justice (High Court Jurisdiction and Appeals) Act 2010 may be exercised by a single judge in the same manner as it may be exercised by the Court."

    (3) In section 31B (procedural directions: powers of single judge and registrar), in subsection (5), at the end of paragraph (c) add "or

        (d)   section 5 of the Criminal Justice (High Court Jurisdiction and Appeals) Act 2010."

7   In section 22 of the Prosecution of Offences Act 1985 (power to set time limits   *5* in relation to preliminary stages of criminal proceedings), in subsection (6B), after "Criminal Justice Act 2003" insert "or section 5 or 8 of the Criminal Justice (High Court Jurisdiction and Appeals) Act 2010".

SCHEDULE 2   Section 14

REPEALS   *10*

Short title and chapter	*Extent of repeal*
Criminal Appeal Act 1968 (c. 19)	In section 31B(5), the "or" at the end of paragraph (b).
Senior Courts Act 1981 (c. 54)	Section 29(6).
Road Traffic Offenders Act 1988 (c. 53)	In section 40(4), the words from "or" to "Crown Court)".
Licensing Act 2003 (c. 17)	In section 130(5), the words from "or" to "Crown Court)".

15

EXPLANATORY NOTES

CLAUSE 1

A.1 Clause 1 abolishes appeal by way of case stated against any order, judgment or other decision of the Crown Court in any criminal cause or matter. It does this by substituting a new subsection (2)(a) for the existing subsection (2)(a) in section 28 of the Senior Courts Act 1981.

Subsection (1)(a)

A.2 Section 28(1) of the Senior Courts Act 1981 makes appeal by way of case stated possible, and section 28(2) sets out exceptions to subsection (1). The effect of the amendment in subsection (1)(a) is that section 28(1) and (2) will read:

> (1) Subject to subsection (2), any order, judgment or other decision of the Crown Court may be questioned by any party to the proceedings, on the ground that it is wrong in law or is in excess of jurisdiction, by applying to the Crown Court to have a case stated by that court for the opinion of the High Court.
>
> (2) Subsection (1) shall not apply to—
>
> (a) an order, judgment or other decision of the Crown Court in any criminal cause or matter; or
>
> (b) any decision of that court under ... the Local Government (Miscellaneous Provisions) Act 1982 which, by any provision of any of those Acts, is to be final.

A.3 Appeal by way of case stated in civil causes or matters is unaffected.

Subsection (1)(b)

A.4 An order under section 17 of the Access to Justice Act 1999 is an order requiring a publicly-funded defendant to pay some or all of the costs of his or her representation (a Recovery of Defence Costs Order). The effect of section 28(4) of the Senior Courts Act 1981 is that Recovery of Defence Costs Orders can be challenged by way of appeal by case stated. Subsection (1)(b) amends section 28(4) of the Senior Courts Act 1981 so that it reads:

> (4) In subsection (2)(a) the reference to a decision of the Crown Court in any criminal cause or matter does not include a decision relating to an order under section 17 of the Access to Justice Act 1999.

A.5 The effect of subsection (1)(b) is to preserve the current position. The amendment made is purely consequential on that made by subsection (1)(a).

Subsection (2)

A.6   Subsection (2) distinguishes between the position under the unamended law and the point when clause 1 comes into force. The amendments contained in subsection (1) only apply to orders, judgments or other decisions of the Crown Court made or given after clause 1 has come into force. It is irrelevant when proceedings were begun or whether they are continuing: the relevant date is the date when the order, judgment or other decision is made or given.

CLAUSE 2

A.7   Section 29(3) of the Senior Courts Act 1981 simultaneously grants the power of judicial review of decisions of the Crown Court to the High Court and prohibits judicial review by the High Court in relation to certain decisions of the Crown Court. Clause 2 amends section 29(3), with the effect that section 29(3) makes judicial review by the High Court in relation to decisions of the Crown Court possible, but it draws the boundaries of the prohibition in a different place.

Amendment of section 29 of the Senior Courts Act 1981

A.8   Subsection (1)(a) amends section 29(3) so that it reads:

> In relation to the jurisdiction of the Crown Court, other than such of its jurisdiction as is excluded by virtue of section 29A, the High Court shall have all such jurisdiction to make mandatory, prohibiting or quashing orders as the High Court possesses in relation to the jurisdiction of an inferior court.

A.9   Subsection (1)(b) has the effect of removing subsection (6) from section 29. Section 29(6) concerns Recovery of Defence Costs Orders. These orders are orders for a defendant to repay the costs of representation, made against a defendant after conviction. Exceptionally they may be made against an acquitted defendant. Section 29(6) takes such orders outside the scope of the prohibition on judicial review and judicial review is therefore possible in respect of Recovery of Defence Costs Orders.

A.10   Subsection (1)(b) preserves this position when section 29 is amended as provided for by subsection (1)(a) and sections 29A and 29B are inserted into the Senior Courts Act 1981 by subsection (2). The effect is to take Recovery of Defence Costs Orders outside the exclusion period and it is therefore no longer necessary to make specific provision about them.

A.11   Subsection (2) inserts the new sections 29A and 29B into the Senior Courts Act 1981.

The new section 29A of the Senior Courts Act 1981

A.12   Section 29A(1) links section 29(3) to section 29A, stating that the excluded jurisdiction of the Crown Court mentioned in section 29(3) is its jurisdiction in proceedings on indictment, but only so far as provided in section 29A(2).

A.13   Section 29A(2) states that the excluded jurisdiction, when applied to a particular trial on indictment, extends only to any decision falling within an exclusion period (unless it is excepted by section 29A(4) or (5)), and to any decision mentioned in section 29A(3).

A.14　An exclusion period is as described in the new section 29B.

A.15　The exceptions to the excluded jurisdiction in subsection (4) and subsection (5) relate to refusals of bail and to hospital orders under section 51(5) of the Mental Health Act 1983 respectively.

Section 29A(4): the bail exception

A.16　The effect of section 29A(4) is that judicial review is possible in relation to a refusal of bail if it relates to a defendant and he or she cannot support an application for bail in the Crown Court with any argument that he or she desires. This will be the case where the Crown Court need not entertain arguments as to law or fact which it has heard previously (see paragraphs 2 and 3 of Part 2A of Schedule 1 to the Bail Act 1976) and there has been no change in circumstances.

A.17　The effect of section 29A(4) is also that judicial review is possible in relation to a refusal of bail if it relates to a witness.

Section 29A(5): the hospital order exception

A.18　The effect of section 29A(5) is that judicial review is possible in relation to a decision by the Crown Court to make a hospital order under section 51(5) of the Mental Health Act 1983. This subsection preserves the position under the current law.

Section 29A(3)

A.19　Section 29A(3) brings the following within the excluded jurisdiction: any decision made in connection with the consideration of any of the following.

> where the Crown Court
>
> > corrects a minor mistake in sentencing
> >
> > amends a suspended sentence or orders that a suspended sentence should take effect
> >
> > revokes or amends a community order, or otherwise deals with a defendant who is subject to a community order
> >
> > imposes a sentence on breach of a conditional discharge under section 13 of the Powers of Criminal Courts (Sentencing) Act 2000
> >
> > varies or rescinds a sentence under section 155 of the Powers of Criminal Courts (Sentencing) Act 2000
> >
> > or reviews a sentence where a case has been referred back to the Crown Court under section 74 of the Serious Organised Crime and Police Act 2005.

A.20   These are all ways in which a sentence passed by the Crown Court might be revisited, and the effect of section 29A(3) is that judicial review is not available in respect of any of them, nor in respect of any decision made in connection with the court's consideration of any of them.

Section 29A(6): meaning of "sentence"

A.21   Section 29A(6) has the effect that "sentence", where it appears in sections 29A and 29B, is to be construed as it is in section 50 of the Criminal Appeal Act 1968 except that, whereas "sentence" in section 50 includes an order deferring sentence, in sections 29A and 29B it does not. The result is that an exclusion period ends immediately after the passing of the sentence which was deferred, not immediately after the deferral of a sentence.

A.22   The effect of section 29A(7) is that, no matter how "sentence" is construed, judicial review is available in respect of a decision by the Crown Court to make a hospital order under section 51(5) of the Mental Health Act 1983.

New section 29B

A.23   Section 29B(1) sets out circumstances which trigger the beginning of an exclusion period, and section 29B(2) sets out when an exclusion period ends.

Section 29B(1): the beginning of an exclusion period

A.24   An exclusion period begins with the earliest of the following:

> a defendant is committed to the Crown Court for trial by a magistrates' court,

> a defendant is transferred to the Crown Court for trial by a magistrates' court,

> a defendant is sent to the Crown Court for trial by a magistrates' court,

> a voluntary bill of indictment is preferred by the direction of the Criminal Division of the Court of Appeal, or by the direction or with the consent of a High Court judge, or

> a voluntary bill of indictment is preferred by the direction of the appropriate person in the prosecuting authority, either within 3 months (or within such longer period as the court may allow) after the proceedings were stayed

A.25   The earliest of the above steps is itself within the exclusion period, and therefore may not be the subject of judicial review.

Section 29B(3)

A.26   If a court orders that a charge may not be pursued without the leave of the court, a new exclusion period will begin if a court gives leave to proceed.

A.27   If a stay of proceedings is ordered but the stay is lifted subsequently, then a new exclusion period begins.

Section 29B(2): the end of an exclusion period

A.28 The exclusion period ends immediately after the earliest of the following events to happen in relation to the last of the charges to be dealt with at the trial. The event itself may not therefore be the subject of judicial review. The events are:

the indictment, or the relevant count, is quashed,

the defendant is found to be unfit to plead or to be tried,

the defendant is acquitted or sentenced (and here, "sentence" is construed as prescribed by section 29A(6)),

the charge is ordered to lie on file,

a *nolle prosequi* is entered by order of the Attorney General, which is an order that the prosecution shall not be pursued,

the proceedings on the relevant count or the whole proceedings are ordered to be stayed or discontinued,

the charge is dismissed, or

any other order is made by the court which puts an end to the proceedings, such as where the judge accepts a plea in bar.

A.29 A Recovery of Defence Costs Order is one kind of order which is made after sentence (or, exceptionally, acquittal) and it therefore falls outside the exclusion period and may be the subject of judicial review proceedings.

A.30 If the jury is discharged and the judge orders a retrial, the proceedings continue and the exclusion period does not come to an end.

A.31 Where a new exclusion period begins because a stay of proceedings is lifted or a court gives leave for proceedings to be pursued (see section 29B(3)), it ends immediately after the earliest of the above events to happen in relation to the last of the charges to be dealt with at the trial, by virtue of section 29B(4).

CLAUSE 3

Subsection (1)

A.32 Section 39 of the Children and Young Persons Act 1933 allows any court to make a direction prohibiting publication of details calculated to lead to the identification of any child or young person concerned in the proceedings. The court may specify an exception to the direction.

A.33 Clause 3 creates a new appeal for children and young persons in relation to a decision permitting reporting of matters which will identify a child or young person in a trial on indictment. It does this by inserting new sections 159A and 159B into the Criminal Justice Act 1988.

New section 159A of the Criminal Justice Act 1988

A.34   The new section 159A applies only to proceedings relating to a trial on indictment. If, in such proceedings, the Crown Court refuses to make a direction under section 39, revokes a direction that has already been made, or makes a direction in certain terms, then a person under the age of 18 who is concerned in the proceedings may appeal against that refusal or revocation, or against the terms (such as the terms of an exception) of any direction that is made by the Crown Court (section 159A(1))

A.35   The appeal is made to the Criminal Division of the Court of Appeal ("the CACD"), but leave must be obtained. Initially, leave is to be sought from the Crown Court. If the Crown Court refuses leave, then leave may be sought from the CACD (section 159A(2)).

A.36   Section 159A(3) and (4) place a limit on the time within which the leave of the CACD must be sought, but they do not specify what that limit is. The time period is to be specified by rules of court, and to be calculated from the time when the Crown Court refuses leave.

A.37   The effect of section 159A(4) is that there may be no appeal from the CACD to the Supreme Court.

A.38   Section 159A(5) states what the CACD may do on hearing an appeal for which leave has been given. As well as powers to deal with the direction, refusal or revocation under appeal, the section gives the court power to stay any proceedings until the appeal is disposed of.

A.39   Section 159A(6) gives the CACD discretion to make orders for costs as it thinks fit in relation to the appeal.

A.40   Section 159A(7) applies subsections (2), (4) and (6) of section 159 of the Criminal Justice Act 1988 for the purposes of section 159A. The effect is:

that the jurisdiction of the Court of Appeal shall be exercised by the Criminal Division for the purposes of section 159A;

that any party to an appeal may give evidence before the CACD orally or in writing, unless it is specified in rules of court that this is not to be the case;

and that, in relation to trials satisfying specified conditions, rules of court may make special provision as to the practice and procedure to be followed in relation to hearings in private and appeals from orders for such hearings. In particular, the rules may provide that parties to an appeal may not give evidence before the CACD orally or in writing.

A.41   If a direction is made or confirmed on appeal under section 159A, then it is to be treated as if it had been made under section 39 of the Children and Young Persons Act 1933 for the purposes of section 39(2) of that Act, by virtue of section 159A(8)(a). The effect of a direction being made under section 39(2) of the 1933 Act is that if a person publishes any matter in contravention of such a direction, that is an offence, which is triable in the magistrates' courts and for which the maximum penalty is a level 5 fine (currently £5000).

A.42   Section 39 of the 1933 Act applies to publication in newspapers, but by virtue of section 57(4) of the Children and Young Persons Act 1963 and paragraph 3(2) of Schedule 20 to the Broadcasting Act 1990 it applies also to sound, television, digital and cable broadcasts.

A.43   Sections 159A(8)(b) and (c) state that a direction made or confirmed on appeal under section 159A is to be treated as made under section 39 of the CYPA 1933 for the purposes of section 57(4) of the Children and Young Persons Act 1963, and of paragraph 3(2) of Schedule 20 to the Broadcasting Act 1990. The effect is that any direction made or confirmed on appeal also applies to sound, television, digital and cable broadcasts.

New section 159B of the Criminal Justice Act 1988

A.44   If the Crown Court has revoked a direction, or refused to make one, or made one in terms which permit some publication, publishers may publish details identifying a child or young person. The purpose of the right of appeal would be defeated if there could be publication while an appeal was pending, and therefore the provisions of section 159B protect the child or young person from the consequences of publication while the appeal under section 159A is resolved.

A.45   A person intending to appeal under the new section 159A must seek the leave of the Crown Court. Once that person indicates to the Crown Court an intention to seek leave, then section 159B applies, by virtue of section 159B(1), and the Crown Court is to be treated as having made a direction under section 39 of the 1933 Act, prohibiting publication without any exception (section 159B(2)).

A.46   If leave is granted by the Crown Court, then the direction remains in effect until the appeal is determined or abandoned (section 159B(4)).

A.47   If leave is refused by the Crown Court, the direction remains in effect until either the period of time referred to in section 159A(3) expires without leave being sought, or, if sooner, the person indicates that they will not be seeking leave from the CACD, or the CACD grants or refuses leave (section 159B(3)).

A.48   If leave is granted by the CACD, then the direction continues to remain in effect until the appeal is determined or abandoned (section 159B(4)).

Clause 3, subsection (2)

A.49   The effect of subsection (2) is that for the purposes of a direction made or confirmed on appeal under section 159A, or treated as made by the Crown Court by virtue of section 159B(2), sections 159A and 159B are to be treated as having the same extent as section 39 of the 1933 Act, which also extends to Scotland. The effect of this is that such a direction, like one made under section 39 of the 1933 Act, is also effective in Scotland, not just in England and Wales. See also subsections (8) and (9) of clause 15 below.

CLAUSE 4

A.50   Clause 4 applies to proceedings before the Crown Court in a trial on indictment and provides a right to make representations to the judge in specified circumstances.

Subsection (1)

A.51 If, in proceedings before the Crown Court in a trial on indictment, any person applies to the court for an opportunity to make representations about a ruling which the court has made or is proposing to make, the court must grant that opportunity if the circumstances are as described in subsection (2).

A.52 The person making the application may be concerned in the proceedings, but need not be.

Subsection (2)

A.53 The circumstances are that it appears to the court that the ruling which the court has made or is proposing to make could result in a real and immediate risk to the life of the person making the application from the criminal act of another person.

Subsection (3)

A.54 Subsection (3) specifies that "ruling", in clauses 5, 7, 9 and 12, includes a variety of kinds of decision that a court may make: decision, determination, direction, finding, notice, order, refusal, rejection or requirement. It thus encompasses a refusal to make an order (or any other kind of decision) which is sought or a rejection of a request, for example.

CLAUSE 5

A.55 Clause 5 creates a right of appeal to the CACD against a ruling which the Crown Court has made which could result in a real and immediate risk to someone's life from the criminal act of another person. The effect of subsection (3) of clause 4 is that this right of appeal extends to all the kinds of decisions described in that subsection, including refusals to make orders sought by those making representations to the court.

Subsection (1)

A.56 The right of appeal may only be exercised:

by a person who made representations to the Crown Court at the time it was considering the ruling in question, or one which related to the same issue;

if leave is given;

if the conditions set out in subsections (5) and (6) are satisfied; and

on the grounds set out in subsection (7).

Subsection (2)

A.57 The effect of subsection (2) is that the person must apply to the Crown Court for leave and that, if the Crown Court refuses leave, the person may apply to the CACD for leave.

Subsection (3)

A.58 If a person decides to pursue an appeal, he or she must ask the Crown Court for leave immediately the ruling is made or refused.

Subsection (4)

A.59   If the Crown Court refuses leave, the applicant may seek the leave of the CACD (see clause 5(2)(b)). If the applicant does so, he or she must do so within a specified time period. That time period is not specified in the Bill, but would be specified in rules of court. The time period is to be calculated from the time when the Crown Court refuses leave.

Subsection (5)

A.60   Subsection (5) states the first condition to be satisfied. It provides the link between the representations made in the Crown Court and the appeal provided by clause 5: the ruling which is to be the subject of the appeal must either be the same as, or must relate to the same issue as, the ruling about which representations were made to the Crown Court.

Subsection (6)

A.61   Subsection (6) states the second condition to be satisfied: the right of appeal is only available in relation to a ruling which could affect the conduct of proceedings in which the strict rules of evidence apply. Such proceedings are a trial for an offence, and a hearing following a plea of guilty held to establish the facts on which the defendant is sentenced (known as a *Newton* hearing). Bail hearings, sentencing hearings, and confiscation proceedings following conviction are not proceedings in which the strict rules of evidence apply.

Subsection (7)

A.62   Subsection (7) contains the grounds of appeal. The first is in terms of the potential consequences of the ruling: that the ruling could result in a real and immediate risk to the life of the person from the criminal act of another person.

A.63   The second paragraph concerns the legal basis of the ruling: it must be a ground of appeal either that the ruling was wrong in law or that it was not reasonable for the court to have made it.

Subsection (8)

A.64   Subsection (8) states that the Criminal Division of the Court of Appeal is to exercise the Court of Appeal's jurisdiction in relation to this appeal.

CLAUSE 6

A.65   Clause 6 deals with the expedition of appeals from the Crown Court to the CACD under clause 5. Whichever court grants leave for the appeal must consider whether the appeal should be expedited (subsection (1)).

A.66   If a court decides that an appeal should be expedited, then it may adjourn the trial in the Crown Court (subsection (2)).

A.67   A decision of the Crown Court that the appeal should be expedited may be reversed by the Crown Court or by the CACD (subsection (3)), whereas a decision by the CACD that an appeal should be expedited may only be reversed by the CACD (subsection (4)).

A.68   Subsection (5) provides that if an appeal is not to be expedited, because the Crown Court or the CACD decided it should not be, either in the first place or on reversing an earlier decision, then the court which makes that decision may adjourn the trial or, if a jury has already been sworn to try the case, discharge the jury (in the case of the Crown Court) or make an order discharging the jury (in the case of the CACD).

CLAUSE 7

A.69   Clause 7 gives the CACD the powers, on hearing an appeal under clause 5, to:

stay any proceedings in any other court (subsection (1))

confirm, reverse or vary the Crown Court's ruling, make any ruling which the Crown Court could have made, or remit the matter to the Crown Court (subsection (2))

make such incidental or consequential orders as appear to it to be just (subsection (3)), and

make such order as to costs as it thinks fit, both in relation to the appeal and in relation to an application for leave to appeal (subsection (4)).

CLAUSE 8

A.70   This clause provides for a further appeal to the Supreme Court from the determination of the CACD of an appeal under clause 5.

Subsection (1)

A.71   Whereas the appeal to the CACD may only be brought by a person who claims that the ruling could result in a real and immediate risk to his or her life, an appeal from the CACD to the Supreme Court may be pursued by anyone who was a party to the appeal to the CACD.

A.72   The appeal lies against the substantive decision of the CACD on the appeal, not against incidental rulings or rulings on side issues such as reporting restrictions.

Subsections (2) and (3)

A.73   Leave must be obtained for an appeal to the Supreme Court. Leave is to be sought initially from the CACD. If that court refuses leave, the party may apply to the Supreme Court for leave.

A.74   In order to obtain leave, the appellant must obtain a certificate from the CACD that the decision involved a point of law of general public importance. If the CACD will not give this certificate, the appeal may not be pursued: there is no right of appeal against a refusal to give this certificate.

A.75   If the CACD does grant the certificate, it may not grant leave unless it also considers that the point of law is one which ought to be considered by the Supreme Court.

A.76   If the CACD grants the certificate but refuses leave, the appellant may apply to the Supreme Court for leave. The Supreme Court will not grant leave unless it considers that the point of law is one which it ought to examine.

Subsection (4)

A.77   Subsection (4) clarifies the relationship between section 33(3) of the Criminal Appeal Act 1968 and the appeal provided by clause 8: the terms of section 33(3) of the CAA 1968 do not prevent an appeal under clause 8.

Subsections (5) to (7)

A.78   Although the appeal under clause 8 is not one which is pursued under the CAA 1968, provisions in the CAA 1968 may be applied to an appeal under clause 8 by order, and subsection (5) gives the Lord Chancellor power to make such an order. The order would be in the form of a statutory instrument, and would be made by the negative resolution procedure. This means that the instrument is laid before Parliament and remains the law unless it is annulled by Her Majesty following a resolution passed by the House of Commons or the House of Lords asking Her to do so.

A.79   The order could make provision for matters like the time limit within which leave should be sought and any power to extend that time.

CLAUSE 9

A.80   Clause 9 provides that a ruling which is the subject of an appeal under clause 5 or under clause 8 will be suspended pending the determination of that appeal.

A.81   Throughout clause 9, "ruling" includes decision, determination, direction, finding, notice, order, refusal, rejection or requirement, by virtue of clause 4(3).

Appeal to the CACD

A.82   The ruling in question will be of no effect from the moment leave to appeal under section 5 is asked for until the appeal cannot be pursued any further or is no longer pursued.

Subsections (1) and (2)

A.83   If the Crown Court gives leave to appeal then the ruling is of no effect until the appeal to the CACD is determined by the CACD or, if the appellant abandons the appeal, until it is abandoned.

A.84   If, however, the Crown Court does not give leave to appeal, then the ruling is of no effect until

    the period within which the leave of the CACD may be sought expires and the appellant has either indicated he or she will not seek leave or simply does not seek leave from the CACD,

    or the CACD refuses leave,

    or, if the CACD grants leave, the appeal is determined by the CACD or abandoned.

Appeal to the Supreme Court

Subsection (3)

A.85   Following determination of the appeal by the CACD, the ruling continues to be of no effect until a party applies for leave to appeal to the Supreme Court, or the period for doing so expires, unless a party asks the CACD to rule otherwise.

A.86   The practical effect is that the parties have a period within which they can consider whether to appeal to the Supreme Court and the ruling in issue is suspended for that time, but the opportunity for a party to bring the matter before the CA means that if no party is genuinely contemplating appealing to the Supreme Court, the suspension of the ruling can be brought to an end, and the case will proceed according to the decision of the CACD.

Subsections (4) and (5)

A.87   Once a party seeks leave to appeal from the CACD, then the ruling continues to be of no effect until

the CACD refuses to grant a certificate as required by clause 8(3)(a), or

if the CACD does grant the certificate required by clause 8(3)(a) but refuses leave, until

the period within which the leave of the Supreme Court may be sought expires and the appellant has either indicated he or she will not seek leave or simply does not seek leave from the Supreme Court,

or the Supreme Court refuses leave,

or, if the Supreme Court grants leave, the appeal is determined by the Supreme Court or abandoned.

A.88   If the CACD gives leave to appeal then the ruling is of no effect until the appeal to the CACD is determined by the Supreme Court or, if the appellant abandons the appeal, until it is abandoned.

A.89   The cumulative effect of clause 9 is that, if a person appeals to the CACD and pursues the appeal to the Supreme Court – or a person appeals to the CACD and another party appeals to the Supreme Court – the ruling in dispute is suspended until the appeal is finally dealt with.

CLAUSE 10

A.90   In some circumstances, the person who claims his or her life is at risk will still potentially be at risk, despite the ruling in dispute being of no effect as provided for by clause 9, and so a specific order will need to be made in order to safeguard that person pending the conclusion of the appeal under clauses 5 and 8 (called a "safeguarding order"). Clause 10 gives the Crown Court and the CACD the power to make safeguarding orders.

A.91 Subsection (1) defines a safeguarding order: it is an order made for the purpose of safeguarding the "appellant" and it lasts only for the duration of any appeal proceedings under clauses 5 and 8. Subsection (1) also defines the "appellant", for the purpose of clause 10, as the person appealing under clause 5.

A.92 When a court makes a safeguarding order, it may make it in such terms as it thinks fit.

A.93 Subsections (2) and (3) give the Crown Court power to make a safeguarding order if a person seeks leave to appeal under clause 5, either when leave is sought or subsequently, before any appeal proceedings in the CACD. Subsection (4) allows the Crown Court to vary or revoke a safeguarding order which it has made.

A.94 If the Crown Court refuses leave to appeal, the appellant may seek leave from the CACD. In that event, the CACD may make a safeguarding order under subsection (5)(a). If the CACD grants leave to appeal under clause 5, it may make a safeguarding order at any stage of the proceedings before it (subsection (5)(b)).

A.95 If there is a subsequent appeal to the Supreme Court, which may be made by any party to the appeal under clause 5, the CACD may make a safeguarding order when a party seeks leave, from the CACD or from the Supreme Court, for that further appeal under subsection (5)(c). If leave is granted, the CACD may make a safeguarding order at any later stage of the proceedings before the Supreme Court, by virtue of subsection (5)(d). The order will be for the protection of the person who was the appellant in the appeal *to* the CACD, who might not be the party appealing to the Supreme Court.

A.96 Subsection (6) gives the CACD power to vary or revoke a safeguarding order, whether it is one made by the Crown Court, by itself on appeal under clause 5, or by itself where a party is pursuing an appeal under clause 8.

A.97 Thus, for the appeal under section 5, both the Crown Court and the CACD have the power to make orders; the Crown Court can vary or revoke its own orders; the CACD can vary or revoke its own orders and those made by the Crown Court. For the appeal under section 8, the CACD alone has the power to make orders, and to vary or revoke them.

CLAUSE 11

A.98 Normal practice is for parties to proceedings to be informed of applications to the court by any other party and of appeals by any other party, to receive documents and material which have to be disclosed to them by other parties by law, and to be present or represented at any hearing in the proceedings. Clause 11 makes it possible for there to be exceptions to these practices, but only to the extent reasonably required to protect the safety of any person concerned in the proceedings relating to the application for leave or the appeal (by virtue of subsection (3)).

A.99 Clause 11 provides authority in primary legislation for rules of court to prescribe circumstances in which various steps in relation to the appeals in clauses 5 and 8 may be made:

without giving notice to any other party to the proceedings

without disclosing material which the applicant would otherwise have to disclose to any other party to the proceedings

at a hearing at which another party to the proceedings is neither present nor represented.

A.100 Those steps are: an application for leave to appeal to the CACD or to the Supreme Court, an application to the CACD for a certificate that a point of law of general public importance is involved in the ruling, and any appeal following the granting of leave to appeal.

CLAUSE 12

A.101 Clause 12 provides the Crown Court, the CACD and the Supreme Court with the power to restrict reporting of any matter relating to the ruling which is being challenged, an application for leave to appeal, an appeal under clause 5 or clause 8, and the person in question.

A.102 "Ruling" here includes decision, determination, direction, finding, notice, order, refusal, rejection or requirement, by virtue of clause 4(3).

Appeal from the Crown Court to the CACD

A.103 Subsection (1) provides the Crown Court with the power to restrict reporting. It applies from the point when leave to appeal is sought from the Crown Court (which must be immediately the ruling is made: see subsection (3) of clause 5 above).

A.104 If leave to appeal to the CACD is given (by the Crown Court or by the CACD), a reporting restriction made by the Crown Court has effect until the appeal is determined by the CACD or abandoned.

A.105 If however, leave to appeal is refused by the Crown Court, the reporting restriction remains in effect (unless revoked) only until

the time for seeking leave from the CACD expires and either the appellant does not seek leave or indicates that he or she will not do so, or

the appellant does seek leave from the CACD but it is refused by the CACD.

A.106 Subsection (2) allows the Crown Court to vary or revoke a reporting restriction which it has made.

A.107 When the CACD hears the appeal, it may vary or revoke a reporting restriction made by the Crown Court (subsection (4)).

A.108 On determining an appeal, the CACD may make a reporting restriction as it thinks fit in the interests of justice (subsection (5)). Its power to do so does not depend on any reporting restriction having already been made in the case. The CACD may vary or revoke its own reporting restriction (subsection (6)).

Appeal from the CACD to the Supreme Court

A.109   If a party decides to appeal from the CACD to the Supreme Court, then any reporting restriction made by the CACD when it determined the appeal continues in effect (unless revoked) until

the CACD refuses to grant a certificate as required by clause 8(3)(a), or

if the CACD does grant the certificate required by clause 8(3)(a) but refuses leave, until

the period within which the leave of the Supreme Court may be sought expires and the appellant has either indicated he or she will not seek leave or simply does not seek leave from the Supreme Court,

or the Supreme Court refuses leave,

or, if the Supreme Court grants leave, the appeal is determined by the Supreme Court or abandoned.

A.110   The CACD may still vary or revoke its own reporting restriction: see subsection (6).

A.111   When the Supreme Court hears the appeal, it may vary or revoke a reporting restriction made by the CACD (subsection (8)).

A.112   On determining an appeal, the Supreme Court may make a reporting restriction as it thinks fit in the interests of justice (subsection (9)). Its power to do so does not depend on any reporting restriction having already been made in the case.

A.113   The Crown Court, which may continue to try the case following determination of the appeal by the Supreme Court (and which may have continued to try the case while the appeal was pursued) may find it necessary to vary the reporting restriction made by the Supreme Court, or to revoke it entirely, and subsection (10) provides it with the power to do so.

General matters

A.114   Subsection (11) states that other reporting restrictions that may be made, by any other court about any matter, are unaffected by this clause. The powers to restrict reporting provided by clause 11 are tied to an appeal under clause 5 or clause 8. There may be a reason for publication to be restricted which holds good whether a person seeks to appeal under clause 5 or not, and so, for example, a judge may make a direction prohibiting reporting under section 11 of the Contempt of Court Act 1981. The power to make such a direction, and the terms or duration of such a direction, are not affected by the powers provided by clause 11.

A.115   Subsection (12) defines "publication" and "relevant programme" for the purposes of this clause and clause 13.

CLAUSE 13

A.116   Clause 13 creates offences if a publication includes any matter in breach of a direction given under clause 12.

A.117   Subsections (2) and (3) state who is to be guilty of the offence if publication is in a newspaper or periodical, or a relevant programme respectively.

A.118   Subsection (4) states that, in respect of any publication which is not a newspaper, periodical or relevant programme, any person publishing it commits the offence.

A.119   Subsection (5) states that the offence is triable in the magistrates' courts, and sets the maximum level of penalty, which is a fine at level 5 on the standard scale (currently £5000).

A.120   Subsection (6) imposes a restriction on prosecutions for an offence under this clause: prosecution may only be begun with the Attorney General's consent.

CLAUSE 14
A.121   This clause introduces Schedule 1 (minor and consequential amendments) and Schedule 2 (repeals).

CLAUSE 15

Subsections (2) to (6)
A.122   This clause enables the Lord Chancellor by order to make incidental, supplementary, consequential, transitional or saving provision in connection with the coming into force of any provision of this Bill brought into force by the order.

A.123   Clause 15 comes into force on the day the Bill is passed, by virtue of subsection (2). The other clauses will come into force on such day or days as are appointed by order made by the Lord Chancellor, and different days may be appointed for different purposes.

A.124   An order made under this provision will be made by statutory instrument.

Subsections (8) and (9)
A.125   The Bill extends to England and Wales only, except for clause 3(2), paragraphs 1(1) and (3) and 5 of Schedule 1, and the corresponding repeal and consequential amendments.

A.126   Clause 3(2) concerns a direction made or confirmed on appeal under section 159A of the Criminal Justice Act 1988, or treated as made by the Crown Court by virtue of section 159B(2) of the Criminal Justice Act 1988. Clause 3(2), and clause 15 so far as it relates to clause 3(2), extend also to Scotland. The effect is that a direction made or confirmed on appeal under section 159A, or treated as made by virtue of section 159B(2), which are treated as having been made under section 39 of the CYPA 1933, will be effective in England and Wales and in Scotland, as is a direction made under section 39 of the CYPA 1933.

A.127   The extent of paragraphs 1(1), 1(3) and 5 of Schedule 1 is described below.

SCHEDULE 1

Paragraph 1(1)

A.128 The effect of removing appeal by way of case stated from the Crown Court in criminal matters is that the High Court's power in section 40(4) of the Road Traffic Offenders Act 1988 to suspend a disqualification from driving would be redundant. Paragraph 1(1) and Schedule 2 therefore repeal the words "or section 28 of the Senior Courts Act 1981 (statement of case by Crown Court)" from section 40(4).

A.129 By virtue of paragraph 1(3), this repeal applies only in relation to decisions of the Crown Court made or given after clause 1 of the Bill has come into force.

A.130 Paragraphs 1(1), 1(3), and the corresponding repeal in Schedule 2, extend also to Scotland.

Paragraph 1(2)

A.131 The effect of removing appeal by way of case stated from the Crown Court in criminal matters is that the High Court's power in section 130(5) of the Licensing Act 2003 to suspend an order under section 129 of that Act (ordering the forfeiture or suspension of a licence to supply alcohol) would be redundant. Paragraph 1(3) and Schedule 2 therefore repeal the words "or section 28 of the Senior Courts Act 1981 (statement of case by Crown Court)" from section 130(5).

A.132 By virtue of paragraph 1(3), this repeal applies only in relation to decisions of the Crown Court made or given after clause 1 of the Bill has come into force.

Paragraph 2

A.133 Section 22 of the Prosecution of Offences Act 1985 enables the Secretary of State to set time limits for the completion of preliminary stages of proceedings, and an appropriate court may extend the time limit or stay the proceedings. By virtue of section 22(13), where the court does so, its decision may be the subject of judicial review. The effect of paragraph 2 is to preserve that position, despite the amendment to section 29(3) of, and insertion of section 29A into, the Senior Courts Act 1981.

Paragraph 3

A.134 Paragraph 3 amends the Criminal Appeal Act 1968 with the effect that the powers of the Court of Appeal exercisable by the single judge, and the powers to make procedural directions exercisable by the single judge and by the registrar, apply in relation to an appeal under section 159A of the Criminal Justice Act 1988.

Paragraph 4

A.135 Section 39 of the CYPA 1933 has been amended, but the amendments have not yet been brought into force. In place of a direction under section 39 of the CYPA 1933 prohibiting publication (which may include an exception or exceptions to that direction), the court would make a direction under section 45(3) of the Youth Justice and Criminal Evidence Act 1999, with or without an excepting direction under section 45(4) or (5).

A.136   When section 39 of the CYPA 1933 is amended and section 45 of the 1999 Act comes into force, sections 159A and 159B of the Criminal Justice Act 1988 will be amended as set out in subparagraphs (2) and (3), and this is effected by paragraph 4(1).

A.137   It follows from this that the right of appeal provided by section 159A of the Criminal Justice Act 1988 will be an appeal against a refusal to make a direction under section 45(3) of the 1999 Act, against the revocation of such a direction, or against the making or variation of an excepting direction made under section 45(4) or 45(5) of the 1999 Act.

Subparagraph (4)

A.138   Paragraph 2(2) of Schedule 2 to the 1999 Act, which will come into force on the same date as section 45 of that Act, deals with proceedings which have already begun on that date. Its effect is that if criminal proceedings have already been "instituted", then section 39 of the CYPA 1933 will continue to operate. The powers available to the Crown Court under section 45 of the 1999 Act will only be available in respect of cases where proceedings are instituted after that date.

A.139   Subparagraph (4) produces the same result in relation to appeals under section 159A of the Criminal Justice Act 1988: if criminal proceedings have already been instituted then sections 159A and 159B are to be read without the amendments set out in subparagraphs (2) and (3).

A.140   "Instituted" is defined for all these purposes at paragraph 1(2) of Schedule 7 to the 1999 Act.

Paragraph 5

A.141   This paragraph deals with the extent of sections 159A and 159B of the Criminal Justice Act 1988.

A.142   A direction made or confirmed by the Court of Appeal under section 159A is deemed to be made under section 39 of the CYPA 1933 (by virtue of section 159A(8)). Similarly, by virtue of section 159B(2), the Crown Court is to be treated as having made a direction under section 39 of the CYPA 1933 in the circumstances described in section 159B(1).

A.143   In both these cases, the direction in question is to be effective in the same parts of the United Kingdom as one made under section 39 of the CYPA 1933 (see clause 3(2)).

A.144   Once section 45 of the 1999 Act is in force, in both cases the direction will be treated as having been made under that section instead.

A.145   The extent of section 39 of the CYPA 1933 is not the same as the extent of section 45 of the 1999 Act, and therefore paragraph 5 states that directions made or confirmed under section 159A, and directions which the court is treated as having made under section 159B(2), are to be treated as effective in the same way as directions made under section 45 of the 199 Act. This means that they are effective in Scotland and Northern Ireland as well as in England and Wales (see subsection (9)(c) of clause 15).

Paragraph 6

A.146   Paragraph 6 relates to the appeal provided for by clause 5. It amends the Criminal Appeal Act 1968 with the effect that leave to appeal to the CACD under clause 5 may be granted by a single judge of the Court of Appeal, and that procedural directions in relation to an appeal under clause 5 may be made by a single judge and by a registrar as set out in section 31B of the CAA 1968.

Paragraph 7

A.147   Paragraph 7 amends section 22(6B) of the Prosecution of Offences Act 1985 with the effect that time ceases to run for the purposes of statutory time limits for the completion by a case of stages of the criminal justice process while the appeal under clause 5, and any further appeal to the Supreme Court under clause 8, is pursued.

APPENDIX B
CONSULTEES ON CP 184

We received responses from

Tony Edwards

Ed Rees QC

Roger Elsey DJ (Magistrates)

Master Venne, Registrar of Criminal Appeals and Master of the Crown Office

Justices' Clerks Society

Criminal Sub-Committee, Council of HM Circuit Judges

Wood Green judges

HH Judge Murphy

Crown Prosecution Service

Law Reform Committee of the Bar Council

Council of HM District Judges (Magistrates' Courts) Legal Committee

Better Trials Unit, Office of Criminal Justice Reform

The Newspaper Society

We also held meetings with:

the Administrative Court Office (Lynne Knapman (Deputy Master) and Martyn Cowlin (Senior Legal Manager))

the Criminal Appeal Office (Master Roger Venne and staff)

the Crown Prosecution Service (CPS)

the judges at the Central Criminal Court

the judges at Snaresbrook Crown Court

the judges at Wood Green Crown Court

the Office of Criminal Justice Reform

the Rose Committee (a committee consisting of senior Appeal Court judges which used to be chaired by Lord Justice Rose)

Peter Fisher MBE of the Office of the Judge Advocate General the Ministry of Defence and

Ian Wise QC of Doughty Street Chambers.

We also benefited from the expertise of members of our Advisory Group:

Professor A Ashworth

Lord Justice Auld

Anthony Edwards

Alphege Bell

Professor I Dennis

Deborah Grice of the Ministry of Justice

Gillian Harrison of the OCJR

Bruce Houlder QC, Director of Service Prosecutions

Lord Justice Hughes

Jaswant Narwal of the CPS

Professor D C Ormerod

Mrs N Padfield

David Perry QC

Mr Justice Pitchers

Edward Rees QC

His Honour Judge Jeremy Roberts

Professor J R Spencer QC

Timothy Workman, Senior District Judge

APPENDIX C
OTHER POTENTIAL WAYS OF IMPROVING THE EFFICIENCY OF THE APPEALS PROCESS

C.1   We take the opportunity here to describe the potential for savings in the system. These matters do not fall within our terms of reference and we make no recommendations in respect of them. However, they are worth drawing to readers' attention.

C.2   There are three routes to challenging a conviction in the magistrates' court in addition to case stated and application for judicial review:

       (1)   application to the magistrates' court to have the conviction set aside,

       (2)   application to the magistrates to re-open the conviction,

       (3)   appeal to the Crown Court.

(1) Application to the magistrates to set aside the conviction: section 14 of the Magistrates' Court Act 1980:

C.3   Where a defendant is convicted at the magistrates but did not know of the proceedings, there is a procedure whereby the conviction can be set aside. Although the governing provision refers to a time limit within which the defendant must take particular steps, it also allows the conviction to be set aside after the time limit has expired if it appears that it was not reasonable to expect the accused to serve a statutory declaration within the time limit.

> *Section 14 Proceedings invalid where accused did not know of them*
>
> (1) Where a summons has been issued under section 1 above and a magistrates' court has begun to try the information to which the summons relates, then, if-
>
> > (a) the accused, at any time during or after the trial, makes a statutory declaration that he did not know of the summons or the proceedings until a date specified in the declaration, being a date after the court has begun to try the information; and
> >
> > (b) within 21 days of that date the declaration is served on the designated officer for the court,
>
> without prejudice to the validity of the information, the summons and all subsequent proceedings shall be void.
>
> (2) ...

(3) If on the application of the accused it appears to a magistrates' court ... that it was not reasonable to expect the accused to serve such a statutory declaration as is mentioned in subsection (1) above within the period allowed by that subsection, the court may accept service of such a declaration by the accused after that period has expired; ...

C.4 Crown Court judges commented to us that this provision is under-used. The result is that defendants use the appeal process to the Crown Court where they need not.

(2) Application to the magistrates to re-open the proceedings: section 142 of the Magistrates' Court Act 1980:

C.5 Stones' Justices' Manual says, "the purpose of s 142 is to rectify mistakes. It is generally to be regarded as a slip rule and the power under the section cannot be extended to cover situations beyond those akin to a mistake."[1]

> Section 142 Power of magistrates' court to re-open cases to rectify mistakes etc
>
> ...
>
> (2) Where a person is convicted by a magistrates' court and it subsequently appears to the court that it would be in the interests of justice that the case should be heard again by different justices, the court may so direct.
>
> (2A)   The power conferred on a magistrates' court by subsection (2) above shall not be exercisable in relation to a conviction if—
>
> > (a)   the Crown Court has determined an appeal against—
> >
> > > (i)   the conviction; or
> > >
> > > (ii)   any sentence or order imposed or made by the magistrates' court when dealing with the offender in respect of the conviction; or
> >
> > (b)   the High Court has determined a case stated for the opinion of that court on any question arising in any proceeding leading to or resulting from the conviction.

C.6 Section 142 is only applicable where there has been a conviction, and therefore, if no evidence is offered or charges are withdrawn, section 142 is not relevant.[2]

---

[1] *Stones' Justices' Manual* (2008) footnote 6 to para 1-2235. The interpretation of s 142 as only available to correct mistakes has been disputed (see P Rule, "The Power to Re-Open the Case in the 'Interests of Justice' and Croydon" (2009) 173 Criminal Law & Justice Weekly 213) but recently confirmed in *Zykin v CPS* [2009] EWHC 1469 (Admin), [2009] All ER (D) 303. Note: s 142 is only available in criminal cases.

[2] *R (Green and Green Scaffolding) v Staines Magistrates' Court* [2008] EWHC 1443 (Admin), [2008] All ER (D) 211.

C.7   There is no time limit for seeking to have a conviction set aside under section 142, but the decision is a matter for the magistrates' discretion, and delay in making the application would be a factor for them to take into account. An increase in the take-up of set-aside procedure for convictions in the magistrates' court where the defendant did not know of the proceedings would reduce the Crown Court judges' workload.

(3) Appeal to the Crown Court against conviction and/or sentence: section 108 of the Magistrates' Court Act 1980:

C.8   A defendant convicted in the magistrates' court can appeal against conviction (if he or she did not plead guilty) and/or sentence to the Crown Court. Leave to appeal does not have to be obtained. Any appeal has to be lodged within 21 days of the date that the defendant was sentenced in the magistrates' court[3] although the Crown Court can extend the period for appealing.

C.9   The appeal takes the form of a rehearing before a Crown Court judge sitting with at least two and not more than four justices of the peace.[4] The Crown Court may affirm, reverse or vary any part of the magistrates' decision appealed against or may remit the matter back to the magistrates' court with its opinion as to how the matter should be disposed of.

C.10   If notice of appeal is lodged in time, then leave is not required. If it is lodged out of time, then the Crown court may give leave to appeal out of time.[5]

C.11   Some Crown Court judges suggested to us that this time limit of 21 days could usefully be extended, to save their time in having to consider applications for leave which is almost invariably granted. This would save judicial time at Crown Court level considering applications for leave.

---

[3]   Criminal Procedure Rules, r 63.2(2) and (3).

[4]   Supreme Court Act 1981, s 74. Criminal Procedure Rules 2005, r 63.8 sets out certain special circumstances where this rule need not be adhered to.

[5]   Criminal Procedure Rules, r 63.9.

Title: **APPENDIX D** **The High Court's jurisdiction in relation to criminal proceedings**	Impact Assessment (IA)	
	IA No: LAWCOM0001	
	Date: 16/06/2010	
Lead department or agency: Ministry of Justice	**Stage:** Final	
	Source of intervention: Domestic	
Other departments or agencies: Law Commission	**Type of measure:** Primary legislation	
	Contact for enquiries: Christina Hughes 020 3334 0278	

Summary: Intervention and Options

What is the problem under consideration? Why is government intervention necessary?

There are different ways in which a party to a criminal case can challenge a Crown Court decision. This variety makes the criminal justice system complicated, which leads to inefficiency and waste of financial resources. It is not clear to a party to a case which route to use, which leads to unnecessary litigation, which is costly to individuals and to the public purse. Finally, the law does not provide rights to challenge rulings of the Crown Court in some circumstances where it should. The combined effect is to undermine public confidence in the fair and efficient operation of the system.

What are the policy objectives and the intended effects?

The aims of the policy are (i) to produce just results for defendants, witnessess and victims; (ii) that criminal cases should not generate satellite litigation; (iii) to avoid delay and interruptions to Crown Court trials; (iv) the reduction of unnecessary litigation; and (v) giving effect to important rights. The ways in which the recommendations would achieve these aims are: by reducing the number of routes of appeal from the Crown Court; to make clear when judicial review of rulings by the Crown Court is and is not possible; to provide additional specific rights of appeal where needed.

What policy options have been considered? Please justify preferred option (further details in Evidence Base)

Do nothing has been considered (option 0), as have option 1 - targeted change - and option 2 - large-scale change. The preferred option is option 1 (targeted change) because it offers an improvement on the current law and, relative to option 2, is a proportionate response to the problem.

When will the policy be reviewed to establish its impact and the extent to which the policy objectives have been achieved?	It will not be reviewed
Are there arrangements in place that will allow a systematic collection of monitoring information for future policy review?	No

SELECT SIGNATORY Sign-off For final proposal stage Impact Assessments:

I have read the Impact Assessment and I am satisfied that (a) it represents a fair and reasonable view of the expected costs, benefits and impact of the policy, and (b) the benefits justify the costs.

Signed by the responsible Chair: .... Date:...........................

Summary: Analysis and Evidence

Policy Option 1

Description:

Targeted change

Price Base Year 2009	PV Base Year 2009	Time Period Years 10	Net Benefit (Present Value (PV)) (£m)		
			Low: Optional	High: Optional	Best Estimate: -£19.316

COSTS (£m)	Total Transition (Constant Price) Years	Average Annual (excl. Transition) (Constant Price)	Total Cost (Present Value)
Low	£0	£0.239	Optional
High	Optional	£17.975	Optional
Best Estimate	£0	£2.559	**£22.027**

Description and scale of key monetised costs by 'main affected groups'

Increased costs for court and parties (including legal aid) for small number of additional appeals. SEE ASSUMPTIONS. SEE ALSO PAGES 17- 19.

Other key non-monetised costs by 'main affected groups'

Potential delay to Crown Court trials and potential knock-on delay on cases at the Criminal Division of the Court of Appeal affecting witnesses, defendants and all users of criminal courts.

BENEFITS (£m)	Total Transition (Constant Price) Years	Average Annual (excl. Transition) (Constant Price)	Total Benefit (Present Value)
Low	£0	£0.023	Optional
High	Optional	£4.700	Optional
Best Estimate	£0	£0.315	**£2.711**

Description and scale of key monetised benefits by 'main affected groups'

Some potential savings to the state and to litigants due to reduced litigation and possibly fewer defendants in prison. Each defendant not in custody could save between £7,715 and £11,750 in the cost of a prison place, assuming 3 months as the time spent awaiting trial. SEE ASSUMPTIONS. SEE ALSO PAGE 19 BELOW

Other key non-monetised benefits by 'main affected groups'

Some court rulings which are unsustainable in law would be corrected, leading to greater protection against publicity for children, liberty for defendants who should be on bail, and increased confidence in the criminal justice system. Potential benefit for acquitted defendants who are able to recoup their costs.

Key assumptions/sensitivities/risks	Discount rate (%)	3.5

Assume: all reforms implemented; more defendants will pay for their defence; most court rulings are lawfully made. Risks: number of additional appeal/review cases is underestimated. These variables will affect the costs and make them hard to predict: venue, complexity, length of hearing, and, with judicial review, whether the prosecution will be represented. Other legal changes could affect take-up.

Impact on admin burden (AB) (£m):			Impact on policy cost savings (£m):	In scope
New AB: 0	AB savings: 0	Net: 0	Policy cost savings: 0	No

Enforcement, Implementation and Wider Impacts

What is the geographic coverage of the policy/option?	England and Wales
From what date will the policy be implemented?	unknown
Which organisation(s) will enforce the policy?	Criminal Justice System
What is the annual change in enforcement cost (£m)?	
Does enforcement comply with Hampton principles?	Yes
Does implementation go beyond minimum EU requirements?	Yes

What is the CO$_2$ equivalent change in greenhouse gas emissions? (Million tonnes CO$_2$ equivalent)	Traded: 0	Non-traded: 0
Does the proposal have an impact on competition?	No	
What proportion (%) of Total PV costs/benefits is directly attributable to primary legislation, if applicable?	Costs:	Benefits:

Annual cost (£m) per organisation (excl. Transition) (Constant Price)	Micro	< 20	Small	Medium	Large
Are any of these organisations exempt?	No	No	No	No	No

Specific Impact Tests: Checklist

Set out in the table below where information on any SITs undertaken as part of the analysis of the policy options can be found in the evidence base. For guidance on how to complete each test, double-click on the link for the guidance provided by the relevant department.

Please note this checklist is not intended to list each and every statutory consideration that departments should take into account when deciding which policy option to follow. It is the responsibility of departments to make sure that their duties are complied with.

Does your policy option/proposal have an impact on…?	Impact	Page ref within IA
Statutory equality duties[1] Statutory Equality Duties Impact Test guidance	No	18
Economic impacts		
Competition Competition Assessment Impact Test guidance	No	
Small firms Small Firms Impact Test guidance	No	
Environmental impacts		
Greenhouse gas assessment Greenhouse Gas Assessment Impact Test guidance	No	
Wider environmental issues Wider Environmental Issues Impact Test guidance	No	
Social impacts		
Health and well-being Health and Well-being Impact Test guidance	No	
Human rights Human Rights Impact Test guidance	No	19
Justice system Justice Impact Test guidance	Yes	8
Rural proofing Rural Proofing Impact Test guidance	No	
Sustainable development Sustainable Development Impact Test guidance	No	

---

[1] Race, disability and gender Impact assessments are statutory requirements for relevant policies. Equality statutory requirements will be expanded 2011, once the Equality Bill comes into force. Statutory equality duties part of the Equality Bill apply to GB only. The Toolkit provides advice on statutory equality duties for public authorities with a remit in Northern Ireland.

Summary: Analysis and Evidence

Policy Option 2

Description:

Large scale change

Price Base Year 2009	PV Base Year 2009	Time Period Years 10	Net Benefit (Present Value (PV)) (£m)		
			Low: Optional	High: Optional	Best Estimate: -£23.572

COSTS (£m)	Total Transition (Constant Price) Years	Average Annual (excl. Transition) (Constant Price)	Total Cost (Present Value)
Low	Optional	£0.320	Optional
High	Optional	£16.000	Optional
Best Estimate	£0	£5.539	£47.674

Description and scale of key monetised costs by 'main affected groups'

Assuming 640 appeals per year, maximum annual cost to courts and parties could be £16m (if every case meant 1 day's hearing costing £25,000) and minimum cost could be £320,000 (if leave to appeal is refused in every case at £500 each). If leave were granted in one third of cases, the annual cost would be 427*£500+213* £25,000 = £5,538,500. SEE ASSUMPTIONS BELOW

Other key non-monetised costs by 'main affected groups'

Potential delay to Crown Court trials and potential knock-on delay on cases at the Criminal Division of the Court of Appeal affecting witnesses, defendants and all users of criminal courts.

BENEFITS (£m)	Total Transition (Constant Price) Years	Average Annual (excl. Transition) (Constant Price)	Total Benefit (Present Value)
Low	Optional	Optional	Optional
High	Optional	Optional	Optional
Best Estimate	£0	£2.800	£24.102

Description and scale of key monetised benefits by 'main affected groups'

Saving of cost to state (court service and legal aid budget), defendants and prosectuing authorities through abolition of case stated and judicial review in relation to criminal proceedings in the Crown Court. Assuming 350 cases per year at £8,000 each this could be £2.8m per year. SEE ASSUMPTIONS BELOW AND PAGE 8

Other key non-monetised benefits by 'main affected groups'

Simplification of the criminal appeal system by removing two routes of appeal and replacing with a new statutory appeal, and improved access to human rights for defendants and all directly affected by a Crown Court ruling in a criminal case.

Key assumptions/sensitivities/risks	Discount rate (%)	3.5

The assumed number of new appeals generated (640 per year) could be an underestimate. £25,000 for a day's hearing in Court of Appeal could be overestimate - see p 14 - and many cases would not take that long. 350 fewer judicial reviews could be an underestimate, and the cost of each case could vary greatly from the estimate of £8,000 .

Impact on admin burden (AB) (£m):			Impact on policy cost savings (£m):	In scope
New AB: 0	AB savings: 0	Net: 0	Policy cost savings: 0	No

nforcement, Implementation and Wider Impacts

What is the geographic coverage of the policy/option?	England and Wales
From what date will the policy be implemented?	
Which organisation(s) will enforce the policy?	Criminal Justice System
What is the annual change in enforcement cost (£m)?	
Does enforcement comply with Hampton principles?	Yes
Does implementation go beyond minimum EU requirements?	Yes

What is the CO₂ equivalent change in greenhouse gas emissions? (Million tonnes CO₂ equivalent)	Traded: 0	Non-traded: 0
Does the proposal have an impact on competition?	No	
What proportion (%) of Total PV costs/benefits is directly attributable to primary legislation, if applicable?	Costs:	Benefits:

Annual cost (£m) per organisation (excl. Transition) (Constant Price)	Micro	< 20	Small	Medium	Large
Are any of these organisations exempt?	No	No	No	No	No

Specific Impact Tests: Checklist

Set out in the table below where information on any SITs undertaken as part of the analysis of the policy options can be found in the evidence base. For guidance on how to complete each test, double-click on the link for the guidance provided by the relevant department.

Please note this checklist is not intended to list each and every statutory consideration that departments should take into account when deciding which policy option to follow. It is the responsibility of departments to make sure that their duties are complied with.

Does your policy option/proposal have an impact on…?	Impact	Page ref within IA
Statutory equality duties[2] Statutory Equality Duties Impact Test guidance	Yes/No	
Economic impacts		
Competition Competition Assessment Impact Test guidance	No	
Small firms Small Firms Impact Test guidance	No	
Environmental impacts		
Greenhouse gas assessment Greenhouse Gas Assessment Impact Test guidance	No	
Wider environmental issues Wider Environmental Issues Impact Test guidance	No	
Social impacts		
Health and well-being Health and Well-being Impact Test guidance	Yes/No	
Human rights Human Rights Impact Test guidance	Yes/No	
Justice system Justice Impact Test guidance	Yes	17
Rural proofing Rural Proofing Impact Test guidance	No	
Sustainable development Sustainable Development Impact Test guidance	No	

Race, disability and gender Impact assessments are statutory requirements for relevant policies. Equality statutory requirements will be expanded 2011, once the Equality Bill comes into force. Statutory equality duties part of the Equality Bill apply to GB only. The Toolkit provides advice on statutory equality duties for public authorities with a remit in Northern Ireland.

Evidence Base (for summary sheets) – Notes

Use this space to set out the relevant references, evidence, analysis and detailed narrative from which you have generated your policy options or proposal. Please fill in **References** section.

References

Include the links to relevant legislation and publications, such as public impact assessment of earlier stages (e.g. Consultation, Final, Enactment).

No.	Legislation or publication
1	Scoping Paper (2005)
2	Law Commission Consultation Paper No 184
3	
4	

+ **Add another row**

Evidence Base

Ensure that the information in this section provides clear evidence of the information provided in the summary pages of this form (recommended maximum of 30 pages). Complete the **Annual profile of monetised costs and benefits** (transition and recurring) below over the life of the preferred policy (use the spreadsheet attached if the period is longer than 10 years).

The spreadsheet also contains an emission changes table that you will need to fill in if your measure has an impact on greenhouse gas emissions.

Annual profile of monetised costs and benefits* - (£m) constant prices

	Y_0	Y_1	Y_2	Y_3	Y_4	Y_5	Y_6	Y_7	Y_8	Y_9
Transition costs	£0	£0	£0	£0	£0	£0	£0	£0	£0	£0
Annual recurring cost	£2.559	£2.559	£2.559	£2.559	£2.559	£2.559	£2.559	£2.559	£2.559	£2.559
Total annual costs	£2.559	£2.559	£2.559	£2.559	£2.559	£2.559	£2.559	£2.559	£2.559	£2.559
Transition benefits	£0	£0	£0	£0	£0	£0	£0	£0	£0	£0
Annual recurring benefits	£0.315	£0.315	£0.315	£0.315	£0.315	£0.315	£0.315	£0.315	£0.315	£0.315
Total annual benefits	£0.315	£0.315	£0.315	£0.315	£0.315	£0.315	£0.315	£0.315	£0.315	£0.315

* For non-monetised benefits please see summary pages and main evidence base section

Microsoft Office
Excel Worksheet

Evidence Base (for summary sheets)

EVIDENCE BASE

A party may challenge a ruling by the Crown Court in a variety of ways: appeal to the Court of Appeal, asking the Crown Court to state a case for the High Court by case stated, and applying to the High Court for judicial review. Different rules apply to the different routes of challenge.

One of those routes of challenge is to ask the High Court for permission for judicial review of the Crown Court's decision. The statutory provision, section 29(3) of the Senior Courts Act 1981, which makes this possible states that it may not be done in matters "relating to trial on indictment".

Section 29(3) of the Senior Courts Act 1981 has generated litigation for over twenty years, and the difficulties of interpretation that it throws up have not been resolved by judgments in cases over that period. Section 29(3) has been described by senior judges as "extremely imprecise".

The Government asked the Law Commission to look at these problems and to examine how the High Court's jurisdictions are best transferred to the Court of Appeal, simplified and, if appropriate, modified; and to draw out the implications for the High Court's criminal jurisdiction over the magistrates' court, and for the Court Martial.

Giving effect to the policy objectives

(i) The objective of producing just results means providing a way of challenging a court ruling where it is claimed the ruling was made unlawfully, such as where a defendant who has been acquitted is refused an order of costs in his or her favour at the end of the case.

(ii) The objective of preventing satellite litigation means a system which does not allow cases to be interrupted by litigation on side-issues, and allows the trial judge to get on with the trial.

(iii) The avoidance of delay and interruption to trials is important because every time a case is adjourned, it becomes less likely that the witnesses will return to give evidence, and the quality of their evidence will suffer. Each case that is adjourned leads to additional delay in other cases. Every delay means additional cost to the public and to the individuals involved.

(iv) Making the law clearer should in itself mean less litigation, and less litigation frees up the time of the judiciary and court staff for other cases, and reduces the costs, for individuals and the public.

(v) Part of the responsibility of the courts is to give effect to individual's rights. The recommendations are for a way of challenging rulings which could affect specific important rights, such as a child's right of privacy, a person's right to life, and a defendant or witness's right to liberty.

The rationale for Government intervention is that these aims can only be achieved by primary legislation.

Scale and context

The problems under consideration in this Impact Assessment are a small part of the whole criminal review/appeal picture. Most appeals from Crown Court trials are appeals against conviction and/or sentence to the Court of Appeal (Criminal Division) ("CACD"). The CACD received 7240 applications for leave to appeal conviction and/or sentence in 2008. The CACD also handles other forms of appeal, from trials at the Crown Court, and between 2005 and 2008 there have been between 184 and 305 of these each year.

The kinds of appeal under consideration in this Impact Assessment are judicial review of, and appeal by way of case stated against, criminal cases in the Crown Court. In the years 2000 to 2008 the Administrative Court received between 246 and 337 applications for permission for judicial review in criminal cases each year (298 in 2008). In the same time period it received between 12 and 23 appeals by way of case stated against the Crown Court each year (but it receives far more appeals by case stated against magistrates' courts).

(Source: Judicial Statistics 2008 (Sept 2009) Cm 7697.)

Consultation

A scoping paper was published in 2005 and comments received on it. A consultation paper was published in 2007 and written responses received from academics, the judiciary and practitioners. Meetings were also held with academics, the judiciary (Crown Court judges and Court of Appeal judges), court staff from the Criminal Appeal Office and the Administrative Court Office, and practitioners.

Policy options and option appraisal

Option 0: Do nothing

Doing nothing is not a cost-free option, as the confusion of choice of appeal route (case stated versus judicial review) persists, as does the lack of clarity over the kinds of rulings related to a Crown Court trial which can be the subject of a judicial review. The risk of unlawful rulings which cause injustice would also continue. Such rulings potentially include an unlawful refusal of costs to a defendant who has been acquitted; an unlawful refusal of bail; a wrongful refusal to impose reporting restrictions for the protection of a child or young person; and a ruling which entails a real and immediate risk to a person's life from the criminal acts of another.

Because the do-nothing option is compared against itself, its costs and benefits are necessarily zero, as is its Net Present Value (NPV). (The Net Present Value shows the total net value of a project over a specific time period. The value of the costs and benefits in an NPV are adjusted to account for inflation and the fact that we generally value benefits that are provided now more than we value the same benefits provided in the future.)

Option 1: targeted change

The preferred option is targeted change. The recommendations would (i) establish a protective boundary around trials on indictment so that rulings of the Crown Court in such trials may not be challenged by judicial review other than exceptionally; (ii) provide an exception to that boundary so that some refusals of bail may be challenged by judicial review; (iii) provide that rulings after the end of the trial may be challenged by judicial review; (iv) provide for a right of appeal to the Court of Appeal for a child or young person against a ruling which lifts or does not impose reporting restrictions in a trial on indictment; and (v) provide for a limited right of appeal to the Court of Appeal for a person whose life is put at real and imminent risk by a ruling of the Crown Court in a trial on indictment.

This would be achieved by removing appeal by case stated from the Crown Court in criminal cases; by amending section 29(3) of the Senior Courts Act 1981; and by introducing two new statutory rights of appeal for specific circumstances.

212

The individual recommendations

The preferred option puts forward the recommendations as a complete package. It is possible, however, for some of the specific recommendations to be enacted individually. The costs and benefits of each recommendation are therefore described individually.

1. ABOLITION OF APPEALS BY CASE STATED FROM THE CROWN COURT IN CRIMINAL CASES

This recommendation would mean removing one route of appeal: there would no longer be the option of appealing a Crown Court ruling by case stated. Those who would have taken this route may choose to apply for judicial review instead.

The impact of this proposed recommendation on numbers of cases would be small because the Administrative Court only receives around 12 to 23 appeals by way of case stated against the Crown Court each year, and that number may decrease following the introduction of means testing for criminal cases in the Crown Court.

Costs

It may be that a procedure will need to be developed for providing the Administrative Court with essential facts or findings for some judicial review determinations, and that in itself would entail some costs.

Benefits

This recommendation would reduce the choice and variety of appeal procedures available and thus simplify one aspect of criminal procedure.

Under the current law a convoluted process is occasionally needed: if the Crown Court refuses to state a case an appellant might then seek (and obtain) judicial review of the refusal to state a case. This complication would be avoided.

We anticipate that some of the cases which currently proceed by way of case stated will be pursued by way of judicial review instead. However, whereas neither leave nor permission is needed for an appeal by way of case stated, permission is needed to pursue an application for judicial review. Permission acts as a filter and the result may be to reduce the number of cases pursued in total. This means less litigation and consequently less cost, to individuals and to the public.

2. MAKING IT CLEAR WHEN JUDICIAL REVIEW OF THE CROWN COURT IN CRIMINAL PROCEEDINGS MAY AND MAY NOT BE APPLIED FOR

We recommend legislation to make clear that judicial review of anything done by the Crown Court from when a case for trial reaches the Crown Court until the end of the case is not permissible. We recommend that this is done by amending section 29(3) of the Senior Courts Act 1981.

Under the current law, judicial review is not permissible in relation to matters relating to trial on indictment, but it has not been clear what this means. The consequences have been litigation, up to the House of Lords (now the Supreme Court) in some cases, and persistent lack of clarity.

Our recommendation would set the boundaries of when judicial review was permissible by reference to identifiable events (such as when the case is sent from the magistrates' court to the Crown Court, or, at the other end, after sentence).

Benefit

We anticipate that our recommendation would make it clearer when judicial review was permissible and when it was not, and thus reduce the amount of litigation (judicial review). An additional effect should be increased confidence in the criminal justice system.

3. MAKING JUDICIAL REVIEW POSSIBLE IN RELATION TO RULINGS AFTER THE END OF THE CASE

Under the current law, judicial review is not permissible in relation to rulings made after the conclusion of any trial. Our recommendation on judicial review would have the effect that judicial review of rulings made after sentence or after a not guilty verdict or after the case has ended in some other way would be possible, which would represent a change in the law.

This recommendation is only about rulings made after the end of a case and therefore cannot lead to the trial or sentencing being held up.

Where a defendant is convicted and sentenced, he or she can appeal any order made against him or her (including a costs order) to the CACD. We do not propose any change to those rights of appeal.

Costs

Some of our recommendations would reduce litigation (judicial review); some would make it possible where it is not currently possible. These impacts are explained below. The following costs are relevant to judicial review.

Where a reform results in an application to a court or a hearing before a court, the costs of providing that court service fall on HMCS (court facilities, staff, judiciary), the prosecutor (generally, but not always, the CPS), the Criminal Defence Service (in the majority of cases), and individuals (applicants who are not publicly-funded).

Using an average immigration and asylum application for judicial review, an average cost for judicial and staff time to process an application for permission for judicial review is £126. We have used the figure of £200 as a working figure for an application for judicial review where permission is refused. If permission is granted, the cost of judicial and staff time for a substantive hearing is £487. If permission is refused, the applicant might renew the application, which would incur staff and judicial costs of £183. If the renewed application is successful, the matter proceeds to a substantive hearing. All figures are for 2009 and are averages, but any one case may be cheaper or more expensive than an average. These costs do not include overheads such as accommodation, ushers, stationery and so on, nor do they include the costs incurred by the parties.

Turning to costs of the parties, an average figure for the cost to legal aid of a judicial review in criminal proceedings in 2004/5 to 2008/9 could be between £2882 and £4400 (assuming the matter proceeds to a hearing). The prosecutor's costs for a substantive hearing could be assumed to be similar, but the prosecutor is not always present at a substantive hearing, and if they are not present then their costs are significantly less. On the other hand, some judicial review matters are complicated and require extensive preparation.

Using these figures, we have taken £8000 as a rough figure for a judicial review hearing, including court costs and defence and prosecution costs, but any individual case could vary a great deal from this estimate.

Care should be taken when comparing this notional cost of a judicial review hearing with the cost of a day at the CACD (see page 12 below) because the judicial review figure assumes a single judge only and a 3-hour hearing.

Specific examples

Our recommendation would affect the rights of acquitted defendants and of the prosecution as regards some costs orders, as now described.

(a) Judicial review of a refusal of a costs order: defendants

The Prosecution of Offences Act 1985 gives the court the power to order the prosecution to compensate defendants who are acquitted of offences brought by the state for reasonable costs they have incurred in their defence. The court may refuse to make such an order if the defendant's own conduct has brought suspicion on him or her and has misled the prosecution into thinking that the case is stronger than it is.

Under the current law, if a defendant is acquitted but the Crown Court refuses to make a costs order in his or her favour, the defendant has no way of challenging that refusal. Our recommendation would allow the defendant to seek judicial review of the refusal.

Costs

If defendants who are not currently awarded their costs become entitled to them, there are cost implications for the court system as a whole of an application for and hearing of a judicial review, as described above.

In addition, defendants who succeeded on judicial review would cause additional cost to Central Funds, from which their costs orders would be paid. In the period 2004 to 2008 the costs borne by the Central Funds budget for payments to acquitted defendants was over £60 million each year. The total additional cost to Central Funds in any one year would be low, but it is hard to say what it might be.

During 2007, 61% (17,226) of the defendants who pleaded not guilty at the Crown Court (28,299) were acquitted, representing almost 20% of the total 88,296 dealt with who recorded a plea. During 2008, 60% (16,786) of the defendants who pleaded not guilty (27,923) were acquitted, representing almost 18% of the 93,494 dealt with who recorded a plea.

Under the current law, a publicly-funded defendant is not going to seek a defence costs order, whereas a privately-funded defendant who is acquitted will.

Estimates for the proportion of defendants in the Crown Court who are publicly funded vary between 91% and 97% (Ministry of Justice (MoJ), Judicial and Court Statistics 2007 (September 2008) Cm 7467 p 190 and MoJ, Judicial and Court Statistics 2008 (September 2009) Cm 7697 pp 191 and 202) Therefore, under the law up to 2009 between 3% and 9% of those acquitted, i.e. under 1,700 defendants (and maybe as few as 50) were probably seeking their costs.

Means testing in the Crown Court for entitlement to legal aid has recently been introduced. There have also been recent changes to the rules on payments from Central Funds in the Crown Court. The combined effect of those changes may be more people seeking an order for payment from Central Funds, but each of them receiving less. (With regard to payments from Central Funds for acquitted defendants, the amount that will be repaid will be capped to legal aid rates. Currently, defendants who pay for their own representation in the Crown Court and are acquitted are entitled to reasonable costs and expenses, which is not necessarily the same as the amount payable under the public funding scheme.) The Government estimate is that "nearly a quarter of defendants could reasonably be expected to contribute towards, or pay for all of, their defence costs" as a result of means-testing in the Crown Court (MoJ, Legal

Services Commission, Her Majesty's Court Service, Crown Court Means Testing (June 2009) CP(R) 06/09) p 9.

If a quarter of defendants are privately-funded, as a result of means-testing, then potentially 25% of those acquitted will be seeking their costs (in the region of 4,250). It is unknown what proportion of that number will be refused a costs order.

There is no information available on how many of those acquitted defendants who are refused their costs would be likely to obtain permission for judicial review, but judicial review will only be possible on established grounds, and in many cases, the defendant will not obtain permission.

In summary, there would be some cases where a defendant would seek to challenge a refusal of costs; not all challenges would succeed; and there would be a costs impact but it would be low.

Benefit

Those defendants who succeeded in judicial review would recoup some of the costs they had spent on their defence. If they succeed then, by definition, the original decision needed to be corrected, and justice would have been served. If mistaken decisions are corrected, then public confidence in the judicial system is enhanced.

(b) Judicial review of a refusal of a costs order: prosecution and defence

The Crown Court may make an order for costs incurred as a result of an unnecessary or improper act or omission by, or on behalf of, another party to the proceedings (made under section 19(1) of the Prosecution of Offences 1985 and regulation 3 of the Costs in Criminal Cases (General) Regulations 1986). The order may be made for the benefit of the prosecution or the defence.

There is no right of appeal or review available in respect of these orders under the current law. If the order was made after the end of the Crown Court trial, our recommendation would change this state of affairs and an application for judicial review could be made against an order or against a refusal to make one. Thus the prosecution or the defence could recoup costs in cases where currently they cannot.

These kinds of orders are not a common feature of trial proceedings, so the number of cases in which an applicant would be able to obtain permission for judicial review of such an order (or a refusal of one) after the end of the case would not be great.

4. EXCEPTION: JUDICIAL REVIEW OF REFUSALS OF BAIL – DEFENDANTS AND WITNESSES

(a) Witnesses and refusals of bail

We recommend that there should be an exception to the bar on judicial review where the Crown Court remands a witness in custody. In other words, that judicial review should be possible by a witness when he or she is remanded in custody during the trial by the trial judge.

This would be a new right for witnesses. (The recommendation does not affect the law on contempt proceedings.)

In practice it is very rare for a witness to be remanded in custody (leaving contempt proceedings to one side) so the impact would be very low. The costs impact (falling on HMCS, the judiciary and the legal aid budget) would therefore be very low.

Benefit

The benefit of the recommendation as regards witnesses is that it would provide a clear means of challenging the lawfulness of a ruling which deprives a person of his or her liberty. Supporting the rights of witnesses in this way accords with the commitment of the UK under the European Council Framework Decision 2001/220/JHA on the standing of victims in criminal proceedings.

If a person is wrongfully remanded into custody it can have very negative effects on their health, and adverse effects on their family – a witness who succeeds in judicial review proceedings and is not therefore remanded into custody might not experience these negative effects.

(b) Defendants and refusals of bail

We also recommend that there should be an exception to the bar on judicial review where the court refuses bail to a defendant, unless the defendant could renew the bail application in the Crown Court.

This right of challenge could be exercised at any stage of the trial (unlike under the current law).

Factors which limit use of this right of challenge are:

  that there is no automatic right of appeal: the defendant would have to obtain permission;

  that it is only available as against refusals of bail, not as against the imposition of conditions on bail;

  that the refusal of bail could only be challenged on the grounds that it was unlawfully made; and

  that the refusal of bail could only be challenged if the defendant could not challenge it via any other route such as by making a repeat or fresh bail application to the Crown Court.

Defendant's bail pre-trial

The current law already allows judicial review of Crown Court bail decisions at "an early stage of proceedings" (undefined in the case law). Therefore the recommendation does not represent a change to current practice except to avoid the lack of clarity in the case law.

Defendant's bail during trial

Judicial review of a remand in custody made in the course of the trial is not currently permissible and the recommendation therefore represents a change in the law.

Judicial review would not be permissible as of right: the defendant would have to show that the refusal of bail was unlawful. We assume this is rarely likely to be possible and most applications for permission for judicial review will be dealt with on the papers. If permission is given, there could be a hearing before a judge of the Administrative Court, following the practice currently adopted for judicial reviews of bail refusals at an early stage of proceedings.

Defendant's bail between verdict and sentence

The current law already permits judicial review of Crown Court bail decisions at this stage of proceedings, but it does not occur in many cases. If the law were changed so as to make it clear that judicial review of a refusal of bail between verdict and sentence is permissible, then there would probably be more applications for permission to review than is currently the case, but it is hard to say how many more.

Costs of the recommendation as regards defendants and refusals of bail

The costs of providing a court service fall on HMCS (court facilities, staff, judiciary), the prosecutor (generally, but not always, the CPS), the Criminal Defence Service (in the majority of cases), and individuals (applicants who are not publicly-funded).

Benefits of the recommendation as regards defendants and refusals of bail

If an application for judicial review is successful and the result is that a defendant is released then there would be the benefit of an unlawful refusal of bail being corrected.

There would be a direct saving to the state of not having to keep a person in custody. That cost may be estimated as between £7,715 and £11,750 per person, assuming (a) the cost of a prison place as between £30,860 and £47,000 per year, and (b) a saving of 3 months' custody (average waiting time to Crown Court trial is 15.2 weeks). (Source: Criminal Justice System Cost – benefit Framework, OCJR, February 2010) There might also be indirect savings in that negative effects on health and employability associated with remands to custody would be avoided. A further benefit would be the easing of pressures on prison capacity.

5. NEW APPEAL AGAINST A REFUSAL TO ORDER REPORTING RESTRICTIONS FOR A CHILD OR YOUNG PERSON ON TRIAL IN THE CROWN COURT

The situation in which it is most likely that reporting restrictions for the protection of a child or young person would be lifted is where the child or young person in question is a defendant and has been convicted. In that circumstance judicial review is already permissible.

The recommendation is that a child or young person could appeal to the Court of Appeal (Criminal Division) against a decision to lift or a refusal to impose reporting restrictions.

Judicial review is probably not permitted under the current law in respect of a ruling pre-conviction and this is the point where the recommendation represents most change.

The impact of this recommendation is likely to be very low because it is very rare for reporting restrictions not to be imposed or to be lifted where a child or young person is a defendant or witness in a trial at the Crown Court.

There is a potential impact on media organisations which would have an interest in the outcome.

Costs

Potential direct costs of this change (financing an appeal) would fall on HMCS, the judiciary and staff of the Court of Appeal, the prosecuting authorities, and the legal aid budget. As is stated, the anticipated impact is very small, so the potential costs are estimated to be very low. (The estimated cost of a day's sitting for the CACD is £14,415; The estimated average cost to the legal aid budget for an appeal to the CACD is £5000; The cost for a prosecuting authority is not known but could be similar. The total cost would be £25,000.)

We do not have a notional length of time for an appeal at the CACD, so have used the day for the purposes of these figures. (If leave is refused on the papers, the court will not sit and the cost will be far lower.) Cases which proceed to a hearing at the CACD may take less or more time than a day.

Care should be taken when comparing this notional cost of a day at the CACD with the notional cost of a judicial review hearing (see page 8 above) because the judicial review figure assumes a single judge only and a 3-hour hearing.

Benefit

If the identity of a child or young person who is a defendant or witness at a Crown Court trial is made public, publication cannot be undone. Public policy generally is to protect the privacy of children and young people and to promote their welfare. It is therefore important that if a child or young person's identity is about to be made public, that there is an opportunity for that decision to be reconsidered at a higher level in the judiciary.

6. A NEW STATUTORY APPEAL AGAINST A RULING WHICH LEADS TO A REAL AND IMMEDIATE RISK TO LIFE

Under the current law, this kind of appeal is not possible. Such situations are unusual, but might arise if, for example, a judge orders disclosure of a defence statement to co-defendants where the defendant was an informer and can expect retribution from the co-defendants. Currently, a defendant might be able to apply for judicial review of the prosecutor's decision to continue with the prosecution, but this is merely a roundabout way of challenging the judge's decision.

It is very difficult to predict how many challenges there might be in a year to this kind of ruling. One indication might be had from the number of cases in which a "witness anonymity order" is refused. (A witness anonymity order is one made by a court which requires specific steps to be taken with the purpose of preventing disclosure of the witness's identity.) The Crown Prosecution Service Policy Directorate was aware of 397 applications for such orders up to 31 December 2009, of which 26 (approximately 6.5%) were refused. This figure is only a weak indicator, however, because there are many unknown factors behind the figure (such as the basis on which the applications were made), and because the kind of ruling which could lead to a real and immediate risk to life is not confined to witness anonymity orders.

Factors which invite use of this right of challenge are:

that it is available to a third party as well as a defendant;

that the type of ruling which may be made is not specified except according to the result – namely that there could be a real and imminent risk to life;

that it may be made at any stage of the trial.

Factors which limit use of this right of challenge are:

that it is only directly affected third parties who may rely on it, not any third party;

that there is no automatic right of appeal: the applicant (whether defendant or third party) would have to obtain leave;

that the ruling could only be challenged on the grounds that it was wrong in law or one which no reasonable court could have made;

that the ruling could only be challenged where the risk to the applicant's life was real and immediate – this limitation cuts out cases where any threats are vague or incredible; and

that the ruling could only be challenged where the risk to the applicant's life is from the criminal acts of another – this limitation cuts out cases where, for example, an applicant might seek to argue that the stress of prosecution affected his or her health so severely that it should not proceed.

Any appeal which needs to be heard urgently – as this kind of appeal probably would – has a knock-on effect on other cases pending appeal.

Any proposal which incorporates a leave stage potentially increases the workload for those who handle the leave applications – here the judges and staff of the Crown Court – and for those who handle the appeals against the refusal of leave, namely the judges and staff of the CACD, even if leave is refused. If leave is refused by the CACD, the applicant might go on to seek leave from the Supreme Court, which generates a further amount of costs, for the applicant, other parties, possibly for the Criminal Defence Service, and the court service.

Costs

There would be costs for HMCS, judiciary and staff, the parties to the proceedings, and the applicant if he or she is not already a party. Some of those costs might fall to the legal aid budget. The costs might vary from one case to another, but might be similar to costs in interlocutory appeals by the prosecution under section 58 of the Criminal Justice Act 2003 (which may count as cases falling in the Very High Cost Case scheme: £90 per hour for preparation and £330 per day in court).

Benefits

This recommendation would enable a ruling which put a person's life at serious and immediate risk – say by revealing his or her identity – to be corrected if that ruling had been arrived at unlawfully. The benefit for the individual (and his or her family) is obvious.

An associated right to be heard

A person whose life could be threatened by a court ruling will only be able to appeal under this recommendation if he or she has made representations to the Crown Court at the time of the ruling. We therefore also make an associated recommendation that someone who is not a party to the proceedings should have a right to make representations to the court in that circumstance.

There is the potential additional cost of representation for such a person, which might fall to the legal aid budget. There is the benefit for that person of being heard on a matter where his or her right to life is potentially in issue.

There is a potential impact here for those responsible for victim and witness care: there may need to be more communication with victims and witnesses about potential effects on them of applications to the Crown Court in the trial.

COST/BENEFIT ANALYSIS SUMMARY

All the recommendations promote justice. Recommendations 1 and 2 simplify processes in the criminal justice system. Recommendations numbers 3, 4, 5 and 6 enable unlawful rulings to be corrected in circumstances where there would be no other way of preventing harm, whether loss of anonymity, loss of liberty, loss of money, or risk to life.

Any reform generates costs at introduction and additional costs in implementing it, which in this case includes drafting secondary legislation and procedural rules, devising new procedures, IT processes, and training all those involved in the new procedure. This means cost for HMCS, the Ministry of Justice (funding the Judicial Studies Board for judicial training), and prosecuting agencies. Solicitors and counsel bear the cost of their own training, though any new procedure might be part of obligatory training time in any event and therefore not represent any additional cost.

Training of the judiciary would need to be provided to Crown Court judges and to judges of the High Court and of the Court of Appeal. Small changes in the law are conveyed to judges by the monthly Judicial Studies Board e-letter and the cost is not significant. These reforms might require a training day for judges and that would mean additional cost to the JSB, but it might be that it would be incorporated into existing training programmes and budgets.

Some of the reforms would generate continuing costs. They would fall on all those individuals and organisations in the criminal justice system. The actual costs generated are hard to predict though estimates have been made where possible, but in the case of some of the recommendations, they would be small.

Table 1: Average annual costs of option 1, 2009 prices

Cost Estimates (£)	Judicial Review (£)		Appeal against no reporting restriction (£)	Appeal against life-threatening ruling (£)	TOTAL(£)
	Costs	Bail			
Low	80,000	84,000	25,000	50,000	239,000
High	6,800,000	9,800,000	125,000	1,250,000	17,975,000
Best	904,000	980,000	50,000	625,000	2,559,000

Explanation of table

Assumptions:

1. In relation to the abolition of appeal by case stated, many cases will now proceed by way of judicial review and any additional costs will be negligible, if any.

2. In relation to the reforms of judicial review, the two areas which will produce an increase in caseload are review of costs refused to an acquitted defendant, and review of refusal of bail. These situations are indicated in columns two and three.

Column 4 provides the estimates for the new right of appeal against a refusal of reporting restrictions by children and young people.

Column 5 provides the estimates for the new right of appeal against a ruling which leads to a person's life being under immediate threat.

Refusal of costs: low estimate: If 50 acquitted defendants seek their costs each year and the majority of the refusals are reasonable and uncontested. Permission for judicial review would either not be sought or be refused. Assume 10 cases in which permission is given. 10 cases at £8,000 per case = £80,000 (See page 10 for case cost explanation)

Refusal of costs: high estimate: The maximum number of cases in which a defendant is privately funded and acquitted and therefore might be seeking costs is 1700 per year. Assume permission for judicial review is sought and given in half of those cases: 850. 850 cases at £8,000 per case = £6,800,000

Refusal of costs: best estimate: Assume acquitted defendants are generally awarded their costs, and if costs are refused, that they are reasonably refused. The best guess is that 20% of defendants are refused their costs and that permission for judicial review would be given in a third of those: 113 cases at £8,000 per case = £904,000

Refusal of bail: Approximately 33,000 defendants await Crown Court trial in custody each year (Source: Judicial Statistics, tables 6.14 and 6.15, which corresponds to the statement by the National Audit Office that "Around ⅓ of defendants in trial cases are in custody" in its report on the Administration of the Crown Court (2009) HC 290 page 15).

The situations where the reform would bring an increased caseload are the review of refusal of bail to a witness, or to a defendant later than at an early stage in proceedings, but before conviction, where there is no change in the defendant's circumstances. There are no figures on how many witnesses are remanded in custody, but the number is likely to be extremely low. As regards defendants, there were 26 applications for judicial review of refusals of bail by the Crown Court at an early stage of proceedings, or between conviction and sentence, in 2005, of which 9 were refused permission, 17 were granted permission, and 8 were successful. It seems reasonable to assume that the reform would bring about an increase in cases where permission for judicial review was given, and an increase in cases where permission was sought but refused. Where the application for judicial review succeeds and the end result is that the defendant is released on bail, there is a saving to the state in the cost of the prison place, and this is represented in the benefits table.

Refusal of bail: low estimate: assume a small change in the number of judicial reviews (say, 10 per year proceed to a full judicial review - 10 x £8,000 = £80,000) and the number of cases where judicial review is sought but refused is 20 per year (20 x £200 = £4,000). Total = £84,000.

Refusal of bail: high estimate: assume large proportion of those remanded in custody seek judicial review (say, 10,000) and 10% of those obtain judicial review (1,000 x £8,000 = £8,000,000) and 90% are refused (9,000 x £200 = £1,800,000). Total = £9,800,000.

Refusal of bail: best estimate: that the number of applications for judicial review increases to 1,000, of which 100 are granted permission (100 x £8,000 = £800,000) and 900 are refused permission (900 x £200 = £180,000). Total = £980,000.

The estimate of 1,000 cases simply presents a scenario.

New appeal against a refusal to make reporting restrictions: low estimate: 1 case per year at £25,000 = £25,000 (See page 14 for case cost explanation.)

New appeal against a refusal to make reporting restrictions: high estimate: 5 cases per year at £25,000 = £125,000. It is assumed that judges rarely refuse requests from children and young people to make reporting restrictions.

New appeal against a refusal to make reporting restrictions: best estimate: 2 cases per year at £25,000 = £50,000

New appeal against a ruling which leads to a real and immediate risk to life: low estimate: 2 cases per year at £25,000 = £50,000. This is based on the cases where the person who claims his or her life is at risk currently seeks judicial review.

New appeal against a ruling which leads to a real and immediate risk to life: high estimate: 50 cases per year at £25,000 = £1,250,000. The estimate of 50 cases simply presents a scenario.

New appeal against a ruling which leads to a real and immediate risk to life: best estimate: 25 cases per year at £25,000 = £625,000. The estimate of 25 cases simply presents a scenario.

Estimate of Benefits
The following monetised benefits are based on hypothesised number of cases.

Low estimate: 3 successful judicial reviews of refusals of bail per year at £7,715, based on serving 3 months in prison, each cost of prison place saved = £23,145

High estimate: 400 successful judicial reviews of refusals of bail per year at £11,750 each cost of prison place saved = £4,700,000

Best estimate: 35 successful judicial reviews of refusals of bail per year at £9,000 per each cost of prison place saved = £315,000

Option 2: large-scale change
This option was rejected. A policy option of creating a new statutory appeal to the Court of Appeal for parties and any directly affected third party in respect of rulings for which there is no existing statutory right of appeal was considered and consulted upon. This was found not to be workable and to have unpredictable resource implications.

The option proposed in the consultation paper (a new statutory appeal) was a large-scale change to criminal procedure. Although hard to quantify, the impact would be considerable, in terms of costs and delays. The Office of Criminal Justice Reform attempted to estimate the number of cases that might be generated and reached the figure of 640 additional appeals per year. They noted also that:

"Taking 'a' as the unit cost of an appeal in court time and 'b' as the unit cost in legal aid time, it may be calculated that the proposals would cost approximately $640 \times a + 640 \times b$ per annum to implement. It will also be necessary to factor in a greater number of appeals to the House of Lords, and prosecution costs.

As noted, these estimates relate only to contested cases. The proposed appeal rights extend beyond the trial itself, applying both after and, more importantly, before the trial, so all 75,000 Crown Court cases are potentially caught. It seems unlikely that there would be many appeals before the trial, but the possibility cannot be excluded. Furthermore, the availability of the potential for delay and disruption may encourage defendants who would otherwise plead guilty to contest cases."

There would inevitably be an increase in the workload of the CACD, and knock-on effects on other cases.

It had been thought that the transfer of work from the Administrative Court to the CACD would bring about some cost saving, but, given the small number of cases in the Administrative Court, this turned out not to be so. This option is not preferred, in part because of the cost implications. Other reasons are that the solution proposed in the consultation paper would have generated increased litigation, making it possible for parties – and others – to appeal different rulings, in ways that could not be predicted. It was not a proportionate solution to the problem.

KEY ASSUMPTIONS

1. The introduction of means testing into legal aid in the Crown Court will result in a greater proportion of people who will be paying for or contributing towards their own representation. There will probably also be a greater proportion of people who will represent themselves.

2. That most court rulings are lawfully made and therefore that leave/permission to challenge a ruling on the grounds that it was unlawfully made will only be granted exceptionally.

3. That those appeals which currently go by way of case stated to the High Court from the Crown Court will be suitable for judicial review.

4. That the number of rulings of the Crown Court which could bring about a real and immediate risk to a person's life is very small.

5. That the number of cases in which the Crown Court lifts or refuses to make reporting restrictions for the protection of a child or young person is very small.

RISKS

1. That we have incorrectly estimated how many people would seek to make use of the new routes of review/appeal we recommend. We assess this risk as very low in respect of all the recommendations (except one) because those routes of review/appeal will only be available in very limited circumstances.

   The exception is the recommendation that judicial review should be available for rulings after the end of the case. Again, we estimate that the number of judicial reviews which result will be very low but the risk that we are wrong about this is slightly higher than for the other recommendations because the recommendation is less tightly limited than the other recommendations. To illustrate: the right of appeal we recommend in respect of reporting restrictions can only apply to restrictions which could be made for the benefit of a child or young person, and the appeal could only be made by a child or young person, whereas the recommendation that judicial review should be available for rulings made after a case has come to an end is not confined to a kind of ruling. It is, however, restricted by the general law of judicial review which means it cannot be used as an appeal on the merits of the ruling nor where another form of appeal is available.

2. That we are mistaken to assume that fixing the boundaries of when judicial review of rulings in trial on indictment by reference to identifiable events (so that judicial review is not possible from when a case has passed to the Crown Court until the end of the case) is a clear way of doing so. We assess this risk as low because there will only be doubt whether a case has gone to the Crown Court from the magistrates' court, or whether it has ended, in a very small number of cases.

SPECIFIC IMPACT TESTS

Legal aid and justice system

The impact on the justice system and specifically on the Criminal Defence Service has been assessed as part of the analysis above.

Equality

Age: There is no evidence that the policy will have any adverse impact based on age.

Gender: There is no evidence that the policy will have any adverse impact based on gender.

Ethnicity: There is no evidence that the policy will have any adverse impact based on ethnicity, except as follows.

Our recommendation that unlawful bail decisions may be challenged by way of judicial review may have a small impact on members of groups which are disproportionately remanded into custody. Those without a permanent address are more likely to be refused bail, and this includes members of the gypsy and travelling communities: source: P Mason and N Hughes and others, Institute of Applied Social Studies, University of Birmingham and A Norman, Celtic Knot, Birmingham, "Access to Justice: a review of existing evidence of the experiences of minority groups based on ethnicity, identity and sexuality" Ministry of Justice Research Series 7/09 May 2009, p 30, citing C Power Room to Roam: England's Irish Travellers, Research Report (2004). Our recommendation will make it more likely that unlawful remands into custody are corrected. If members of those groups are unlawfully remanded (and we do not have evidence on this point) then the policy would benefit them.

Disability: There is no evidence that the policy will have any adverse impact based on disability.

Religious belief: There is no evidence that the policy will have any adverse impact based on religious belief.

Sexual orientation: There is no evidence that the policy will have any adverse impact based on sexual orientation.

Human rights

The proposals are compliant with the Human Rights Act 1998.

Annexes

Annex 1 should be used to set out the Post Implementation Review Plan as detailed below. Further annexes may be added where the Specific Impact Tests yield information relevant to an overall understanding of policy options.

Annex 1: Post Implementation Review (PIR) Plan

A PIR should be undertaken, usually three to five years after implementation of the policy, but exceptionally a longer period may be more appropriate. A PIR should examine the extent to which the implemented regulations have achieved their objectives, assess their costs and benefits and identify whether they are having any unintended consequences. Please set out the PIR Plan as detailed below. If there is no plan to do a PIR please provide reasons below.

Basis of the review: [The basis of the review could be statutory (forming part of the legislation), it could be to review existing policy or there could be a political commitment to review];

Review objective: [Is it intended as a proportionate check that regulation is operating as expected to tackle the problem of concern?; or as a wider exploration of the policy approach taken?; or as a link from policy objective to outcome?]

Review approach and rationale: [e.g. describe here the review approach (in-depth evaluation, scope review of monitoring data, scan of stakeholder views, etc.) and the rationale that made choosing such an approach]

Baseline: [The current (baseline) position against which the change introduced by the legislation can be measured]

Success criteria: [Criteria showing achievement of the policy objectives as set out in the final impact assessment; criteria for modifying or replacing the policy if it does not achieve its objectives]

Monitoring information arrangements: [Provide further details of the planned/existing arrangements in place that will allow a systematic collection systematic collection of monitoring information for future policy review]

Case law could be monitored for decisions at High Court and Court of Appeal; suggest analysis of criminal judicial review cases; suggest obtain views of Circuit judges; suggest keep data of new appeals proposed.

Reasons for not planning a PIR: [If there is no plan to do a PIR please provide reasons here]

It is not the role of the Law Commission to implement legislation and therefore it is inappropriate for us to plan a PIR. We therefore simply make the suggestions for monitoring implementation above.

Add annexes here.